When Tigers Fight

When Tigers Fight

The Story of the Sino-Japanese War, 1937–1945

Dick Wilson

THE VIKING PRESS   NEW YORK

Copyright © 1982 by Dick Wilson
All rights reserved
Published in 1982 by The Viking Press
625 Madison Avenue, New York, N.Y. 10022

Library of Congress Catalog Card Number: 81-52205
ISBN 0-670-76003-X

Printed in the United States of America
Set in Times Roman

Dedicated to George Bull

Contents

Chronology

1937

7 July	Marco Polo Bridge incident
7 August	Beijing captured
9 August	Oyama incident in Shanghai
24 August	Battle of Pingxing pass
	Baoding falls
26 August	Battle of Nankou pass
October	Battle of Dachang
	Xinkou falls
	Battle of Niangzi pass
	Battle of Zhabei
November	Shanghai falls
December	Nanjing falls

1938

March–April	Battles of Taierzhuang and Xuzhou
11 May	Yellow River dykes breached
August	Battle of Wuhan begins
Sept.–Oct.	Battle of De'an
21 October	Guangzhou captured
25 October	Wuhan falls

1939

January	Wang Jingwei defects
27 March	Nanchang falls
May	Battles of Tongbai and Wutai mountains
14 September	First battle of Changsha
December	Battle of Kunlun pass

1940

12 June	Yichang falls
August	Battle of a Hundred Regiments

1941

January	New Fourth Army incident
18 September	Second battle of Changsha
October	Zhengzhou falls
7 December	Pearl Harbor
8 December	Hong Kong invaded
27 December	Third battle of Changsha

1942

January	Stilwell in China
March	Battle of Tounggoo (Burma)
17 April	Battle of Yenangyaung
18 April	Doolittle air raids
8 May	Myitkyina falls

1943

March	Battle of Taihang mountains
May	Battle of west Hubei
2 November	Battle of Changde
23–26 November	Cairo Conference

1944

April–May	Ichi-Go offensive
June	Battles of Myitkyina and Hengyang
October	Last Burma offensive
November	Guilin falls

1945

March–April	Battle of Linhekou
6 August	Hiroshima atom bomb
10 August	Japan surrenders

Main Characters

China

Head of State
Generalissimo Jiang Jieshi
(Gimo for short)
President and C-in-C

Political Leaders
Madame Jiang Meiling
Wang Jingwei (he defected)
Mao Zedong (Communist
Party Chairman)
Zhou Enlai (Communist liaison
with Guomindang)

Generals
1 Guomindang or Nationalist

Chen Cheng
Li Zongren
Bai Chongxi
Hu Zongnan
Tang Enbo

2 Communist

Zhu De
Peng Dehuai
Lin Biao

Japan

Head of State
Emperor Hirohito

Political Leaders
Prince Konoye
(Premier 1937–41)
Gen. Tojo Hideki
(Premier 1941)
Togo Shigenori
(Foreign Minister)

Generals

Katsuki Kiyoshi
Matsui Iwane
Doihara Kenji
Itagaki Seishiro
Hata Shunroku
Isogai Rensuke
Ishihara Kanji

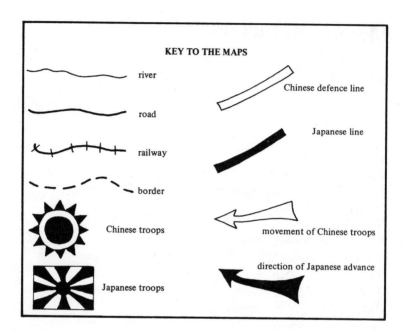

Maps

Illustrations

Major-General Claire Chennault, the 'Flying Tiger', with his dog Joe (Keystone)

'Vinegar Joe' Stilwell with Sun Liren in North Burma (Keystone)

General Hata Shunroku (Keystone)

General Itagaki Seishiro, hanged as a war criminal (Keystone)

General Doihara Kenji, hanged as a war criminal (Keystone)

General Matsui Iwane, hanged as a war criminal (Keystone)

Note on Names

Personal names, both Chinese and Japanese, are given throughout this book in the proper Chinese and Japanese way, i.e. the family name first and the given name second. The Chinese names, including place names, are spelt according to the Pinyin system of romanization, which may seem unfamiliar to some readers but is the form of spelling now followed in China itself and by most Western students of China.

The following list gives principal Chinese place and personal names as they were usually rendered at the time of the war in the English language, with their Pinyin equivalents.

	Pinyin
Kuomintang (Nationalist Party)	Guomindang (GMD)
Amoy	Xiamen
Canton	Guangzhou
Chungking	Chongqing
Dairen (Port Arthur)	Lüda
Mukden	Shenyang
Nanking	Nanjing
Peking	Beijing
Swatow	Shantou
Tientsin	Tianjin
Chiang Kai-shek	Jiang Jieshi
Sun Yat-sen	Sun Zhongshan

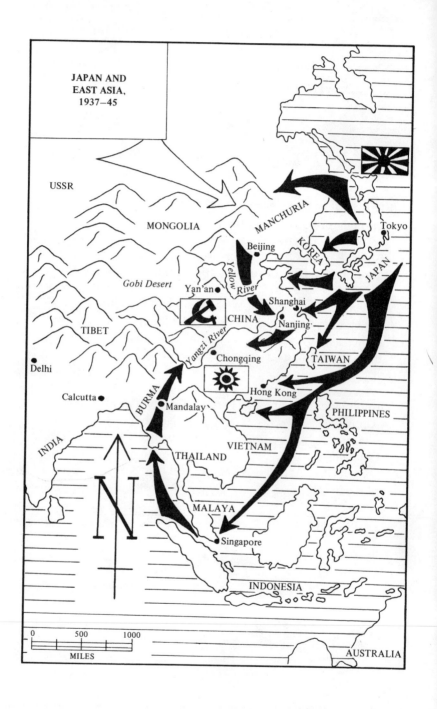

JAPAN AND
EAST ASIA,
1937—45

USSR

MONGOLIA

MANCHURIA

Tokyo

KOREA

Beijing

Gobi Desert

Yan'an

Yellow River

CHINA

Shanghai

Nanjing

JAPAN

TIBET

Yangzi River

Chongqing

TAIWAN

Delhi

Calcutta

Hong Kong

BURMA

Mandalay

PHILIPPINES

INDIA

VIETNAM

THAILAND

N

MALAYA

Singapore

INDONESIA

0   500   1000

MILES

AUSTRALIA

Introduction

When tigers fight, the forest is shattered. The two giant nations of the Far East, China and Japan, waged total modern war against each other from 1937 to 1945, and the official count of soldiers killed on both sides came to 2½ million. There were so many more civilian casualties on the Chinese side, including those from starvation and flooding which might have been avoided but for the war, that some observers put the ultimate toll at 10 million lives – equivalent to the entire population of Greece or Belgium. The homeless reached about 40 million.

Curiously, while the diplomatic and political aspects of this Sino-Japanese War have been well covered by western authors, the actual fighting itself has not been satisfactorily narrated from a non-partisan point of view. This book tries to fill that gap.

It was, said Lin Yutang, China's leading novelist of the day, 'the most terrible, the most inhuman, the most brutal, the most devastating war in all Asia's history'. It was a struggle to the death between the two rival powers of East Asia – one strong in numbers, the other in technology; one in an uneasy double harness of revolutionary democrats and Communists, the other openly fascist; one claiming superiority for past cultural glory, the other for contemporary vigour and modernity.

Sven Hedin described it at the time as a 'trial of strength' which might 'gain the same importance as the appearance of the Huns and Mongols once had on the colossal stage of the old world'. China and Japan together constitute just a quarter of the human race, and if one of the two had made a decisive victory of it, the resulting power concentration would have gravely threatened other continents.

To most of Asia's intellectuals the war furnished the same focus of passionate ideological rivalry between the left and right paths to progress that Spain provided for their western counterparts – with the added complication that Japan, while repelling left-wing critics, attracted many Asians for whom getting the white imperialists out of Asia was a more important goal. On this issue Jawaharlal Nehru, for example, broke with his rival for the leadership of post-war India, Subhas Chandra Bose. One backed China, the other Japan – so that, if Japan had won, Bose might have led independent India instead of Nehru.

Most of the present generation of power holders and leaders in the Far East, not only in China and Japan but also in Korea, Hong Kong and Southeast Asia, were involved in one way or another in the Sino-Japanese War, with which the Second World War ultimately merged. A recent Japanese Prime Minister, Mr Fukuda Takeo, was a young official in occupied China in the 1940s, while the late Ohira Masayoshi, his successor as Prime Minister in 1979, worked in northern China during the war as a junior Treasury official.

Another Prime Minister, Lee Kuan Yew of Singapore, was a humble interpreter for the Japanese in that city, which was treated as Chinese. Ask any businessman or government official in Hong Kong, of whatever race but of the right age, and you are likely to elicit a story of danger, tragedy, bravery or deprivation during those wartime years. For the whole area the war has cast a frame of reference for the dreams and nightmares of hundreds of millions of people.

The national anthem of the People's Republic of China is based on an anti-Japanese wartime song, and ex-Chairman Hua Guofeng's name (a wartime alias) was artificially assembled from three of the nine characters of the organization in which he served – the Anti-Japanese Vanguard Troop for National Salvation.

Ever since the Japanese nation was formed, probably by a union of migrants from north China with others from the Southeast Asian islands, love and hate have been wound together in the two millennia of China-Japan relations. China gave Japan in those early centuries writing, philosophy and many other endowments of culture, but came to look upon Japan in the twentieth century as a provincial backwater enviably modernized but otherwise contemptible.

Japan had the reverse image of China as a respectable centre of ancient civilization grown perilously soft and weak. This was put most vividly by Mr Matsuoka Yosuke, a subsequent Foreign Minister, who told a foreign reporter a few weeks after the opening of the war:

China and Japan are two brothers who have inherited a great mansion called Eastern Asia. Adversity sent them both down to the depths of poverty. The ne'er-do-well elder brother turned a dope fiend and a rogue, but the younger, lean but rugged and ambitious, ever dreamed of bringing back past glories to the old house. He sold newspapers at a street corner and worked hard to support the house. The elder flimflammed the younger out of his meagre savings and sold him out to their common enemy. The younger, in a towering rage, beat up the elder – trying to beat into him some sense of shame and awaken some pride in the noble traditions of the great house. After many scraps the younger finally made up his mind to stage a showdown fight.

Nothing could be more explicit.

The analogy of brothers has a deeper meaning than might at first appear. John Gunther, arriving in Shanghai a few months after the war had broken out, enquired anxiously of a colleague, 'How do you tell a Chinese from a Jap?' Actually the Chinese always seemed to recognize their enemy by his relatively smaller height and tendency to bandy legs. 'East-Ocean pygmies' was a common phrase for the Japanese.

But the Japanese did not always find it so easy. Hino Ashihei, the Japanese novelist whose books about the war are so telling and vivid, described his peculiar feelings on first seeing a group of Chinese prisoners, because 'they look like us'. 'Whenever I see Chinese soldiers and civilians,' he wrote in his diary on the Chinese battlefield in 1938, 'their close resemblance to the Japanese gives me a strange feeling. Moreover, it is not at all rare for me to come across Chinese faces which remind me of Japanese friends. The degree of resemblance is in fact so great that it sometimes makes me feel very uneasy. This may be superficial emotionalism on my part, but leaving aside the high ideas of Japanese and Chinese cultural brotherhood and shared Asian identity, I find it unpleasant that the enemy with whom we are locked in mortal combat should so resemble us as to feel like a neighbour.' It was in the end 'a quarrel between brothers, in order to shake hands more tightly in the end'.

To some extent Hino justified his presence in China by China's obvious need. He and his fellow-soldiers were astonished at the Chinese toleration of their coming, as if the Chinese did not feel that they had a nation worth fighting for. 'The Japanese have their own country, but the Chinese have none.' He was swayed by the somewhat masochistic Chinese intellectuals who rallied to the Japanese, arguing that the Chinese system needed to be destroyed once and for all before the country's revival could be assured. This was Japan's 'mission' in China.

China's story in the decades before the war was one of gradual breakdown of the effete empire of the Manchu Dynasty, overthrown in 1911, and the subsequent inability of provincial warlords and westernized republican leaders to collaborate in a single effective government. During all that time outside powers, including not only Europe and the United States but also Japan, had been nibbling away around the edges of China. Every young Chinese patriot in the first third of the twentieth century dreamed of shaking off foreign imperialism.

But the strongest emotion which China aroused in the Japanese was disappointment, even dismay, at the appalling weakness of the central state in the East Asian system, which was almost inviting European penetration. In the long history of their relationship there had never been a successful invasion of China by Japan, or of Japan by China, until modern times. In the seventh century AD the Japanese Emperor had sent an army to attack the Chinese protectorate of Korea, but it was routed.

The next attempt had come while Marco Polo was residing at the court of Kublai Khan in Beijing in the twelfth century. The Venetian described how his master sent an army through Korea and then in a great armada to Chipangu, 'the land of the rising sun'. But a violent gale wrecked the Chinese fleet before it could land. Three centuries later the great Japanese warrior Hideyoshi led a military expedition to the Asian mainland, but he too failed.

Then in the late nineteenth century Japan, beginning her own process of forced-march modernization on the western model, joined the European and American predators who were gobbling up pieces of China all round that country's long borders. The Japanese began in the 1870s by forcing a treaty on Korea, which until then had been regarded as within the Chinese sphere of influence.

In 1894 the question of control of Korea came to a head, and the Japanese and Chinese armies fought bitterly. China had to sign an ignominious treaty at Shimonoseki, abandoning her rights in Korea and ceding to Japan not only the Liaodong peninsula in northern China but also Taiwan and the Pescadores islands, as well as paying an indemnity of $200 million.

Ten years later Admiral Togo attacked the Russian fleet at Lüda (Port Arthur), and wrested from the Tsar his rights in the southern part of Manchuria, taking over Lüda, with valuable rights over railways and minerals. China placidly endorsed the arrangement, and even granted further concessions to Japan in the cities of Manchuria.

The First World War gave Japan her opportunity to enlarge this foothold. In 1914 she declared war on Germany, demanding the surrender of the German lease of Qingdao on the Shandong peninsula, placing the Chinese in the extraordinary position of having to designate a specified area of their country as a battle-zone between two foreign powers.

Tokyo followed through with the famous Twenty-One Demands of 1915, requiring China not only to cede to Japan all the German rights, but also to give Japan precedence over other foreign powers in all kinds of ways, including advising and supplying the Chinese army, constructing railways and mines and developing a steel industry. The Twenty-One Demands would have made China effectively a Japanese protectorate. But since no other power would come to China's assistance, the new Chinese republic was obliged to accept them.

China also joined the Allies by declaring war against Germany in 1917, but too late; the Japanese had already wrung from those same allies a commitment to support Japan's claims to the former German rights in Shandong. At the Versailles peace conference the Chinese therefore had to resign themselves to a Japanese stake in Shandong, as a reward for her help in the European war.

But this was not the end to China's suffering at the hands of Japan, who in 1931–2 consolidated her occupation of Manchuria in China's farthest north and made the puppet state of 'Manchukuo' out of it. The excuse was a bomb explosion on a railway outside Mukden, the natural capital of Manchuria now known as Shenyang, in September 1931. The Japanese military used this as a pretext for attacking the weak Chinese forces there and to extend their control of Manchuria. Although China appealed to the League of Nations, which in turn called on Japan to withdraw, and although the civilian government in Tokyo wanted to obey, the Japanese army leaders in the field were contemptuous of both authorities and ignored them.

Indeed, they brazenly drove even farther into China's soft body. It was the turn of Shanghai, halfway down China's long coastline, next. A confused incident in which a Japanese Buddhist monk and Chinese policemen were killed led in January 1932 to an all-out clash between Japanese marines and local Chinese soldiers.

At this time there were many Japanese traders and office workers living in Shanghai, about six thousand of them in Zhabei, one of the Chinese districts. The Japanese navy sent men in without warning, to 'protect' them, and when the Chinese resisted the Japanese commander ordered the entire district to be bombed. Within hours it was one vast bonfire.

Arnold Toynbee wrote at the time: 'This bombing of a crowded area, without warning, was bound to cause great loss of life and damage, and it struck terror into the hearts of the hundreds of thousands of civilians whose homes were in Zhabei.'

In the professional fighting, however, the Chinese forces were in the end surprisingly successful. In May Japan sued for peace, accepting the League of Nations cease-fire proposals.

But the new state of 'Manchukuo' was now thoroughly subjugated and the Japanese audaciously summoned the last Emperor of China, Henry Pu Yi, to be the figurehead ruler of a new 'republic' – a device for Japanese imperialism which deceived no one. Pu Yi had been placed briefly on the Dragon Throne in Beijing at the tender age of two, just in time to see the effete Manchu Dynasty collapse.

The League of Nations sent out an investigation team which found Japan at fault in Manchuria, but Tokyo ignored this and actually withdrew from the League in 1933, proceeding immediately to annex Jehol on the north side of the Great Wall of China.

Then the Japanese army began to nibble away at parts of eastern Hebei province by the sea and Mongolia deep inland, as part of an evident programme to swallow up China piece by piece. The mastermind of this plan was Colonel Doihara Kenji, Japan's army intelligence chief in Manchuria. The expansion was legitimized by the so-called Ho-Umezu Agreement between China and Japan, after Japanese troops had fought their way across the Great Wall almost to Beijing itself.

All this had happened under a civilian regime in Tokyo which normally tried to keep its headstrong soldiers under restraint. But in 1936 the militarists seized power by force in Japan, enabling Doihara's plans for China to proceed without let or hindrance from Tokyo, fortified by a new treaty with Nazi Germany.

Such was the position in 1937. Japan's commanders in north China were determined to bring the Chinese to heel, and their voice prevailed over the better counsels of such military experts as Colonel Ishihara Kanji, who pleaded in vain for a more rational and cautious approach. The generals of the Rising Sun in Manchuria sought only a new pretext to march decisively against the main body of China. The summer of 1937 was to provide that pretext.

What was Japan really after? A British observer in Tokyo summarized the Japanese rationalization of their actions in China:

We say to ourselves: 'We must get this China business settled once and for all. The Chinese must be taught a lesson.' And we go forward to do it. And then, afterwards, we say: 'We must have access to China because of our scant resources,' or if you don't like that, 'the Chinese have attacked our army and we must avenge them'. Or if you don't like that, 'our interests by treaty established are threatened and we must protect them'. Or if you don't like that, 'anti-Japanese education is rampant in China and is the spear-head of anti-foreign education and in everybody's interests we must put an end to it'. And if you don't like that, 'well in any case, damn you, we are going to do it, because instinctively we know we must'.

The two armies could hardly have been more different. Japan's was conscript-based but highly professionally led, equipped with all the latest weapons, and imbued with the strongest sense of unquestioning patriotism of any army in history. Traditional *Samurai* ethics combined with Japan's modern sense of nationalism to produce an extraordinary devotion to duty.

An incident from the fighting in China in the early 1930s illustrates this. A certain Major Kuga had been found unconscious on the battlefield in Shanghai by a young Chinese who had earlier been his student in Japan. Moved by the memory of their earlier friendship, the young Chinese carried the Japanese infantry officer away and nursed him back to health. Eventually Kuga returned to his own unit, knowing that he would face a court martial because of his capture by the enemy. In the particular circumstances he would probably have been let off, but the moral disgrace in the eyes of his colleagues would remain. He therefore chose to go back to the battlefield and commit suicide there to atone for his dishonour.

'War,' said a Japanese army pamphlet in 1934, 'is the father of creation and the mother of culture. The testing of one's ability against hardship is the motive and stimulus for the development of life and the creation of culture, both in individuals and competing nations.'

The Chinese army, on the other hand, was professional but loosely organized, badly armed and poorly trained. Generalissimo Jiang Jieshi (Chiang Kai-shek) himself, China's supreme ruler and army commander-in-chief, was a formidable figure, one of the architects of the history of his time. Stilwell, the sour-faced American observer of the war, called him 'Peanut' because of the shape of his skull as revealed by his close haircut. But he was a man of great intelligence and resourcefulness, though never as powerful in controlling China's political forces as his detractors portrayed him. Ironically, he had not only been trained in a Japanese military college, graduating from Shimbo Gokyo in 1909, but actually went to serve in the Japanese Thirteenth Field Artillery. He thus had an excellent preparation for the war, although he had pursued a political rather than a military career thereafter.

Jiang's conduct of the war was marred, however, by his relatively little experience of actual battle conditions or of junior or middle-ranking service in the field. He also placed political obedience before military skills. His wife once put it to him that one particular general was being widely talked about as militarily incapable. Jiang's reply was: 'It is true that Liu Zhi is a bad commander in war. But where can you find a man who is so obedient?'

The armed forces which Jiang commanded were a motley collection, indifferently equipped with an extraordinary variety of weapons. China's air force was quite inadequate – some 400 combat pilots with 300 aeroplanes of varying makes.

There was a reasonably efficient nucleus of modern forces run by graduates of the military training college at Huangpu. These had the benefit of foreign assistance in their training, notably by German officers, and they were loyal to the central government. But the majority of the men under arms whom Generalissimo Jiang had to field against the Japanese invaders owed their loyalty either to a corrupt and old-fashioned military bureaucracy or else to the political leaders of individual provinces, whose generals were usually interested in using their soldiers to further their own political power rather than fight a serious war against Japan. Lung Yun of Yunnan, for example, a tiny man who had made a fortune from opium, issued his own currency and maintained his own army. Whenever he had to go to the capital to meet Jiang Jieshi, he would wait until Madame Jiang had arrived in his own provincial capital to remain as a hostage during his absence. Such was the feudal background to much of the Chinese army.

The divisions even showed in action. A Russian observer told the story of the Japanese bombing of one Chinese headquarters in which more than one faction was represented. There was a direct hit and many officers became casualties. One of the first to be dug out from the ruins was a general, the deputy chief of staff. A senior officer of the guard battalion arrived just at this moment, took one look at the rescued Chinese and barked: 'Bury him! He's not one of ours.' Luckily the Russian adviser came up at this point and saved the general's life, though he later went mad and did not return to his duties. The bad feeling among the Chinese was almost as great as between the Chinese and Japanese.

These were the forces which were now to confront each other in 1937 in the most damaging and bloody war ever to be fought between two nations. China represented the passive, aristocratic element in east Asian civilization; Japan was the brash and energetic newcomer, newly modernized and dying to proselytize. China was a huge reservoir of humanity, Japan a relatively small island state, with only about one-tenth the population of China. It was as if Britain were to try to conquer the entire European continent.

In the pages that follow only the main thread of the war is followed, because otherwise the story would run into several volumes. But what a colourful cast of characters it presents, from the morbidly austere Christian who was China's commander-in-chief, Generalissimo Jiang Jieshi, to his opium-eating, freebooting generals, and from the daring fanatic Doihara (the 'Lawrence of Manchuria') to the honest and painstaking Matsui on the Japanese side – with men like the abrasive Vinegar Joe Stilwell, the Prussian ramrod von Falkenhausen with his pince-nez, and General Claire Chennault of the Flying Tigers also in attendance.

Such was the drama that now began to unfold in an obscure and sleepy town in northern China in the hot summer of 1937.

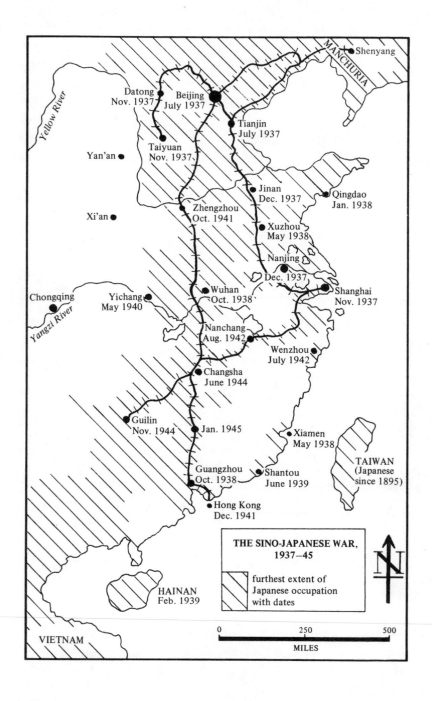

Shenyang

MANCHURIA

Yellow River

Datong
Nov. 1937
Beijing
July 1937

Tianjin
July 1937

Yan'an

Taiyuan
Nov. 1937

Jinan
Dec. 1937

Qingdao
Jan. 1938

Xi'an

Zhengzhou
Oct. 1941

Xuzhou
May 1938

Nanjing
Dec. 1937

Chongqing

Yichang
May 1940

Wuhan
Oct. 1938

Shanghai
Nov. 1937

Yangzi River

Nanchang
Aug. 1942

Wenzhou
July 1942

Changsha
June 1944

Guilin
Nov. 1944

Jan. 1945

Xiamen
May 1938

TAIWAN
(Japanese
since 1895)

Guangzhou
Oct. 1938

Shantou
June 1939

Hong Kong
Dec. 1941

**THE SINO-JAPANESE WAR,
1937–45**

furthest extent of
Japanese occupation
with dates

N

HAINAN
Feb. 1939

VIETNAM

0   250   500

MILES

1

Marco Polo Bridge

Unlike most big capitals, Beijing does not stand on a river. To reach a ship you must ride out ten miles to the west, as Marco Polo did seven centuries ago. There you strike the River Yongding, on which boats carry goods destined for the capital. The Venetian explorer observed here 'a very fine stone bridge, so fine indeed, that it has very few equals.... It is three hundred paces in length and ... ten mounted men can ride across it abreast.'

The bridge still survives, its arches and tiers topped by a marble parapet lined with stone elephants, lions and tortoises. The Chinese name for it is Lugouqiao – Black Moat bridge – but Europeans still call it the Marco Polo bridge, after the man who first described it to the outside world.

This bridge is not only an architectural relic from the twelfth century (though twice restored), but also a vital crossroads of northeastern Asia. Here is the traditional river crossing, for centuries and probably millennia, of travellers between the Yellow River provinces of north-central China and Manchuria in the northeast.

The railway age added another dimension to its importance, because a spur line at nearby Fengtai joins the main Beijing–Wuhan and Beijing–Tianjin lines, enabling trains to connect without having to negotiate the capital itself. It crosses the river parallel with the old stone bridge.

It was here that the war began. Under her earlier agreements with China, Japan had many foot soldiers as well as small units of artillery, tanks, cavalry and engineers headquartered in Tianjin. But one infantry regiment, the First, was based at

Beijing, and that regiment's Third Battalion was at Fengtai near the Marco Polo bridge.

Like other foreign troops stationed there under the old Boxer Protocol, this Japanese battalion used the Lugouqiao area for drilling and manoeuvres. In 1937 its summer manoeuvres gradually became bigger and more frequent, and one of them was in progress on the night of 7 July 1937 – which the Chinese, with their delight in numerology, immediately called the Triple Seventh – at the northeast end of the historic Marco Polo bridge.

Accounts of how the shooting actually started vary. The Japanese found during their night manoeuvre that one of their men was missing, and since they were outside the town of Wanping (whose name means 'obliging peace') at the eastern end of the bridge, they demanded to search it. The Chinese garrison commander refused.

In any case the missing Japanese soldier rejoined his unit about two hours later, having probably spent his time in a brothel. The official Japanese reports made no mention of him, merely referring to an exchange of shots at 10.10 p.m., after the manoeuvres had ended. Another Japanese account claimed that the battalion had only blanks in its rifles, being on training, although its commander had thirty bullets for emergencies.

The evidence does not bear out the respective claims that either the Japanese or the Chinese engineered the Marco Polo bridge incident in order to provoke a war. But once the accident had happened, the extremists in the Japanese army saw the shooting as an excellent excuse to expand their role in China. By 3 a.m. eight truckloads of Japanese under General Terahira, a Chinese-speaking officer of the feared Special Service Corps, appeared at the walls of Wanping demanding restitution for the Chinese 'kidnapping' of their soldier.

Two American correspondents who arrived eagerly at Wanping next day found no one in sight except Chinese sentries alert on the wall with their rifles pointed to the north. The gate, thirty feet high, was shut: 'Soldiers shouted down to us that it could not be opened as we had asked, because it was sandbagged to the top.'

Desultory shelling continued at Wanping for the next day and a half, and for a short time the fate of China and Japan hung in the huge vegetable basket which unceremoniously hoisted negotiators from each side over the wall into the besieged town. They agreed a cease-fire, but neither side was ready to forget the incident.

Japanese reinforcements were sent from Tianjin, while the Chinese government ordered more divisions to move north by rail to the area. What was at stake was not the kidnapping of a sex-starved Japanese soldier but the political control of the whole of northeast China. This was confirmed in the terms of a truce negotiated on 11 July, after twenty hours of strenuous talks between the Japanese garrison command and General Song Zheyuan, commander of the Chinese Twenty-Ninth Army. The Japanese demanded that Song withdraw his troops from all strategic military centres in north China, punish the men 'responsible' for the Marco Polo bridge incident, eliminate anti-Japanese societies in north China and make a strong stand against Communism.

These last two demands made clear that the Japanese command saw the Marco Polo bridge incident as an opportunity to improve its position in the whole of north China.

In Tokyo the Japanese cabinet accused the Chinese of insincerity, alleging that they had planned the incident. The Chinese should urgently apologize for their 'lawless actions and manifestations of antagonism and opposition to Japan' and guarantee against any recurrence. Prime Minister Konoye told journalists: 'China's anti-Japanese attitude ... has become markedly serious of late, and in order to make China reflect upon her attitude, Japan has now decided to despatch troops of due numerical strength ... not in despair of the situation ... but with intent to call for grave reflection on the part of China.'

In fact neither the cabinet nor the War Office really wanted the incident to escalate into war, and General Sugiyama, the War Minister, was not initially allowed to send reinforcements from Japan. But the reluctance of the most senior army commanders, like Ishihara Kanji, now promoted to general, to be drawn into a military expansion in China was outweighed by the enthusiasm of their juniors, typified by the firebrand Colonel Muto who was in charge of army strategy.

But the Chinese central government of Jiang Jieshi also now put demands on the table, calling on Tokyo to acknowledge responsibility for the Marco Polo bridge incident, to apologize for it and to give compensation as well as a promise that such things would not recur. At the same time Jiang ordered General Song not to accept any Japanese demands and not to withdraw his Twenty-Ninth Army, but rather to make 'all sacrifices necessary' to repel the Japanese.

But Song, occupying both military and civilian posts on the complex borderline of Japanese influence in north China as it had built up in the 1930s, felt uncomfortably squeezed from both sides. Reinforcements from the south were inhibited by earlier international agreement. His discomfiture ended when Jiang ordered him to pull back to Baoding, farther down the railway line towards Wuhan.

The cease-fire was ignored all round, and fighting continued spasmodically as new Japanese troops poured in from Tianjin. The Twenty-Ninthers were reputed to be the fiercest Japan-haters in north China, having fought along the Great Wall during the earlier Japanese drive in Manchuria. When the 'old China hands' in the Beijing foreign community went out to the golf course at Babaoshan to find the fire-eating Chinese Thirty-Seventh Division digging itself in on the fairways and greens, they had to admit that this time the fighting was serious.

By 16 July the Japanese had concentrated such force in the Beijing–Tianjin area that Jiang could not procrastinate any longer without losing credibility as a national leader. He issued his famous Guling Declaration proclaiming China's territorial integrity and her sovereign rights as a nation.

China would not allow any restrictions to be placed on the positions held by the Twenty-Ninth Army outside Beijing, and could not allow its local officers in the area to be removed. These were China's 'minimum demands', and they indicated that Jiang Jieshi was ready to commit himself to resisting Japan and would not now be able to retreat from a confrontation if the Japanese should press it. 'Although our country is militarily

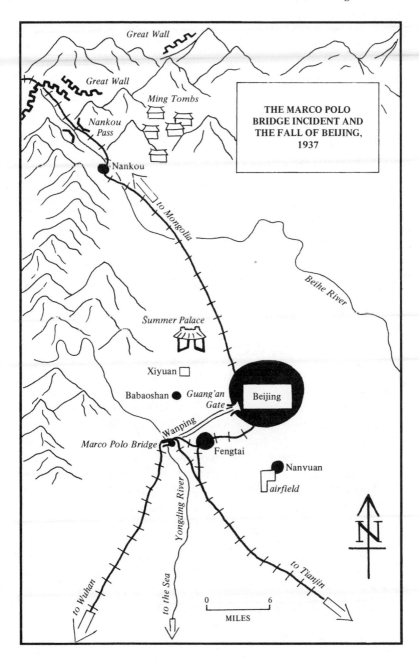

Great Wall

Great Wall

Ming Tombs

Nankou Pass

Nankou

to Mongolia

THE MARCO POLO
BRIDGE INCIDENT AND
THE FALL OF BEIJING,
1937

Beihe River

Summer Palace

Xiyuan

Babaoshan

Guang'an Gate

Beijing

Wanping

Marco Polo Bridge

Fengtai

Nanvuan airfield

Yongding River

to Wuhan

to the Sea

to Tianjin

N

0   6
MILES

weak,' Jiang declared, 'if the time has come where we have reached the last limit of our forbearance, then there is only one thing to do, and that is to throw the last ounce of the energy of our nation into a struggle for national existence.'

The Lugouqiao incident was not a sudden and accidental development, Jiang said. The Japanese demands would allow foreign armies a free run of Chinese soil, while Chinese troops were kept under restriction: 'Any country with the least self-respect could not possibly accept such humiliation....

'Weak nation, militarily, that we are, we cannot neglect to uphold the integrity of our race and ensure our national existence.... Once the war is begun there must be no looking backwards. We must fight to the bitter end.

'If we allow another inch of our soil to be lost, then we are guilty of an unpardonable offence against our race.... At this solemn moment, Japan will have to decide whether the Marco Polo bridge incident is to result in a major war between China and that country.'

Jiang thus threw down the gauntlet and waited to see whether Japan would pick it up. Outwardly he exuded confidence. 'You don't have to bother about the invasion of China by the Japanese,' he wrote to his son, 'for I am sure of finding a way to subdue them.'

Jiang was an extraordinary figure. He 'neither smokes nor drinks', a Chinese author wrote of him. 'He likes water. His personal habits are those of a self-disciplinarian, bordering on spartan asceticism.... Daily, winter or summer, he gets up at 5 or half past 5....' He always went to bed at ten and could not tolerate unpunctuality, dirt or sloppiness. At the same time there was a mystical side to his Methodist nature. The year before the war he had had a kind of vision while escaping from Chinese captors at Xi'an. At the worst moment, when his recapture and certain execution seemed imminent, he prayed to God and asked Him if He had indeed chosen him to lead China, for a sign to safety. When he opened his eyes he saw before him two white hares: they were the sign, and he followed them to safety.

General Song returned to the scene on 18 July to negotiate in

Tianjin with Lieutenant-General Katsuki Kiyoshi, commanding the China Garrison Army. Song was happy to offer the apology which Tokyo demanded. But his senior officers, doubtless fortified by the Generalissimo's speech from Guling, would not now go along with his conciliatory moves.

In the end it was control over telephone lines which led to the mutual commitment to full-scale war. Some Japanese soldiers got off the train at Langfang, midway between Beijing and Tianjin, and demanded the use of a military telephone at the Chinese barracks there. The Chinese asked them to leave their arms outside, but the Japanese pushed their way in and occupied the exchange.

This led to a full-scale Japanese attack on the barracks, followed on 25 July by a surprise Chinese attack on the Japanese signal unit repairing the Langfang telephone lines, and also on Japanese infantrymen protecting the station.

The final Japanese ultimatum was that Chinese forces should withdraw from Luguoqiao and its area within twenty-four hours. But it was impossible even for Song to accept this, and he cabled the central government in Nanjing that he intended to reject it. 'The continued despatch of Japanese troops,' he explained next day, 'and repeated provocations, have left no alternative to the Chinese troops but to defend the country to the best of their ability and resources.'

The Japanese demand was ignored. That sunset a Japanese battalion returning from Fengtai to Beijing, under routine arrangements agreed earlier with the Chinese authorities, was attacked as it passed through the Guang'an gate. Some Chinese felt that this arrival of 300 Japanese troops at the gates of Beijing was an attack, although the 'invaders' had previously come and gone as they pleased, and were technically within their rights by international law.

The Chinese guard, responding to the new mood, opened the main gate to the Japanese but then immediately closed it behind them, trapping them in the narrow area between the outer and inner gates. The Chinese then fired trench mortars at them and lobbed hand grenades from the walls. In the end, the Chinese accepted a temporary truce, allowing the surviving Japanese to march with their arms into their legation quarter to join the Japanese legation guard.

Now there was no turning back. General Song ignored the Japanese ultimatum, commanded his Twenty-Ninth Army to fight Japan and begged Jiang Jieshi for reinforcements. General Katsuki declared to the world at large that the Japanese now reserved 'freedom of action' in dealing with the Chinese Twenty-Ninth Army. Everyone knew what he meant. It was the nearest the Japanese ever came to a formal declaration of war.

For all his brave words, however, General Song's situation was untenable. To face the division and three brigades which Japan now threw, under strong aerial support, into a general attack on Beijing, he had in the Beijing area only 10,000 troops with modest weapons, only a few pieces of light artillery and no tanks or aeroplanes at all.

The Chinese Twenty-Ninth Army had not only been prevented from erecting permanent defences of any kind, as the last-minute resort to the golf course underlined, but were apparently told by Song to dismantle what street barricades had been put up. The Chinese, engaged until now in policing duties, were scattered in small groups and could not use the railways to concentrate themselves, since these were now controlled by Japan. Reinforcements promised from the south never materialized.

The Japanese columns marched out of Fengtai on 28 July and encircled Beijing by sunset. The foreign diplomats hid behind their sandbags in the legation quarter, telegraphing their capitals that the war had started. Song's main forces were in suburban barracks, at Nanyuan to the south of the main walls, and Xiyuan to the west. Both places were death traps and both were immediate targets for the Japanese.

The second was hastily evacuated, but at Nanyuan, despite their complete exposure to attack from the air and their lack of anything more effective than trench mortars and machine-guns, the Chinese held to their positions all day.

About 5000 of them died, including two divisional commanders, and only a handful of the raw Beijing student volunteers in the Hebei militia survived their baptism of fire. Without a single anti-aircraft gun, the Chinese futilely defended at Nanyuan an airfield with no planes.

Meanwhile an extraordinary drama began to unfold at Tong-xian, the old terminus of the Grand Canal a dozen miles east of Beijing. This was the administrative capital of east Hebei, which was in fact controlled by Japan.

Tongxian itself, however, was now a part of the 'demilitarized zone', and, because it was so close to Chinese territory, a small garrison of 800 men of the Chinese Twenty-Ninth Army was allowed to remain: if Japan had turned them out, it might have provoked an incident, and so they were tolerated. The Chinese equally tolerated what they regarded as the illegal stationing of a small number of Japanese soldiers at Tongxian, so each side was pretending that the other did not exist.

But once the Japanese decided to move openly against Beijing, their 500 men in Tongxian were needed to join the advance, and the 800 Chinese Twenty-Ninthers had to evacuate or be disarmed. The Japanese commander on 27 July gave them three hours to lay down their arms.

The Chinese flatly refused, and a contemporary Japanese account noted that they displayed 'an ugly mood' and an 'insolent attitude' when told to withdraw or disarm. It also admitted that 'some resistance was offered' to the disarming – which in other accounts became eight hours of fighting in which the Japanese artillery played havoc with the Chinese contingent equipped only with light arms.

The Chinese version had it that the Japanese commander, not content with disarming the Twenty-Ninthers, 'herded them into a corner of the city walls – and machine-gunned the defenceless men until not one of them was left alive'.

The Japanese-recruited Chinese militiamen, whom the Japanese expected to take over routine garrison duties in the city when the Japanese army marched to the main theatre of war, were on the spot. The experience of seeing their own compatriots murdered in cold blood inspired them to revenge two nights later.

The Japanese now set off for battle in Beijing leaving only a skeleton garrison in Tongxian. But at three o'clock on the

morning of 29 July the local Chinese militiamen, encouraged by
false reports of a Chinese victory in Beijing, mutinied against
their Japanese superiors.

More than 2000 Chinese turned on their former masters in a
night of shooting and pillaging which quickly became as notorious throughout Japan as the Black Hole of Calcutta had been in
Britain. Two in three of the 380 Japanese in the city were killed,
and the Japanese were shocked by the horror and cruelty of the
attack. All Japanese buildings were sacked and burned, and the
day became known in Japan as the Black Day of the 'Tongchou
(Tongxian) massacre', the work of 'monsters and animals' in a
mutiny comparable to those of Cawnpore and Delhi against
Britain. The Japanese cabinet described it as 'an act which
neither God nor man can forgive'.

But in northern China the event highlighted the very deep
resentment which local people had against the puppet regime of
the Japanese, strongly associated in the minds of Chinese
residents with smuggling and dope-peddling.

The *Asahi* correspondent who reached the city a few days
later reported that: 'The bodies had been so mutilated that
there was no telling men from women.' One of the survivors
told the *Yomiuri Shimbun*:

I chanced to see a man being dragged along by a wire. At that time I
thought that he was only bound with it, but now I know that it was
pierced through his nose. After all that I have witnessed, I cannot help
having a deep hatred for the Chinese soldiers who were indeed devils
incarnate.

A girl who was the only Japanese to be employed in a local
bank woke up that night to find the Chinese employees who
lived in the same quarters evacuating. 'They had been kind to
me before, but now they refused to take me with them.' She had
the presence of mind to hide in a dustbin in the backyard, and
after forty-eight hours was rescued by Japanese soldiers.

The rising at Tongxian may not have been entirely spon-
taneous. Lin Yutang, in his historical novel *Vigil of a Nation*,
remarked that the Chinese resistance leaders in Tianjin 'had

knowledge of a mutiny planned to take place at Tongxian the following day among the east Hebei troops, which had been equipped and trained by the Japanese'. Certainly the Tongxian story was to be re-enacted in Tianjin, only with less success.

It was said that General Song in Beijing had been promised reinforcements by Jiang Jieshi if he could only hold out for forty-eight hours. But after a day of fighting he lamely left Beijing 'with tears in his eyes', handing over his civilian authority to a pro-Japanese successor.

One of the mysterious factors in this Japanese victory was the role of the commander of the Thirty-Eighth Division of the Twenty-Ninth Army in Beijing, General Zhang Zhizhong. Zhang was an able soldier who had spiritedly fought the Japanese control on the Great Wall in 1933, but in the twilight years of peace under Japanese control in northeast China he appeared to have been seduced by Japanese bribery.

While Beijing was still being fought over, General Zhang surrendered it to the Japanese, out of a desire, he claimed, to save it from destruction. He was then damned by Chinese opinion as a traitor, although it has been claimed that he was deliberately courting the Japanese under superior orders, in order to gain their confidence for the benefit of the Chinese High Command. In any case, General Song's retreat gave Zhang little choice.

Later his own division denounced Zhang's actions and elected a new commander rather than go over to the Japanese. The story went that General Zhang had to hide in the German quarter in Beijing for a while, but then slipped out on a bicycle and gave himself up to the Chinese army outside the walls. Some people expected that he would be shot, or reduced to the ranks, but he vowed to make amends for his treachery in Beijing, and was eventually decorated for his part in subsequent military victories over the Japanese.

General Zhang's division gave the Japanese a tough time at the Tongxian airfield on the day Beijing fell, destroying many Japanese aircraft, but nothing could prevent the rout of the Chinese forces as a whole in the Beijing–Tianjin area.

The Japanese now executed in Beijing their favourite tactic, to be repeated time and again in north China, of surrounding the Chinese on three sides and laying an ambush along the apparent way out on the fourth. The false escape route here was the road to the southernmost gateway out of the capital, Yongdingmen.

Shattered by the day's bombardments and paralysed by the absence of any further orders from their headquarters, the Chinese soldiers at last abandoned Nanyuan. But their cars and trucks were caught in enfilading fire from machine-gun nests on either side of the road. The Japanese lost only about fifty men at Nanyuan, but in just one place on the Yondingmen road there were as many as 800 Chinese bodies piled up together. Jacques Guillermaz, who was there afterwards, recalls that he could not walk on the road without stepping on corpses. 'No veteran of the world war,' a British spectator commented, 'could remember such a slaughter.'

The invaders had overwhelmingly superior equipment. Each Japanese division had over 600 machine-guns, twenty-four 37 mm artillery guns, twenty-four 70 mm howitzers, twenty-four 70 mm field guns and the same number of anti-tank guns, as well as a dozen 105 mm howitzers and four anti-aircraft guns.

This impressive armament, contrasting with the meagre weapons of the Chinese, encouraged the Japanese commanders to rely on an initial massive demonstration of materiel to break the heart of the defenders at the outset. In these opening stages of the war Japan's generals modelled their strategy on that of the Germans at Sedan, dreaming of a Cannae or a 'three months' war won by rapid encirclement of China's main forces.

The risk was, of course, that deep Japanese penetration of China's huge land mass might disperse the main Chinese forces without conquering them. Japan could win the great fixed battle, but final political success might still elude her. China's two assets were superior numbers and extensive space, and if her leaders could so utilize these as to deny the Japanese a satisfactory political exploitation of their military victories then Japan would fail to win the war. General Hayashi, for one, warned his colleagues of this danger and doubted whether a quick victory was going to be easy.

While the Japanese were taking over the ancient Chinese capital of Beijing, Generalissimo Jiang Jieshi reaffirmed the conditions he had laid down in.his Guling Declaration for the settlement of the Marco Polo bridge affair. They were 'unalterable'. It was out of the question that China could make any concessions at this critical juncture, and Jiang pledged to lead 'the masses of the nation ... into a struggle to the last'. To which General Katsuki's reply was that if Jiang's troops came north of the Yellow River, contrary to the previous understanding, 'we shall have to smash the Central Government'.

The Twenty-Ninthers thus had to take the brunt of the Japanese attack alone, and their bodies, clad in their grey Mongol uniforms, were seen floating in ever larger numbers down the rivers to the Yellow Sea. The remnants of their main force were withdrawn to the right bank of the Yongding River, leaving only the Thirty-Eighth Division to defend Tianjin.

The Japanese had already revealed their contempt for Chinese intellectual opinion by bombing the famous Nankai University at Tianjin (*alma mater* of Zhou Enlai, among others) to rubble – although no Chinese soldiers were there at all.

Briefly the heroic Twenty-Ninthers, joined by the rebellious 'puppet' Chinese militia, captured one of Tianjin's railway stations, came very close to storming the second one, and reached within 200 yards of the military airfield from which the Japanese had been carrying out their raids.

After a day of reckless fighting, however, the Twenty-Ninthers were suddenly ordered to withdraw south, and the Chinese militia, lacking arms or support, had to scatter or surrender. The Japanese had at least been put on notice that, even in the two 'safe' areas of Tongxian and Tianjin, and even by the very groups of Chinese which they had taken under their benevolent protection, they were going to be resisted resolutely and with determination.

Three days after the capture and looting of Tianjin, a young Japanese soldier began his journey from home to the China front. He was General Itagaki's bodyguard, and his diary entry for 2 August ran: 'For long have I waited, and looked forward to the time when a man may prove himself before the world.

Such a day has come at last. I bear the fate of my country on my two shoulders. The place I go to is north China, dark under wind and cloud – a land thousands of miles wide. Fighting and again fighting. Although I do not expect to come back alive, yet when I think of my parents, of my wife who will be left after my death, I cannot help feeling sad at heart. . . .'

On 7 August, after a week of mopping up the outlying districts, the Japanese army made its official entry into Beijing, coming in from the southwest for a grand parade along the Avenue of Everlasting Peace. About a thousand Japanese civilians applauded this belated retribution for the insult of Kublai Khan who, seven centuries earlier, had tried to invade Japan. Now the island people marched as conquerors into the Great Khan's old capital. The War Minister, General Sugiyama, told Emperor Hirohito that the war would be over in a month. 'Please kill Chinese people quickly, and then come home again,' was the moving sentence which the little son of one of the Japanese soldiers wrote to his father in China.

About this time a western war correspondent asked a group of Japanese soldiers on a train near Beijing why they thought they were there, and what the war was all about.

'We Japanese are peaceful,' answered one pink-cheeked youngster with jutting teeth, 'but the Chinese keep making trouble for us.'

'The dirty Chinese murdered our people in Tongxian,' said another.

'We came to save China from the Communists,' a third explained.

A peasant boy said that he had been called up to serve the emperor. 'I am not clear,' he admitted, 'about the cause of the war, but Jiang Jieshi is always hurting our people, and we are fighting him, not the good Chinese.'

Finally, the eldest in the group, a sergeant who spoke good Chinese and had been an old campaigner in Manchuria, offered his opinion. 'We came to teach the Chinese a lesson,' he said. 'They were getting too bold.'

One of the thousands of Chinese unexpectedly trapped by the Japanese in Beijing was Madame Deng Yingchao, the wife of the Communist leader and later Premier, Zhou Enlai. She had gone secretly to an isolated temple in the Western Hills near the capital to recuperate from the tuberculosis which she had developed during the Red Army's famous Long March in 1935.

The dry northern spring air, together with good food and rest, had cured her. The first she knew of the outbreak of war was the approach of Japanese soldiers to her temple, whereupon she fled through their lines in the dress of a peasant woman and came to Beijing.

Here Edgar Snow, the American journalist who had met the Communist leaders in Yan'an the year before, offered to accompany her on the train to Tianjin, whence she would be able to travel safely back to the Communist base in the northwest. But it would be better for her to pretend to be Snow's servant.

'Yingchao,' Snow recorded, 'arrived at Qianmen station, looking the complete *amah*; her bobbed hair miraculously disappeared. I saw her safely deep into a car, whence she remained lost to view behind the quite unbelievable mass of legs, heads and elbows which squeezed in after her. Well, there was some safety in numbers, I tritely reflected....

'It was dark when the train arrived in Tianjin. I waited for Deng Yingchao and we had a bad moment passing through the Japanese guards at the station. Or rather I had. Visibly, at least, Yingchao was not at all perturbed. She dropped her jaw in an imbecile attitude and grinned happily at the sullen Japanese sentries who, after giving her a cursory examination and spilling the contents of her straw luggage on the floor, made grunting noises indicating that we could proceed.'

Not everyone was so lucky. As Snow and Deng walked down the platform station they saw a dozen young Chinese girls and boys yanked out of line and hurried off to waiting military trucks. Their soft white hands, contrasting too suspiciously with their peasant clothes, had aroused Japanese suspicions.

How did the conquerors behave? A neutral Red Cross worker operating in the area around Beijing immediately after its capture found that the Japanese troops made a good impression. The worst offences were petty theft and occasional meanness.

Most of them 'were very young, obviously fresh from training school, and it was hard to resent as individuals these hordes of grinning children helping themselves to the benefits of the countryside and only incidentally making life miserable for the Chinese they encountered'.

This observer once drove past the Summer Palace in Beijing, which the Japanese had taken for their headquarters: 'We found every brook and pond full of naked little Japs scrubbing themselves and rinsing their underwear. They were delighted to still be alive and many would laugh and wave at the Red Cross trucks as we passed.'

Once a luxury hotel in the Western Hills outside Beijing was visited by a Japanese patrol, which lined up all the women and after some deliberation selected the wife of a Chinese doctor, marching her upstairs at the point of bayonet. The others feared the worst, but an hour or two later she came down trembling with fury – but intact. The soldiers had only wanted her to scrub their backs in the bath, a duty which any Japanese woman would expect to perform, however shocking to a Chinese.

In the city itself, 'the most serious trespasses were in shopping at Chinese stores and paying for their purchases only what fraction of the price they chose to give. Otherwise, as far as could be seen, their amusements were harmless. They loved to drive about the city in their trucks and motor cycles and like children they drove too fast, in order to show importance.'

Indeed, what appalled this observer was not the brutality of the invader but rather the callous neglect of Chinese for Chinese. He had to go through the battlefield of Nanyuan, just south of Beijing, to tend the remaining wounded. In one cornfield he came across a forgotten Chinese soldier, only four-teen or fifteen years old, who had been sitting there for a month with two wounds, both fatally enlarged by rotting. 'His left arm was shattered below the elbow and he had some sort of hole through his body. The damaged arm was enormously bloated and dangled before him like a misplaced thigh; around it was clumsily knotted a filthy black rag which nevertheless failed to cover the expanse of putrescent grey flesh beneath.'

He had been squatting in this field with no shelter during four weeks of rain, and because of his injuries could not move by himself. For food he had relied on the irregular mercies of neighbouring farmers. Caught like an animal in a trap, this boy could only crouch and wait, 'feeling the decay spread up through his body, swallowing him up by inches,' until the Red Cross took him to the city.

The worst case was a soldier whose flesh had turned a 'greenish mustard colour' and who was covered with thousands of flies and his leg with maggots. 'It was shocking that we should have been able to find these men within a dozen miles of Beijing....'

Yet the local farmers were without anger, and when war was discussed their faces showed only resignation. 'They plainly considered their destiny was to till their own few square feet of soil, whoever ran the nation.... Their cheerful fortitude was a clue to the country's immense resources of resistance. Still the war had flowed over them for weeks and made victims of them, and they were not yet part of it.'

2

Shanghai Falls

While these violent events were taking place in and around Beijing, tension rose in Shanghai, the great central coastal city and focus for foreign interests in China. All the western powers maintained forces and concessions there, as did Japan. Inevitably there were sparks between the Chinese and Japanese forces stationed in Shanghai, any one of which could have been used by either side to spread the fighting to the Yangzi delta.

At one time it looked as if the sexual needs of the Japanese stationed far from home might also play a role in Shanghai. The Japanese navy, jealous, it was said, of the glory being won by the Japanese army in north China, began to raise the case of a missing marine, only to find that he, too, had merely been visiting an off-limits brothel.

The decisive incident came on the evening of 9 August, when a Japanese naval lieutenant, Oyama Isao, with a rating beside him at the wheel, was motoring past the Hongqiao aerodrome to the west of Shanghai. A group of Chinese militiamen objected to what looked like a Japanese inspection of Chinese military facilities, and ordered them to move on. The Japanese stoutly refused, and so the Chinese shot them both.

According to the Chinese version, the two Japanese, together with a Chinese soldier, died 'in a scuffle caused by attempted forcible entry into the aerodrome', and the body of the dead Chinese was produced to back up the story. Not to be outdone, the Japanese displayed the mutilated corpse of their soldier to show that he had been mistreated.

Both sides protested furiously. The Mayor of Shanghai reminded the Japanese naval command that it had already been 'warned' against permitting its men to spy on Chinese positions, and so the airfield shooting should bring home that the warning was serious.

The Japanese did not immediately force the issue. Rear-Admiral Hasegawa, commanding the twelve Japanese warships lying in the stream of the Huangpu River, had only about 7000 sailors on hand. He agreed with the Japanese Consul-General that the matter should be pursued through diplomatic channels. But then the Chinese militia started putting up sandbag fortifications at three road junctions near the aerodrome, and this so infuriated Hasegawa that he put his ships at the ready, guns stripped for action, and radioed for reinforcements from the Third Battle Fleet.

The Chinese regarded Lieutenant Oyama and his companion as having deliberately sacrificed their lives to create a 'pretext' for Japanese action, and there was much speculation as to why the Japanese shifted the fighting from north China to Shanghai and the Yangzi delta.

It was surmised that the hot-blooded Young Officers, the extremists in the Japanese camp, wanted to destroy Nanjing, Jiang Jieshi's capital farther up the Yangzi from Shanghai, as the centre of the Chinese government. The military high command may have believed that a threat to Nanjing would settle the situation in the north. Yet another consideration may have been the knowledge that a strike against Shanghai would directly threaten western interests in China, and thus satisfy the ideological instincts of Japan's war leaders. But in fact it was the Japanese navy, not the Young Officers' clique, which set off the fighting in Shanghai, and by any reasonable yardstick the Japanese self-interest at this stage would surely have lain in keeping the western powers neutral. Japan had only a small force of bluejackets in Shanghai, appropriate for their modest naval garrison role, while in the hinterland of the Yangzi valley they faced the full power of more than a million men in the Chinese army.

Not only did Generalissimo Jiang Jieshi have his best forces and military equipment laid out along the Yangzi, but the tiny new air force, built and trained by the Americans and Italians

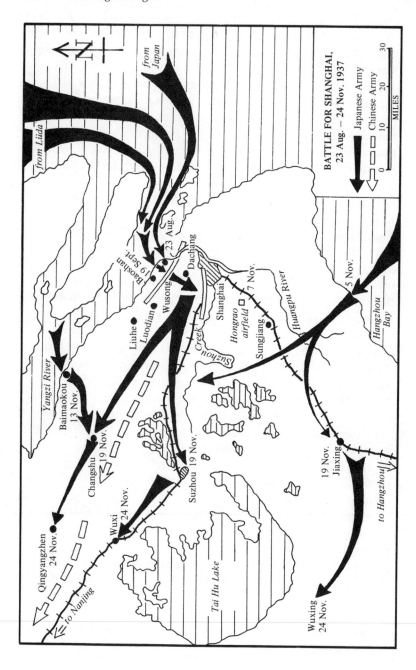

BATTLE FOR SHANGHAI,
23 Aug. – 24 Nov. 1937

Japanese Army
Chinese Army

MILES
0   10   20   30

and under the direct patronage of Madame Jiang, was also there. A Japanese strike at Shanghai could only be welcomed by China since it would strengthen the chance that the Americans and the other western states would be dragged into the fight on China's side.

The most trusted neutral observer – H. G. Woodhead, editor of *China Weekly Review* and *Oriental Affairs* – said categorically at the time that, whatever may have happened in north China, 'the charge that Japan desired or provoked hostilities in Shanghai is absolutely unsubstantiated and is on the face of it extremely improbable'.

The Japanese actions in Shanghai suggested rather that they wanted to avoid a fight. They evacuated their nationals from all the Yangzi ports, and they made no issue of the Hongqiao airport incident. It was perhaps tactless of them to send their fleet and land reinforcements after 11 August, but it could not be seriously argued that another 1000 bluejackets proved Japan's intention to attack Chinese territory. After these reinforcements were landed, the Japanese troops still amounted to a mere 3500 to 4000. They had a community of almost 25,000 to defend, and they would have been mad to seek an offensive against 25,000 of China's best German-trained soldiers.

It appears that they genuinely hoped to be left in peace in Shanghai while taking the offensive in north China, and that hostilities could be 'localized'. It was the Chinese government which decided to elevate the Shanghai tension into becoming a part of the nation-wide war.

Jiang rushed four divisions of his crack First Army Corps, together with an artillery brigade, into Shanghai the moment that fighting broke out. Once Japan was provoked, she would be committed to a debilitating fight in the Generalissimo's own backyard.

To engage so precipitately in Shanghai was a military and political blunder by the Japanese. It was in this region that the waverers among China's ruling class were to be found, men who had betrayed China's national revolution in the past in collaboration with foreign capitalists. Yet Japan set out to smash the interests of this group so decisively as to weaken their influence

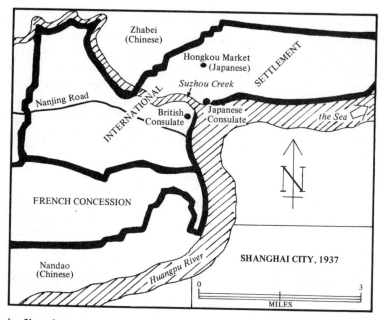

Zhabei
(Chinese)

Hongkou Market
● (Japanese)

Suzhou Creek

SETTLEMENT

Nanjing Road

INTERNATIONAL

British
Consulate

Japanese
Consulate

the Sea

N

FRENCH CONCESSION

Nandao
(Chinese)

Huangpu River

SHANGHAI CITY, 1937

0   3

MILES

in Jiang's government and take away their incentive to make a compromise at the expense of the north.

Some commentators even suggested that Japan would have done better to withdraw from Shanghai altogether, at least for the time being. She could then have concentrated her efforts on thoroughly cleaning up the north, after which she could have negotiated the centre and south of China in her own time. Probably in the end the Generalissimo's gamble was well judged: the Japanese military were too proud to ignore the arrival of his ace troops in the vicinity of Shanghai.

By 12 August there were 50,000 regular Chinese soldiers in the suburbs of Shanghai, in what had until then been the 'unarmed zone', matching the reinforcement of the 5000-strong Japanese garrison at Hongkou, at the northern end of the International Settlement in Shanghai. A special naval landing party brought the Japanese forces up to 9000, all bluejackets and marines.

Japanese guns opened up from Admiral Hasegawa's warships early on Friday, 13 August, and at nine in the morning the

Chinese were machine-gunning the Japanese landing force from Zhabei, one of the Chinese quarters of Shanghai. The Japanese marines tried to land in barges below their consulate, and then sought to link up with the Japanese sector inside the International Settlement by marching through the other sectors.

General Xing Zhennan, commanding the Chinese troops in Zhabei, declared that if they attempted such a march he would take 'immediate measures to stop it'. Both the British- and American-defended sectors of Shanghai's International Settlement were thus endangered, and Anglo-American warships began to converge on the city from the East China Sea.

Meanwhile the Chinese navy and air force moved into action. On 14 August Chinese aeroplanes attacked two crack Japanese naval air squadrons on the ground. The Chinese navy busied itself with blocking channels, laying mines and trying to put Japanese ships out of action.

But so notorious did the Chinese inability to hit the Japanese flagship *Izumo* become that, when one foreign resident nervously asked her husband where she should put her jewels for safety now that war had broken out, he said facetiously, 'aboard the *Izumo*!'

On Saturday afternoon foreign residents sipping cocktails in the Palace Hotel bar saw two Chinese aeroplanes coming towards them high over the river. Someone remarked that they 'were probably going to take another shot at the *Izumo*'. The two planes circled under the clouds and then dropped four bombs, two on a crowded crossroads, one on the roof of the Palace Hotel and another on the neighbouring Cathay Hotel. Over a thousand people were killed, and Vicki Baum based a novel – *Nanking Road* – on the incident.

A few minutes later on this Bloody Saturday, as it came to be known, another Chinese aircraft dropped two more bombs in the crowded square of the International Settlement in front of the Great World Amusement Palace, again killing more than a thousand people.

Why had these Chinese planes attacked their own city? Madame Jiang Jieshi explained that they had been hit by Japanese anti-aircraft shells on their way home from a bombing raid, and the mechanism of the bombing racks had been loosened. She expressed her sorrow for the 'tragic accident'. Cynical observers suggested that the bombs were meant to draw the West into the war, but there was no proof of this.

The Chinese air force, using obsolete Russian, American and Italian aircraft, was indeed inexperienced in these early operations. It did not inspire confidence in Shanghai that August. But several of the Chinese pilots made names for themselves. One, Yan Haiwen, parachuted by error into Japanese lines after he had been shot down, and killed several Japanese soldiers before committing suicide himself. An admiring Japanese put up a tablet in his memory, inscribed: 'Tomb of a Chinese air force warrior.'

On 15 August the Japanese decided to raise the stakes by ordering a so-called Shanghai Expeditionary Army, built around the Third and Eleventh Divisions, under General Matsui Iwane, to assist in the protection of the Japanese naval units. This key reinforcement landed at the mouth of the River Huangpu on the 23rd. On the day the new army sailed, the Japanese air force began the systematic bombing of Nanjing, and from then onwards it kept up a continuous bombing of a wide range of Chinese cities.

General Matsui had ten divisions at his disposal in Shanghai, together with the marine corps, representing a force of about 300,000 men. They were supported by more than 300 guns, 200 tanks, 200 aircraft and scores of warships, to make a combat and firing strength unparalleled at the time.

On the Chinese side there were about fifty divisions embracing 700,000 men, but this enormous force was spread over a front on which there was no truly defensible strategic point.

So fierce was the Japanese fire that the Chinese artillery could not operate in daylight, having to bombard blindly at night, when the targets could not be properly located. Casualties on the Chinese side reached 'a rate of thousands per hour', in the phrase of one officer.

In almost hopeless circumstances, the Chinese under General Feng Yuxiang fought back in Shanghai with surprising fierceness. The Japanese were checked for a while in their own backyard of Hongkou by troops streaming out from the Chinese suburb of Zhabei. But they proceeded to extend operations over a much longer front along the river, stretching all of the twenty miles to the mouth. China could do little as Japan poured more and more of her military power into the Shanghai arena.

'It was no longer,' an eyewitness said, 'a war between armies, but between races. With mounting fury the two giants, like two men who have started a boxing match and who suddenly find themselves convulsed with hate, sprang at each other's throat in a tussle in which the only prize was death.' A Chinese military historian described it as 'the bloodiest battle ... since Verdun'.

Despite the Japanese footing along the entire right bank of the Huangpu and its solid wall of warships backed up by rows of artillery, hundreds of charging tanks and swollen divisions of infantry, the Chinese in the end held out for two months.

'Men stood before tanks', another observer noted. The damage to the city and its protecting armies was indescribable, with indiscriminate bombing by the grey Japanese planes, the unceasing roar of guns and the incessant human slaughter. It was said at the time that never had so much destruction been concentrated within so narrow a space. Perhaps ten Chinese fell for every Japanese.

An American officer went out to the Chinese lines during the fighting to observe the soldiers in their thin cotton uniforms of horizon blue or olive drab, their legs mostly wrapped in khaki, and with rifles of various makes, mainly German, Russian or Czechoslovakian.

'What are you fighting for?' he asked one soldier in the trenches.

'National salvation', the Chinese soldier replied. Asked to elaborate, he thought for a while, and then explained: 'The enemy want to take our homes. If we work together, we can defeat him.'

One Chinese sergeant who was captured during this fighting claimed after his subsequent escape that he had personally seen Japanese soldiers killing the plumper peasants, cutting off their flesh and cooking it to eat as they camped. It was rumoured that they belonged to a particular Japanese 'tribe' accustomed to cannibalism. The story spoke more for the local image of the invader than for his reality.

By the 20th there were about fifteen Chinese divisions in the field, and from then onwards another one or two arrived each day to bring the total at the end up to a staggering eighty-five divisions. Everyone was surprised by the spirit of resistance of the Chinese. In the face of point-blank gunfire from the ships in midstream they drove the Japanese infantry back through the International Settlement almost into the river.

The Japanese found it almost impossible to outmanoeuvre the Chinese right flank, which pivoted on the intervening neutral International Settlement area. They had to land their reinforcements to the north, along the twenty-mile front between Wusong and Liuhe on the Yangzi River.

Yet they took nearly a week to put a landing party ashore under naval and air protection to pass the extremely hasty defence works which the Chinese threw up, and then, having established this new flank at Liuhe and assembled a large force there, the Japanese were not able to make much progress for several weeks. Only after two months of steady naval and artillery shelling did they succeed in making a final breakthrough.

Meanwhile the Chinese hopes that the Americans and Europeans would be fatally provoked were dashed. Not that there was any shortage of incidents. On 20 August an anti-aircraft shell dropped and exploded on the American flagship *Augusta*, killing an American sailor and wounding many others. A few days later the British Ambassador to China was driving to Shanghai for a conference when Japanese aircraft fired on his car, which flew the Union Jack, about forty miles west of Shanghai. The ambassador was hit in the spine. Four days after that an American liner was bombed by Chinese aircraft mistaking it for an enemy transport.

But neither China nor Japan formally declared war. The Chinese government refrained because such a declaration would force the Americans to invoke their Neutrality Act, which would hurt China more than it would hurt Japan. As for the Japanese, they did not wish to appear to be violating the Paris Pact outlawing war.

The Japanese Premier, Prince Konoye, declared on 20 August that until the developments in Shanghai Japan had sought to contain the fighting, but now the campaign against the Chinese would have to be prosecuted with the utmost rigour in order to force the Chinese government to co-operate economically and politically with Japan. It would have to be a fight to the finish without any third-party intervention.

On the night of the 22nd the Japanese Shanghai Expeditionary Army landed at the mouth of the Huangpu River and struck southwards towards the city of Shanghai. The Chinese tried to counter-attack, but found the concentrated fire of the new Japanese forces too much for them. In the first week of September the Japanese took Wusong and Baoshan, defended by the Yue Regiment against overwhelming odds until its last man fell (today, as if in penance, Japan is building a new steel mill for China at Baoshan).

In Tokyo Prince Konoye obtained the Emperor's endorsement for a tough new policy in north China, and the Prime Minister told the Diet on 5 September that Japan's goal was to 'administer a thorough-going blow to the Chinese army so that it may completely lose its will to fight'.

By the middle of September, when Generalissimo Jiang took over direct command of the Chinese defence, the Japanese had thrown about 100,000 men in the Shanghai area into the positional warfare being waged along a line running southeast from Luodian. They broke through this line on 30 September, forcing the Chinese defenders to retire to new positions. The two sides launched a simultaneous attack and counter-attack on 19 October with consequent huge losses on both sides.

Madame Jiang Jieshi almost became a victim of the war at this point when her car was shelled and machine-gunned on the road from Nanjing. The Japanese did not score a direct hit, but in the course of evading the attack the car overturned while going at speed on a corner on the badly damaged highway, and the first lady of China was found unconscious with a broken rib lying in a puddle of mud. The rib eventually healed but a displaced ligament gave her agonizing headaches for the next five years.

In the last part of October the Japanese attack was concentrated on Dachang, a little market town six miles northwest of Shanghai popularly known as 'chicken village', because in normal times it was the city's chief source of poultry. Japan concentrated a huge force which included 700 artillery pieces and 150 bombers to reduce this sector of the Chinese line to rubble, and on 24 October every one of these 150 bombers concentrated on the village itself in what one observer called 'the most savage aerial bombardment in military history, not excelled by any that had occurred in Spain'.

Within two or three days the Japanese forced their way into the 'chicken village', although Evans Carlson, the US assistant naval attaché who saw the battle, noted that the creeping barrage which the Japanese artillery laid down there in front of its own infantry was usually as far as 600 to 700 yards ahead of them, allowing time for the Chinese defenders to re-man their positions.

The loss of this strategic village of Dachang threatened the Chinese flank, so that the defenders had to withdraw to the south bank of the Suzhou Creek. To cover this retreat a 'Lone Battalion' of 800 men from the Chinese Eighty-Eighth Division held positions at the district of Zhabei, in the heart of Shanghai, for four days, from 27 to 31 October. These gallant heroes entrenched themselves in a reinforced-concrete warehouse owned by four commercial banks, surrounded by the eight-mile wall of flame of burning Zhabei, described by a western observer as 'surely one of the most spectacular conflagrations in world history'.

The leader of this Lone Battalion which undertook to die in its tracks rather than join the humiliating retreat was the Sichuanese General Sun Yuanliang, then only thirty-four. He knew his enemies at first hand. Ten years earlier he had attended the Tokyo Military Academy, before being expelled by the Japanese for taking too much interest in politics! The beauty of his Lone Battalion's stand at Zhabei was that the British defence zone lay directly behind it and in the line of fire, so that the Japanese could not launch a frontal attack without involving the British.

The British troops, for their part, remained in position in their sector to form a natural alley through which the Lone Battalion heroes could retreat when they wanted to. But for four days they stood their ground, fed by supplies brought by Chinese girl scouts across the no-man's-land during the night when the Japanese were asleep. One of the girls took a Chinese flag for them to fly.

The British officer in charge, General Telfer-Smollett, urged the Chinese command to bring the Lone Battalion out from Zhabei before international property was damaged. Madame Jiang was said to have commented: 'No, they must die that China may live.' But eventually the Generalissimo accepted the 'friendly' British advice and a night was fixed for the withdrawal of the Chinese survivors into the International Settlement. The Japanese trained machine-guns and searchlights down the Tibet Road, along which the Chinese would have to pass and at the end of which, next to the bridge, stood a British pill-box directly in the line of fire.

General Telfer-Smollett took cover behind the Bank of China godown to receive the Chinese personally as they sprinted to safety between the bursts of Japanese firing. The Chinese, it was claimed, lost only seven men.

'Some people will tell you,' W. H. Auden and Christopher Isherwood wrote afterwards, 'that the British troops in their pill-box, tired of being shot at, returned the Japanese fire and even put a machine-gun out of action. This is officially denied. Anyhow, the Japanese, in the darkness and confusion, could hardly be certain where the bullets were coming from.' By international agreement the Chinese soldiers were interned in the International Settlement until the end of the war.

While the heroes of Zhabei were holding up the Japanese advance into the centre of Shanghai, the main Chinese forces withdrew to avoid capture, crossing the bridges over the Suzhou Creek under cover of darkness, to escape the attention of Japanese pilots.

But in the morning there were still thousands of Chinese

civilians, mainly women and children, swarming over the roads and the single-track railway bridge crossing Suzhou Creek. One western observer noted that 'the opportunity for slaughter was too tempting to resist', since a Japanese pilot repeatedly flew over the bridges and machine-gunned the crowds of terrorized people.

Even so, the Chinese defence could have held out longer if it had not been negligent in relaxing the vigil on the shore of Hangzhou Bay, to the south of Shanghai, where on 5 November the Japanese landed their Tenth Army, under General Yanagawa Heisuke. This landing ended the battle for Shanghai. It began at five in the morning, and a total of about 30,000 Japanese were put ashore from transports.

Jiang Jieshi had changed the command of the local Chinese forces here twice in the course of the six weeks preceding the Japanese landing, and the Manchurian troops which had been assigned there were late in arriving. Japanese intelligence had discovered this interregnum and so the landing was unopposed. The Tenth Army quickly moved north, covering the twenty miles to the south bank of the Huangpu River in twenty-six hours. By the night of the 7th it had torn up the railway lines between Shanghai and Hangzhou, and on the 10th it made contact with the Japanese forces in Shanghai itself.

In the middle of all this the senior Japanese general in the field, General Matsui, was promoted. On the Chinese side, as the steady withdrawal began to tremble on the edge of a rout, the Generalissimo installed yet another new commander, in the person of the Guangxi General Bai Chongxi, a Moslem whom the German adviser, General von Falkenhausen, once described as 'the only general in China to whom I can teach anything . . .'.

Von Falkenhausen was on loan from the German High Command. He could not speak Chinese, and one of the supreme ironies of the war was that he used to converse with Jiang Jieshi in Japanese, their only common language. He was indeed the archetypal Prussian, erect and tall, tight-lipped and using thick pince-nez.

Bai was a brilliant strategist whom Edgar Snow described as

'one of the most intelligent and efficient commanders boasted by any army in the world'. The Americans later pressed Jiang to make him Chief of Staff, but he was not one of the Generalissimo's inner circle and he had a record of sometimes daring to countermand orders from above when circumstances warranted it.

During the first two weeks of November the Japanese poured ever more men and supplies into Shanghai. Hundreds of shallow-draught fishing boats were brought over from Japan and sent up to Lake Taihu by river. Armed with light guns and manned with a crew of thirty, these little boats enabled the Japanese to use their great central lake as well as the Yangzi River itself as a line of offence. Japan added the inland waters to its lines of communications. If the Chinese had defended these inland waters, even with a light armed motor flotilla, this could have been prevented.

Too late in the day, the Chinese tried to push the completion of a strong secondary position along the concrete 'Hindenburg line' stretching eighty miles east of Shanghai from the Yangzi River southwards to Hangzhou.

One of the Japanese soldiers described in his diary an encounter with Chinese prisoners. His unit had been throwing hand grenades into a concrete dugout from which they then ordered the Chinese soldiers to come out. Eventually they did so, surrendering their weapons:

Out they came, one after another, all young and sickly-looking. What was irritating, though, was that they all looked so Japanese. They must have been injured by the hand grenades for they emerged at their last gasp or with faces singed black, jaws blown off or left cheeks torn to shreds. They made fawning bows and joined their hands, their faces pleading for help. One of the first four to come out tried to escape and Lance-Corporal Sakagami shot him.

Most of them came out, but a few refused ... so I went in with Lance-Corporal Nakagawa. The smell of gunpowder pricked my nostrils. I fixed my bayonet and headed into the darkness yelling at them to come out. The only light inside came from the gleam of my bayonet. Frightened faces appeared from against the wooden walls and they trooped out.

I was just thinking that they must all have gone when I heard a loud groaning in the darkness. Straining my eyes I saw dark shapes squirming on the central earthen floor. My bayonet fixed, I approached, imagining they were the writhing bodies of soldiers injured by the hand grenades.... As I got nearer the groaning grew even louder, but it was not so much groaning as crying. I touched the soldiers who were rolling on the ground making this indescribable sound. 'Come on.' At this, two soldiers slowly got up.

The faces which loomed suddenly up at me out of the darkness in the light from a loophole in the wall were so young and beautiful that I felt cut to the quick. They were both about the same age, virtually boys, and of an almost feminine beauty. Their faces swollen with weeping, they clung to my shoulders, one on either side. They started to say something but of course I could not understand. Then one of them produced a notebook from his pocket, turned the pages and showed me a photograph. It seemed to be the picture of a mother. Of course I had a pretty good idea of what they were saying, presumably that they were brothers.

For an instant I wondered if I could let just these two stay behind but I took them outside, clinging on to my shoulders as if they were attached to them. Repeatedly the soldiers mimed at me not to kill them, putting their hands to their necks, and I nodded at them not to worry. A pale shadow of joy seemed to play on the faces of these boy soldiers ravaged by sorrow. There welled up inside me an inexplicable feeling halfway between anger and desolation. When I got outside, the troops were there waiting. I handed over the two boy soldiers....

When I got back to the former village which was our battalion headquarters, the prisoners were lined up in a row. Private Yoshida informed me that my meal was ready and I went into the house.... It was the first meal of rice I had had in a long time and it tasted indescribably delicious.

The instant I lay down I felt sleepy. I slept a little, waking up with the cold. 1 went out, but the captives, who had been tied together with telegraph wire, were no longer to be seen. When I asked the soldiers there what had happened to them I was told that they had all been killed.

The bodies of the Chinese soldiers had been cast into the trenches. Since the trenches were narrow, the bodies were piled on top of one another, half submerged in the muddy water. Had they killed all thirty-six? I sorrowed and yet could feel the anger welling up inside. Sickened and depressed I was about to go off when I noticed something strange.

The corpses were moving. On looking closer, I discovered that it was the squirming of one of the Chinese soldiers, half-dead and covered in blood, on the lower layer of the piled-up bodies. Perhaps he heard me coming, for he raised his head to look at me as if summoning all the strength in his crippled body, The look of suffering on his face made me shudder.

With pleading in his eyes he indicated his chest and mine in turn; I had not the slightest doubt but that he was asking me to shoot him. I did not hesitate. I hurriedly aimed at the chest of the dying Chinese soldier and pulled the trigger. He stopped moving. Platoon Commander Yamakazi came hurrying up and asked me why I had fired into the enemy to no purpose. . . .

The Japanese Tenth Army took Songjiang, behind the Chinese right flank, on 9 November, precipitating a general Chinese retreat. Indulging their usual custom, the Japanese celebrated the victory by flying a captive balloon high over Zhabei dangling a long streamer of self-congratulatory characters.

On the day which Europeans call Armistice Day, 11 November, an American correspondent, climbing a water tower in Shanghai from which the fierce fighting could be most clearly seen, stepped in a patch of red which he thought at first must be paint.

In fact it was the blood of Pembroke Stephens, the *Daily Telegraph* correspondent who had climbed up to the exposed top of the tower in order to get an even better view, but had then been shot through the head and groin by a Japanese machine-gunner on a high building on the other side of the creek. Stephens was the first foreign war correspondent to fall victim to the war. He was still wearing a red Armistice poppy in his buttonhole.

The Chinese general retreat became irreversible on 12 November, and the Japanese Sixteenth Division made a leap-frog landing at Baimaokou a little way up the Yangzi River, in order to cut it off. But Japan's hopes of taking large numbers of Chinese troops out of the war receded. By the 19th the Japanese main force had reached the Changshu–Suzhou–Jiaxing line without managing to engage the main body of retreating Chinese. The strong fortresses which had been constructed along this line proved useless, however, because the retreating Chinese could not find the keys to open them!

Imperial GHQ, newly set up in the Emperor's moated palace in Tokyo, had hoped that Japan would achieve its goals before that line, and had therefore made it the limit for pursuit. A few days later it had to be stretched further to the line Qingyang-zhen–Wuxi–Wuxing. But the Chinese nevertheless escaped to fight another day.

Their casualties were put by the American military attaché at the time at well over 100,000, or a third of their total force. The Chinese figure for Japanese casualties was 60,000, but the American estimate was only 40,000, out of a total force of 90,000, and a European military observer put it lower than that.

As for Shanghai itself, a local editor commented that 'practically nothing escaped in an area estimated at more than three miles square'. A Japanese visitor who came to see Shanghai a few months after the battle was at first 'speechless with astonishment', then exclaiming: 'Just like our earthquake!' (of 1923). The loss of property in the greater Shanghai area was estimated by foreign observers at about US $1 billion.

The battle of Shanghai was thus a story of eight Chinese divisions, unprotected by planes or tanks, being chewed up piecemeal over three months of costly and heroic resistance within the sight of Japanese naval guns.

The engagement was particularly shattering to the élite modern sector of China's army. About three-fifths of the 80,000 first-rate fighting troops, equipped with German weapons, who constitued the best Chinese divisions, had been unwisely deployed around Shanghai and Nanjing, to form the backbone of the 450,000-strong force which Jiang ordered to make a life-or-death stand.

About 60 per cent of China's modern army was thus lost at Shanghai, with particularly high casualties among the junior officers. At one blow, China lost 10,000 junior officers and many hundreds of thousands of her best troops who would have provided the potential junior officers to take their place.

The loss in one battle of so many of the élite officers whom

China had taken nearly two years to train was a grievous error. But it was also a demonstration that China intended to fight for her independence, and that her army could not only absorb punishment but hand it out as well.

The Soviet advisers, who maintained a low profile in the war but were nevertheless influential, criticized the way in which Chinese infantry attacked in close formation. 'Close formations,' said one of them to the Chinese staff officers, 'are good food for machine-guns, flame-throwers and artillery. We recommend that the commanders shift to small group tactics. This would diminish the losses.'

To which General Bai Chongxi, who was present, replied, 'Chinese soldiers are used to close formations and the feeling of close fellowship. Besides, such a close order ensures better control.'

'All that is true,' one of the Russians maintained, 'but close fomations are as appropriate to modern warfare as the battle order of Tsar Kir's horse chariots are for modern tanks.'

The Chinese officers laughed and one of them, showing off his knowledge of military history, commented, 'Tsar Kir was a great general, and he knew all his troops by name.'

'Yes,' another Russian interjected, 'but he didn't leave us rules for training troops in the tactics of contemporary warfare.'

The Japanese underestimated China's spirit of nationalism, which showed itself in its true colours only as a result of their own threat to it. The Japanese soldiers proved themselves brave in the field, but their officers often betrayed an unexpected lack of resourcefulness and initiative. Observers formed the impression that the Japanese army had been trained to fight by rote, following a formula of infantry advancing only after preliminary aerial and artillery bombardment. In Shanghai the Chinese had shelters to hide behind, and once the artillery fire had lifted they were able to pour out and resume their defensive fire.

Another weakness noted was Japan's inability to organize a creeping artillery barrage ahead of advancing infantry (an exception being at Dachang where, however, it was deployed too far ahead of the Japanese front line).

Captain Carlson, the American observer, even concluded

that the Japanese military machine, regarded as so formidable since its victory over Russia in 1905, had been revealed as a 'third-rate army when judged by European standards'. This was an exaggeration, but Edgar Snow, who was also there, argued that the offensive spirit of the Japanese infantry was not, when faced in Shanghai with a brave and determined enemy on roughly equal terms, 'nearly as formidable as widely advertised'.

If Jiang had gambled on bringing the West into the war, he was disappointed. But the Shanghai battle had steeled Chinese will and rallied Chinese opinion around an erstwhile partisan leader. As for the Japanese, they still did not recognize the trap they were walking into.

3

Down to the Yellow River

Neither the Chinese nor the Japanese in north China stood still to await the outcome of the battle of Shanghai. Only a week before the shooting began in that city, Generalissimo Jiang Jieshi sent Chinese units to reinforce Hebei province and ordered the Second Army Corps of General Tang Enbo to mass in the mountains northwest of Beijing to stop the Japanese from crossing the Great Wall into Mongolia.

The Japanese government responded with a nation-wide mobilization on 15 August, and three divisions were ordered into the north Chinese theatre under Lieutenant-Generals Itagaki Seishiro, Tani Hisao and Isogai Rensuke.

The Japanese immediately marched along the line of the railway from Beijing to Mongolia, in the expectation of cutting off supplies to China from the Soviet Union. The Chinese conducted what their official war historian lamely described as 'piecemeal resistance', but by mid September had been pushed behind the inner Great Wall.

The key battle was at the pass of Nankou, near the ancient Ming tombs, and a Chinese machine-gunner told an American correspondent a few weeks later that in that battle he had 'fought one whole day and one whole night without rest or food'. Some of their Japanese prisoners were students of only fifteen or sixteen.

'I fought in that position for twenty days and twenty nights. Often we were without food except sweet potatoes which the peasants brought us. We were ... exhausted. After twenty days we fought hand-to-hand battles with the enemy. Three Japanese attacked me at one time, and I fought with a sword. I killed two of the men and drove off the other, but they injured me here on the skull, and here, they shot me in the leg, just above the ankles. . . .

'Even after they wounded me I fought them; then I realized I could not stand. The blood was streaming all over me and I was nearly blinded. But the enemy had taken our position. I began to roll down the mountainside to find our comrades. No, we had no doctors, no nurses, no first-aid workers on the battle-field. . . .'

This was the nearest pass from Beijing to Inner Mongolia. It was difficult terrain at the best of times, but in August it was drenched in rain, which delayed the arrival of Japanese supplies and troop reinforcements. The Chinese resisted General Itagaki's mechanized siege guns, but were finally taken by surprise by a small Japanese unit which went round behind their position.

Once they were over the pass, on 23 August, the Japanese marched rapidly along the railway to Huhhot, the capital of Inner Mongolia. They now controlled the ancient caravan route to Mongolia and Russia. Here the Japanese forces divided, one army continuing westwards to take Baotou in the middle of October, the other veering southwards towards Shanxi and the main focus of the war.

On 4 September General Terauchi, commander of the North China Area Army embracing the Japanese First and Second Armies, arrived in Tianjin to take up his new command. His personal difficulties in reaching his post were an indicator of things to come. The weather was too bad for him to land at Tianjin airport, and so his plane from Tokyo landed at Lüda on the opposite side of the Bohai Gulf instead. From there he had to take a destroyer to Tanggu and a train finally to Tianjin.

General Terauchi immediately outlined his plans to trap and destroy the Chinese forces which had advanced to Baoding and Cangxian on the two vital railways south of Beijing. 'The decisive battle,' his orders explained, 'will be waged in the area along the Beijing–Wuhan railway and the time for this operation will be early October.'

The preliminary to the big ground battles which were now to

unfold was a series of air engagements in the middle of September. Japan's full-scale aerial presence for the war in the north had begun at the end of July when Lieutenant-General Baron Tokugawa Yoshitoshi's Provisional Air Group took up duties at Tianjin airfield. The Baron had six squadrons of reconnaissance aircraft, five of fighters, four of light bombers and two squadrons of heavy bombers at his disposal.

The Chinese air force struck back with British Gloucester Gladiator fighters, Russian Ilyushin-15 biplanes and Ilyushin-16 fighter monoplanes and American Curtiss Hawk biplane fighters – all single-seaters. The opening battle between these two air forces was the Japanese bombing and strafing of a new Chinese air base at Yangshu, from which the Chinese pilots had been making things difficult for the Japanese invaders in the area northwest of Beijing. The Japanese claimed to have destroyed seventeen Chinese planes in this first direct dogfight of the war.

The advance down the Beijing–Wuhan railway began earlier than General Terauchi had envisaged. The opening shots were heard on 14 September, between three concentrations of rival forces facing each other along a quarter-circle in the semi-marshy land south of the Yongding River where it flows from Marco Polo bridge to Tianjin. On the Japanese side stood the formidable First Army of General Katsuki.

Katsuki's Twentieth Division faced General Sun Lianzhong's Twenty-Sixth Army on the western sector of this line. In the centre was Katsuki's Fourteenth Division, fresh from Japan, while the left flank was held by the Sixth Division. These latter two groups of Katsuki's men were opposed on the Chinese side by the armies of Generals Feng Zhenhai and Wan Fulin.

It was later alleged that Katsuki and Feng, who were already acquainted, had secretly agreed on a safe Chinese withdrawal. At any rate the Japanese attack went well on the first day. Katsuki told his middle and left groups to strike forward boldly and veer to the right in order to cut off the retreat of the Chinese Thirtieth and Fifty-Third Armies, which were combining to fall back on prepared positions.

At 1.40 p.m. on 15 September a delighted General Katsuki

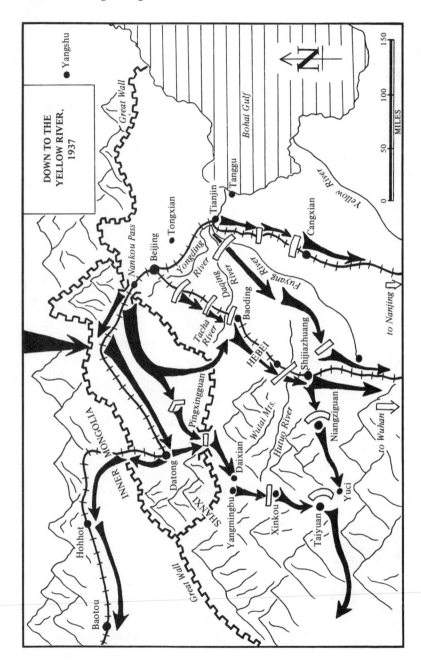

DOWN TO THE
YELLOW RIVER,
1937

put out the order: 'The majority of the enemy has been put to rout by the heroic efforts of each group. The army will pursue the enemy towards ... Baoding without let-up....' He soon went further, exploiting the First Army's success by sending it directly against Baoding, the first major stop on the railway to Wuhan, without bothering first to prepare east–west lines in support.

The three Japanese forces pursued the Chinese inexorably south, to reach a line at the River Dasha, on the south bank of which the Chinese had prepared a strong defensive position to protect Baoding. Katsuki told his men on the evening of the 18th: 'The enemy is retreating in confusion to the south and west.'

By the 20th, as they began their assault on Baoding, the Japanese for the first time came up against their real enemy in China, namely their own lengthening supply lines. Their rear units of motorized transports, faced with earth roads not yet recovered from the summer rains, could not catch up with the men at the front, so that the soldiers had to rely on getting supplies locally. The occupation of Baoding itself on the 24th was delayed because artillery units could not get there on time. On the same day the Second Army took Cangxian.

The Japanese capture of Baoding gave the Chinese and foreign observers in China their first glimpse of what the Japanese military occupation was going to be like. About 30,000 Japanese soldiers embarked on a week's rampage of rape, murder and pillage. The Japanese themselves admitted that they killed 25,800 Chinese in the course of capturing this city.

Yet the American military attaché, Colonel Joseph Stilwell, could not detect a few days later the kind of damage to walls and buildings which would suggest that the Chinese had put up a strong defence. He cabled to Washington that the Chinese would not stem the Japanese advance 'until they lose their inherent distaste for offensive combat'.

Meanwhile the Japanese were fatally drawn into the mountainous terrain of Shanxi province, directly west of their main area of operations down the railways which ran north–south through Hebei province. Here the Red Army of the Chinese Communist General, Zhu De, known as the 'Red Napoleon', had made a novel compact with its old enemy, the central government and central armies of Jiang Jieshi.

In August the Generalissimo had invited Zhu De to a national military conference at Nanjing, assigning the Communist Eighth Army, many of whose units had two years earlier completed its famous Long March from Jiangxi to Yan'an, to operate as part of the Central Government forces on the Shanxi front under the Guomindang General Yan Xishan. Zhu, a one-time opium addict and then Mao Zedong's legendary military partner in the early 1930s, remained commander-in-chief of the newly-designated Eighth Route Army, with Peng Dehuai (once described as having 'a mouth big enough to grin until his face is split ear to ear') as his deputy.

The Guomindang generals in Shanxi were not trusted by the Communists. Agnes Smedley, the American correspondent, described General Yan, who was provincial governor as well as commander, as 'somewhat the worse for age, and utterly ignorant of the youth, virility and ruthlessness of the Japanese army' (actually he had been a cadet in the Tokyo Military College).

Before the Marco Polo bridge incident the Communists and Guomindang had been deadly enemies. But now, at least for the opening months of the war with Japan, they collaborated out of a new-found sense of patriotism, and nowhere more effectively than in Shanxi.

Here, wrote Auden, '... danger works a civil reconciliation,/Interior hatreds are resolved upon this foreign foe ...'

The Chinese troops in Shanxi, especially those under Communist leadership, now began to operate on highly mobile lines, going deep into Japanese-occupied territory and often losing contact with their own headquarters. They sliced Japanese communications, annihilated forward detachments and wiped out many outposts.

The Red Army offered a constant threat along the flank of Japan's southward drive from Beijing along the railway to Wuhan. The Japanese, distracted from their real goal, were forced up into the Western Hills where they were vulnerable to guerrilla ambush, instead of proceeding quickly down into the soft valley of the Yangzi.

Meanwhile another Japanese army, led by the notorious 'Samurai' Fifth Division under General Itagaki Seishiro (later War Minister in Prince Konoye's cabinet), swung confidently southwards into Shanxi province in September after its successes in Inner Mongolia.

Itagaki had won his spurs in Manchuria in the early 1930s. It was he who had drawn up the blueprints for the army-dominated puppet state of Manchukuo. Now he met little resistance from the demoralized Shanxi provincial troops of the Guomindang General Yan Xishan.

The principal divisions of the Communist Eighth Route Army under General Zhu De had, however, crossed the Yellow River into Shanxi early in September. The Shanxi provincial troops were supposedly resisting the initial thrust of Japanese forces from the north, although General Itagaki's bodyguard commented in his diary on 12 September: 'Threatened by our guns, the enemy retreated yesterday to Datung. Oh my Chinese soldiers, sooner or later you must die! Why did you retreat? I cannot understand the minds of troops like these.'

Zhu sent his 115th Division under Lin Biao to the Wutai mountains in the northeast of Shanxi. Unknown to the Japanese columns, Lin's men took up positions to the south side of the Pingxing pass on the Great Wall, having secretly worked round to the rear of the Itagaki division.

The terrain at the Pingxing pass was rugged. The Japanese column had to march along an old trail sunk beneath the floor of the valley, winding between hills. The Chinese plan was for one group under an anti-Communist general to block the main route of the Japanese advance, while two brigades of Lin Biao's Communists launched a surprise attack from the rear.

As Zhu De afterwards explained: 'It was decided that we would wait until the Japanese were well within the pass, then attack with the [non-Communist] Shanxi regiments moving from the west towards the enemy, while our division moved in from the south flank and from the rear.'

At midnight on 24 September General Lin Biao gave his orders for the day, to destroy the Japanese as they marched along the seven-mile stretch of ridges between the Pingxing pass and Laoyemiao. Lin was a very thin man, and one of the regimental commanders at this briefing commented afterwards: 'He looked as if a mere gust of wind could fell him.'

At seven o'clock next morning the Japanese entered the pass. A Chinese officer, Colonel Li, described the scene. 'The distant drone of motors was heard from the canyon. A fleet of vehicles carrying Japanese troops and military supplies was moving up toward Pingxing pass. Someone was counting in a low voice, "One . . . two . . . fifty . . . a hundred."

'Following the lorries were more than 200 animal-drawn carts, and mules and horses were drawing large-calibre guns. Behind them was the cavalry. Vehicles and animals were stretched in an unbroken line. With cars honking and hoofs clanging, they were a very imposing sight indeed.

'The Japanese troops riding on horseback or sitting in lorries wore leather boots, steel helmets and woollen overcoats. They had rifles slung diagonally across their shoulders. They were quite at ease, talking and laughing.

'Some were eating, while others were whipping the press-ganged porters. . . . The slimy black mire was ankle-deep at some places on the highway.'

At this point some lorries began to turn back, presumably because of the difficulties on the road ahead, so that the section which Colonel Li's men faced soon became 'clogged with scores of lorries. . . . Men and horses and lorries were all held up by the congestion. It was an ideal moment for us to attack. I grabbed the phone and asked the lookout post: "Hello, are all the enemy troops in the trap?"

'"No more are visible on the highway. . . ."

'In that case,' Colonel Li thought, 'this was the tailend of the Itagaki division.'

He sent a messenger for his general's instructions. In the various Chinese headquarters there was a certain lack of co-ordination. The Shanxi troops made no movement, but the Communists decided to move immediately if the advantages of

surprise and position were to be utilized. The order to attack
went out.

'The moment the fighters had long awaited,' Colonel Li
remembered, 'had come at last. The ridges south of the highway
roared and rocked under the impact of the explosion of
hand-grenades, trench mortars and the rat-tat-tat of machine-
guns. The enemy who cluttered the highway went down in large
numbers. One lorry . . . caught fire, others collided.'

Colonel Li was summoned by General Lin Biao for new
orders.

'We have encircled one enemy brigade of over 4000 men,'
Lin explained, 'but one big group is hard to tackle. We have to
cut it up into several sections. Your men should cross the
highway and divide the enemy at that point, then use one
battalion to take Laoyemiao. Once we have taken that commanding point, we could easily annihilate the enemy down
there.'

Colonel Li gave his men the order to charge. 'But the
Japanese proved to be a formidable foe. They showed no
inclination to quit. Their shooting was quite accurate. Despite
heavy casualties, they remained in the ditches and depressions
of the road, or behind lorries, making a stubborn stand. Their
bullets kept whizzing over our heads. I was furious. I looked
through my field glasses and saw that the wheat stalks were
being mowed down by the enemy's fire. It was clear that their
fire-power was superior to ours.'

Eventually, after a bout of hand-to-hand fighting, the Japanese were forced to take shelter underneath their lorries.

'We didn't know that the right thing for us to do at that time
was to burn the lorries to deprive them of their shelter. . . . We
thought that, if we pressed them hard, they would surrender.'
The Chinese shouted to the Japanese soldiers: 'Put down your
arms! We won't kill you!'

'Not only did they not understand what we said, for of course
we shouted in Chinese, but they were a batch of beasts who had
been trained in the code of the *Bushido*. They were instilled
with the idea of conquering China, slaughtering the Chinese
people and exploiting them.

'As our soldiers had had no previous experience fighting the Japanese, many were killed or wounded by these desperate fiends. I remember a telephone operator of the First Battalion who was going along the highway examining the telephone lines when he saw a dying Japanese soldier lying beside a lorry. He ran up to him and urged: "Give up your weapon; we won't kill you. We give magnanimous treatment to prisoners of . . ."

'Before he had finished, the Japanese raised his hand and thrust the bayonet into his chest.

'One comrade, carrying back a seriously wounded Japanese soldier, had his ear bitten off. Some comrades were killed or wounded while trying to bandage wounded Japanese soldiers. . . . Even the wounded fought each other like devils until one was killed or both were locked in a death embrace.'

The Japanese did not understand the tactics of mountain warfare: except for the small group holding out at Laoyemiao, they stayed on the road where there was no cover. Colonel Li's men crossed the highway and made for the mountainside whose strategic heights they at last managed, with the help of a neighbouring battalion, to occupy. Then: 'We attacked the highway from the Laoyemiao Temple which dominated it from both sides. The enemy troops were fully exposed to our raking fire. They finally understood what mountain warfare meant. Their commanders, realizing their mistake, waved their sabres and shouted curses and orders, directing their men to scale the barren summit. Now the enemy's guns and cavalry were useless. Infantrymen in heavy, clumsy boots were climbing up helter-skelter. We trained our guns on them and waited. When they were quite close, gasping heavily for breath, the order of "Fire!" was given.'

But enemy numbers began to tell, and Colonel Li could count 500 or 600 enemy soldiers, with Japanese planes now hovering overhead. Everything depended upon the arrival of the expected Chinese reinforcements on the left flank.

'We stood firm before the enemy onslaughts until about one o'clock in the afternoon. The 687th Regiment arrived at last. I noticed a faltering in the rear of the enemy lines. I instantly knew the time had come. I ordered my troops to close in for the kill. We set upon the Japanese from both directions and succeeded in completely annihilating them along the mountain ravine....'

General He Long admitted afterwards that the Red success at Pingxingguan created its own problems. 'We actually captured,' he recalled, 'a number of those tanks and armoured cars, but we could only destroy them because – well, I've got to admit – because we didn't know how to drive the damn things. Anyway, we could have done nothing with them.

'They would have been a nuisance: tanks aren't much use except on level ground, and there's not much level ground in north China. What level ground there is, we can and do easily cut up to make it almost impossible for tanks to get around.'

The scene which greeted Colonel Li's eyes on the morning after the battle was forever engraved on his memory. 'Scanning the battlefields, you could see that the gully stretching for about three miles in length was littered with "Imperial Army" bodies, dead horses, carts and lorries. The road was spattered with blood and several thousand disfigured Japanese bodies were lying about. They had got what they richly deserved.

'The Twenty-First Japanese Brigade had suffered a fatal defeat. The Japanese aggressors experienced the might of the Chinese people for the first time.... When I trod on the battered rifles and the torn flags with the "Rising Sun" and stepped over Japanese corpses strewn about the fields, I thought: "So this is the so-called Invincible 'Imperial Army!'"'

The Reds captured Itagaki's headquarters, and forced the Japanese to retreat in disorder, having lost about one man in three, all their transport and all their supplies. It was not a decisive battle, but it meant that no Japanese commander would advance quite so recklessly into hilly country again.

And at this early stage of the war the battle of the Pingxing pass heartened the Communist faction, stiffened Chinese resistance in the northwest, and advertised to the Japanese almost for the first time what kind of opposition they would be up against in the years to come.

General Zhu De, who put the Japanese losses at more than 3000, explained the victory on three grounds. First, it was hill fighting in which the Japanese could not use their tanks or aeroplanes; secondly, it was a surprise attack; and thirdly, the Chinese regular and Communist armies were collaborating. Incredibly, the Japanese commander had moved without air cover and without long-range reconnaissance.

'We engaged the enemy infantry right at the start, so that they had no chance to use their artillery; they could not even use their machine-guns. It was a running fight in the hills, and our troops, of course, are much more mobile than theirs. The Japanese, we found, do not like this kind of fighting. They had learned to rely on their tanks and on their heavy artillery . . . and they were very uncomfortable without them. We killed many of them here with hand-grenades.

'But even though they were defeated, they fought to the last,' Zhu added, 'and none of them would surrender. Why? Because they knew that if they lost their arms they would be killed by their own commanders; this is a rule of the Fifth Division. . . . Partly, too, it was because they were afraid of being killed by the Chinese if they were taken prisoner.'

The Japanese also disliked leaving their dead behind on the battlefield, preferring to take them for cremation so that the ashes could be sent home to Japan in small white boxes. Knowing this, one Chinese Red Army officer planted a mine under a Japanese corpse, and was gratified when a Japanese platoon came back after nightfall to recover the body. An officer and five soldiers were killed when the mine blew up.

Zhou Enlai claimed afterwards that some of the Japanese dead at Pingxing pass had manifestos of the Japanese Communist Party in their pockets calling on them to resist the war. 'You know,' he told a British journalist, 'we captured many diaries and records from the Japanese troops, and some of these showed quite clearly their opposition to the war.

'The rank and file do not know why they are here in China. They hate the country and the climate. They cannot eat the local food; and wherever their armies come, the countryside is deserted. They have had some hard fighting – much harder than they expected and they really do not know what it is all about.'

One Japanese colonel killed in action in Shanxi in September wrote in his diary just before dying: 'The Red Army gives me a headache. We Japanese can only fight during the daytime, but the Red Army can fight anytime ... around here even these Chinese women join the war and throw hand-grenades. I have received orders from my superior officer that every person in this place must be killed.'

Another Japanese officer confided to his diary during this Shanxi campaign: 'The Chinese soldiers, even when wounded, do not leave the front. They wait for us to come near and then they use their bayonets to kill our men. Some of them save a cartridge in their pistols to kill themselves. Though these men are our enemies, they are great men.'

This observation should not be generalized: not every Chinese was a superman. Although the ideals were not always lived up to, both sides had fearsome standards of military honour. One Japanese captain captured by the Chinese during fighting earlier in the 1930s and later released went hopefully to the nearest Japanese consulate after his release, only to be told that he was officially dead. 'Your ashes,' the Consul-General told him, 'have been taken to Tokyo and the clothes in which you died have been buried in your coffin outside Shanghai. I suggest that you go to your grave.' The captain listened politely, bowed before the Emperor's portrait, went to his grave and shot himself – in order, as the Chinese say, 'to rejoin his clothes'.

As for the Chinese, there were many who shared the feelings of General He Long, the Communist and secret society leader, when he told a foreign correspondent: 'All my life I have wanted to fight the Japanese and I could never get at them! But now they have come to me....'

One of the exploits of the Chinese guerrillas in north Shanxi during October was a daring raid on the Japanese airfield of Yangmingbu. 'You have heard,' the guerrilla base commander told a correspondent afterwards, 'how we destroyed twenty-four enemy aeroplanes at Yangmingbu? Our army had watched the airfield for several days, from the top of a high mountain – the Japanese never troubled to reconnoitre. One day, we saw that many aeroplanes came – more than twenty. That night we attacked.'

When they reached the airfield, some of them had never seen an aeroplane before. They banged on the aircraft with bewilderment, shouting, 'Are these planes?'

On the Hebei front the Japanese had noted 'a marked decline in the enemy's fighting power and spirit' after the fall of Baoding and Cangxian on the track of the main Beijing–Wuhan railway. They decided to continue the pursuit southwards and seek to encircle and destroy the Chinese army. The Japanese First Army continued down the railway, while the Second Army followed broadly the course of the River Fuyang.

In Shanxi, however, to the east, there was a fiercely fought battle for the provincial capital, Taiyuan, parallel with Shijiazhuang. As the Japanese moved south along the railway line towards Taiyuan, four divisions under General Wei Lihuang were rushed from Hebei to take up defensive positions at Xinkou. General Itagaki's Fifth Division, recovered from its setback at Pingxingguan, came into contact with these forces in mid October, and for three weeks there was a stubborn fight.

This, incidentally, was another phase of the war in which Chinese aircraft were successful. One Japanese ace fighter pilot, Major Miwa Hiroshi, was captured. Here also for the first time the Japanese army received a decisive check in positional fighting, and it is usually said that more than 30,000 died in the battle of Xinkou – pretty well equally distributed between the two sides.

When the Japanese vanguard first engaged the Chinese defences here, it was around a mountain pass and so it began as a case of mobile warfare, as at the Pingxing pass earlier. But this time the Chinese had concentrated 100,000 troops, including not only General Wei's Fourteenth Army but also two central divisions and several Shanxi units which for the first time in the war showed up very well indeed. The Japanese had about 60,000 very much better equipped men.

With these numbers, and with the Chinese concentrating their troops on both sides of the valley through which the Japanese wished to pass, a positional battle developed with the Eighth Route Army making guerrilla attacks on the Japanese rear and flank. This was perhaps the high point of Communist–Guomindang co-operation against the Japanese invader.

The Communists' role was to attack and sever the Japanese lines of communication, and this they did on three main routes: only the road remained open, and that was repeatedly attacked.

One of the Red Chinese officers involved was Colonel He Bingying, described by a British correspondent as 'a brisk little man who always wore a helmet and a blue sleeveless cape; only when I offered to shake hands did I discover that his right arm was missing'. Colonel He, a brusque and explosive Hunanese, described afterwards how his unit struck at a bend in the road, on an uphill gradient between high banks.

'First we ambushed forty Japanese trucks there, and destroyed many of them with hand-grenades – killed about 300 of the enemy. We got out when their planes arrived. Next time, about sixty trucks came, with three tanks leading. But the night before we had destroyed the bridges, so that the whole column jammed. Then we attacked from above and below, and destroyed about half of the trucks.

'After that, they sent out their next column with 500 infantry as escort. But we ambushed the escort, and attacked all along their line with machine-guns. All together we killed about 500 Japanese in under a week – that's their own hospital report! And we had less than 100 casualties.'

General Zhu De, in charge of the Communist troops, explained that as a result of this action the Japanese 'could get no supplies, for we held the roads, and trucks and munitions trains had to turn back. They had no supplies of petrol, so could not use their mechanized units. For a while, this invading Japanese force was in a really desperate position.'

Meanwhile the Japanese brought in a pincer attack from the east. The indispensable Fifth Division spearheaded a drive to the right from Shijiazhuang into Shanxi province towards Taiyuan, and the Chinese correspondingly moved men from the Wutai mountains in the north to the area of the Niangzi or Ladies' pass on the Shanxi–Hebei border. The Japanese GHQ thereupon ordered its Twentieth Division to occupy the plain just inside Shanxi province, involving a preliminary attack on the Chinese positions at the Great Wall near the Niangzi pass.

Zhu De for the Eighth Route Army admitted afterwards that he had moved too slowly to cut off the Japanese rear. 'One important strategic town before the Niangzi pass unaccountably fell with scarcely any resistance; and so it proved difficult for Chinese troops to hold the eastern pass.'

The Red Army fought twice against the Japanese near the Niangzi pass, although General Zhu De complained that he had 'a much smaller force, and no support at all: the other Chinese troops had withdrawn on Taiyuan'. But the Japanese forced their way along the railway to Taiyuan all the same. The Guomindang counter-complained afterwards that the Communists' Eighteenth Army Group had 'sat idle' during the three weeks' fighting for Taiyuan.

Actually the Japanese advancing on Taiyuan from the east outnumbered the Chinese Eighth Route Army by nine to one, and in equipment by a hundred to one. General Zhu De had hoped desperately for reinforcements from Tang Enbo's crack Thirteenth Army and Liu Xiang's Sichuan Army.

Lin Biao of the Eighth Route Army confided to a reporter on 6 November: 'We cannot fight the Japanese. There are too many of them. Our forces in this region are relatively few. We are the only army in the rear of the enemy, where the enemy has 20,000 and more men at Xinkou alone.

'What we can do is split the enemy up in smaller groups wherever possible, and destroy them. We can harass them, cut their communication routes so they can get no reinforcements, no food, no supplies of any kind....' (Lin was to survive the war and attempt in 1970 the assassination of Chairman Mao Zedong.)

The Japanese did not have everything their way. One of their units was ordered to support the Taiyuan operation by advancing, on a path slightly south of the main force, via Yuci. But it quickly encountered the factor which was eventually to dictate Japan's failure, the inability to keep the front lines constantly supplied over the vast distances of continental China. The unit's departure from Tangshan was delayed because of a shortage of horses.

The eastern front crumbled so swiftly that the main Chinese

defence had to give up Taiyuan, which the Japanese captured on 8 November. It was a grave loss to China, with heavy casualties including the death of General Hao Menglin, who fell in the front line.

The rearguard action in Taiyuan was carried out by General Fu Zuoyi with 6000 men. Everyone else in the city, including Zhou Enlai, the Eighth Route Army's liaison officer with the northern command, was evacuated on the night of 5 September.

For three days and two nights General Fu and his men fought without stopping. The city wall ran with blood and the bodies of the defenders piled up around their machine-guns. By the evening of the 8th, 4000 of his 6000 men had been killed and he left the city with the few survivors.

No sooner were the Japanese inside Taiyuan than Chinese recriminations broke out. The Communists complained that their men had been sent out in too small numbers, with inferior arms and without sufficient support to hold up the Japanese advance. They said that General Wei Lihuang had retreated too soon at Xinkou, and that his troops' withdrawal became a rout in which they threw down their arms in order to escape more quickly: the Communist General He Long, following on their heels, was able, it was said, to rescue 10,000 rifles and large numbers of machine-guns.

But the arguments were academic. The formal Chinese defence fell back swiftly after the capture of Taiyuan, and by the end of the year the Japanese were at the Yellow River.

4

The Rape of Nanjing

With a quarter of a million troops at the mouth of the Yangzi controlling Shanghai, the Japanese were bound to set their sights next on Nanjing, the city only 200 miles away which served as the Chinese government's capital of the day. In anticipation, the Chinese government moved on 20 November, first to Wuhan and then a year later to Chongqing, declaring to its people: 'For the sake of our national existence, of the status of our race, of international justice and of world peace, China finds no grounds for submission. All those who have blood and breath in them must feel that they wish to be broken as jade rather than remain whole as tile.'

Generalissimo Jiang summoned his leading commanders and von Falkenhausen to a conference in Nanjing to discuss the city's defence. General Li Zongren advocated declaring it an undefended city so that Japan would have no excuse to slaughter civilians. Nanjing was actually indefensible and its capture by Japan, whatever the psychological gain, would not affect the overall military situation.

General Bai Chongxi agreed, and so did von Falkenhausen. Other Chinese generals prevaricated, and only General Tang Shengzhi ventured a different opinion. Reminding the others that Nanjing contained the mausoleum of former President Sun Zhongshan (Sun Yat-sen), father of the nation, he asked in an outburst of emotionalism: 'If, when the enemy is at our door, Nanjing does not sacrifice one or two big generals, how can we account for ourselves before the soul of the father of the nation in heaven, and how can we discharge our duties before the supreme commander? I advocate defending Nanjing to the end and fighting the enemy to the death.'

The Generalissimo was delighted. He immediately appointed Tang as commander-in-chief for the defence of Nanjing, preferring his lone voice of dissent to the more cautious counsel of the other commanders.

Meanwhile the devastation of the war gradually spread inland from the Shanghai metropolis. The Japanese air force approached the systematic bombing of these lush areas, often densely populated, in an almost festive mood.

One foreign journalist saw them terrorizing a farming village north of Shanghai at the end of October. On the day that he was there, eighteen planes dropped 350 large bombs over an area easily encompassed by the naked eye. The Japanese aviators, he reported, 'staged a veritable field-day of destruction, going through most of the antics they would perform had it been a public exhibition for entertainment purposes. Squadrons of three or four planes would power-dive from high altitudes dropping missiles of great weight and explosive character upon Chinese farmhouses made of bamboo and mud-plaster with tile roofs, the whole structure probably not costing more than the equivalent of a few dollars.'

According to Commander Mizuno, the Japanese bomber-pilots, true to the *Samurai* tradition, 'carried swords instead of parachutes, preferring death to capture in the event of accident'. But the Japanese code had no thought for the innocence or otherwise of the victims of these attacks. Generalissimo Jiang Jieshi conceded that: 'The cruel and inhumane, indiscriminate bombing of non-military objectives and of civilians by Japanese has dealt a hard blow to China's progress.... If such barbarous acts were expected by Japan to break the morale and destroy the fighting spirit of China, the results have been just the reverse....'

Wuxi, the industrial city midway between Shanghai and Nanjing, suffered especially. An American doctor working there kept a diary. 'A Chinese', he wrote on 16 October, 'was brought to the hospital today, his intestines badly torn by machine-gun bullets.... The subsequent loss of blood made his case hopeless. When the Japanese planes approached, he ran for cover in a mulberry grove. The plane followed and machine-gunned him. At the same time, three other farmers were killed and four wounded. There were no Chinese soldiers within miles. Why, or for what purpose, could these Japanese attack poor country people who are perfectly harmless?'

November 10 was described by this doctor as 'our worst day so far for bombings. Conservatively, 160 of them were dropped, causing heavy damage and terrible fires.... Civilians brought to our hospital were terribly mangled. A man had his left ear torn to shreds, his left bicep muscles almost severed, a long penetrating wound in his left thigh, his right foot almost torn in half (amputation will be necessary) and his genitals badly mutilated. He had a dozen other smaller wounds. Goodness knows where we will put patients if this bombing round here continues.'

On the next day, after further raids, 'four horribly wounded civilians were brought in with legs and arms dangling grotesquely and all requiring amputations'.

General Matsui and the other professional soldiers in the Japanese field command knew that their best chance of winning a political settlement with Jiang Jieshi was before embarking upon the capture of Nanjing. But they were overruled by the strategists in Tokyo whose ideas were based on Japanese feudal history, where capturing the seat of power automatically led to one's installation as the new ruler.

This forward school was helped by the fact that, in the words of a Japanese correspondent on the spot, 'the Chinese ran away from Shanghai to Nanjing too fast'. Besides, the generals who were directing the war from Tokyo had got used to the two-timing inefficiency of the northern Chinese warlord commanders, and saw no reason to believe that Jiang would be different.

The Japanese Imperial GHQ sent out the order to march on Nanjing on 1 December. The Shanghai Expeditionary Army was to move directly to Nanjing, but one of its units was to cross the Yangzi to 'sever' the Grand Canal and cut the Tianjin–Nanjing railway. Meanwhile the Japanese Tenth Army was ordered to Anqing by a southerly route to cut off any Chinese retreat, by sending one unit to cross the Yangzi near Dangtu and then move up to Pukou, the railhead opposite Nanjing.

Suzhou was taken at dawn on 19 November by a Japanese advance guard marching through the gates in the pouring rain, with waterproof hoods over their heads. The somnolent Chinese sentries did not recognize them. Two days later an American missionary arrived in the city, driving carefully to avoid running over the dead bodies which lined the roads. He found looting in progress from every bank, shop and house. 'Japanese soldiers were passing in and out ... , like ants loaded down with bales of silk, eiderdown quilts, shop goods and household effects of every description.'

The Japanese left wing was in sight of Nanjing by 5 December. While the Chinese systematically destroyed whatever petrol and ammunition could not be saved, as well as hangars, the Generalissimo flew out on 7 December, as the Japanese vanguard began to engage the primary Chinese positions in the city outskirts.

'I intend to defend Nanjing to the last man,' General Tang Shengzhi, the Chinese commander, boasted to an American military observer on the eve of the assault. 'The Japanese may eventually capture the city, but they will pay a heavy price for it.' The Americans formed the opinion, however, that Nanjing would not last long, for once the Japanese were inside the walls with their tanks and mechanized equipment, the city would be theirs.

At midday on the 9th, a Japanese plane dropped a letter from General Matsui to General Tang calling for a surrender within twenty-four hours. When no reply was received, a fierce bombardment of the city from air and ground began. An American civilian watched the shells falling inside the city walls: 'They formed a perfect pattern, the explosion advancing in regular rows about twenty-five yards every half minute'. One by one the gates fell, and by 13 December the Japanese capture of the former Chinese capital was complete, with a claimed loss of 40,000.

The triumphal entry of the victors into Nanjing was led by General Matsui, but very close behind him was the unabashed Colonel Hashimoto riding a prancing white horse. The general represented the traditional restraint which outsiders expected of the Japanese army, but the colonel was the symbol of the younger super-patriots who were to prevent Matsui from keeping control over the Japanese soldiers.

The Chinese army of over 100,000 had been routed in barely four days. It was alleged that the withdrawal was completely unplanned, and that both officers and men were allowed to flee as they wanted. Acting without orders, a small nucleus of passionately patriotic Chinese troops put machine-guns on top of the city walls in order to strafe the men leaving the city, presuming that they would be few. In fact heavy casualties resulted from this internal slaughter.

Thousands of Chinese in Nanjing tried to escape through the Xiaguan gate to the river. But all thirteen gates of the city had been closed and locked as part of the defence. Access to this particular gate was through a seventy-foot-long tunnel, inside which two military vehicles collided and burst into flames, blocking the tunnel. The refugees from the city fought desperately to get out, trampling and killing each other, while more and more soldiers pressed into the tunnel from behind. Thousands were suffocated or trodden underfoot. Two days later two Americans who went through the tunnel found that they had to drive 'over the bodies of dead men who lay where they fell two or three feet deep'. Japanese machine-gunners added to the toll.

The Japanese air force had already scattered pamphlets pledging that the invading troops would protect good citizens in cities occupied by Japan and enable them to live in peace. General Matsui had promised his opposite number in Nanjing in his surrender demand that, while his men would be 'harsh and relentless to those who resist', they would also be 'kind and generous to non-combatants and to Chinese troops who entertained no emnity to Japan'.

Events after 13 December were to show the full meaning of the 'harsh and relentless' treatment which the citizens of Nanjing had earned because of their refusal to surrender. This proud and elegant city was now brutalized in a way never before seen in warfare. The field commander of the occupying troops was a 'royal', Lieutenant-General Prince Asaka Yasuhiko, who had married the Emperor's aunt. It was he who gave the initial orders for the general massacres which now took place.

A Swedish orientalist's verdict was: 'With a blindness and absence of psychological judgement that astonishes the westerner who is at all familiar with Chinese mentality, the Japanese soldiers sullied their march to victory with repeated acts of cruelty, ruthlessness and bloodshed on innocent people. Actions unparalleled in modern times and perpetrated by no civilized nation.'

The Japanese approached the gates of Nanjing in a spirit of euphoria verging on abandon. Two celebrated fighters in the old *Samurai* tradition actually waged a contest, highly publicized in the Japanese press, to see who could kill more Chinese on the road to Nanjing. 'Sub-lieutenants in Race to Fell 100 Chinese Running Close Contest', the *Japan Advertiser* headline ran on 7 December. The two officers, Mukai and Noda, had a 'friendly' competition, the newspapers explained, to see which could be first to fell 100 Chinese in individual sword combat. A week later the Tokyo press reported that both had exceeded the target, but could not decide who had passed the 100 mark first, so they decided to go on to 150.

'Mukai's blade was slightly damaged in the competition. He explained that this was the result of cutting a Chinese in half, helmet and all. The contest was "fun", he declared. . . .'

Once they were inside Nanjing, the Japanese behaved as if the war were won, staging a prolonged victory celebration. Inside the city were twenty-seven foreign missionaries, doctors and teachers who had chosen occupation rather than flight. They organized what they hoped would be a 'Safety Zone' within the city where the majority of the 250,000 refugees from Shanghai and the towns between were packed into temporary accommodation.

A Japanese diplomat confided that the Japanese generals were angry at having to complete their occupation under the eyes of neutral observers, and if it had not been for those few men the carnage would have been far worse.

One of the Germans in Nanjing unashamedly used his Nazi

armbands and decoration to make Japanese soldiers and officers abstain from atrocities in his presence, and one of the other (non-fascist) Europeans confessed to his friends that the 'three Germans had done splendidly, and I'd almost wear a Nazi badge to keep fellowship with them'.

A westerner who met the Japanese on their first arrival at the Safety Zone reported: 'They showed no hostility, though a few moments later they killed twenty refugees who were frightened by their presence and ran from them. For it seems to be the rule here that anyone who runs . . . must be shot or bayoneted.'

For the next seven weeks or more those courageous foreigners interceded repeatedly for the lives of the refugees who, since the Chinese municipal authorities had fled, and the Japanese had not appointed any successor administration, were morally in their charge. One of them who had spent almost all his life in China wrote on Christmas Eve to his friend outside. Two weeks before, he explained, Nanjing had still been ' . . . the beautiful city we were so proud of, with law and order still prevailing: today it is a city laid waste, ravaged, completely looted, much of it burned. Complete anarchy has reigned for ten days – it has been hell on earth.

'Not that my life has been in serious danger at any time; though turning lust-mad, sometimes drunken soldiers out of houses where they were raping the women, is not altogether a safe occupation; nor does one feel, perhaps, too sure of himself when he finds a bayonet at his chest or a revolver at his head and knows it is handled by someone who heartily wishes him out of the way. For the Japanese army is anything but pleased at our being here after having advised all foreigners to get out. They wanted no observers.

'But to have to stand by while even the very poor are having their last possession taken from them – their last coin, their last bit of bedding (and it is freezing weather), the poor ricksha man his ricksha; while thousands of disarmed soldiers who had sought sanctuary with you together with many hundreds of innocent civilians are taken out before your eyes to be shot or used for bayonet practice and you have to listen to the sounds of the guns that are killing them; while a thousand women kneel before you crying hysterically, begging you to save them from the beasts who are preying on them; to stand by and do nothing while your flag is taken down and insulted, not once but a dozen times, and your home is being looted; and then to watch the city you have come to love and the institution to which you have planned to devote your best deliberately and systematically burned by fire – this is a hell I had never before envisaged....

'Every day we call at the Japanese Embassy and present our protests, our appeals, our lists of authenticated reports of violence and crime. We are met with suave Japanese courtesy, but actually the officials here are powerless. The victorious army must have its rewards – and those rewards are to plunder, murder, rape, at will, to commit acts of unbelievable brutality and savagery on the very people they have come to protect and befriend, as they have so loudly proclaimed to the world. In all modern history surely there is no page that will stand so black as that of the rape of Nanjing.'

Auden listed the city among the places 'Where life is evil now:/Nanjing; Dachau.'

The catalogue of complaints made pathetic reading. On 18 December the following reports were lodged:

'One tea house master's daughter, age 17 years, was raped by seven Japanese soldiers and she died on the 18th. Last night three Japanese soldiers raped four girls between six and ten o'clock. In number 5 Moh Kan Road, one old man reported his daughter was brutally raped by several Japanese soldiers.

'There are about 540 refugees crowded in number 83 and 85 on Guangzhou Road. Since the 13th instant up to the 17th those houses have been searched and robbed many times a day by Japanese soldiers in groups of three or five. Today the soldiers are looting the places mentioned above continually. At present, women of younger ages are forced to go with the soldiers every night by sending motor trucks to take them. They are released the next morning. More than thirty women and girls have been raped. The women and children are crying the whole nights through. Conditions inside the compound are worse than can be described.'

One girl clawed with her nails at the Japanese soldier who was raping her. 'Her reward was a bayonet thrust which cut away half the muscles on one side of her neck.'

Two days afterwards a seventeen-year-old married girl, nine months pregnant, was raped by two Japanese soldiers at 7.30 in the evening. An hour and a half later her labour pains began, and the baby was born at midnight. 'Mother is hysterical,' the report laconically concluded, 'but the baby is doing well.'

On 23 December the sole survivor of 140 refugees who had been led to the hills came back for medical treatment. 'They were first sprayed with gasolene, then set afire. His eyes are burned out.'

On Christmas Day itself the registration of refugees by the Japanese authorities began, on the university campus. Ex-soldiers were invited to volunteer for the labour corps, but were then machine-gunned or used for bayonet practice in groups.

On 3 January the following complaints were lodged with the Japanese by the western residents:

'A woman who was taken with five others from number 6 Chien Ying Hsian ostensibly for washing clothes for Japanese officers, ...came to the University Hospital. She stated that they were taken by Japanese soldiers to a house in the west central portion of the city which she thought must be a Japanese military hospital. The women washed clothes during the day, and were raped throughout the night. The older ones were raped from ten to twenty times; the younger and good-looking ones as many as forty times a night.

'On 2 January two soldiers took our patient with them to a deserted school house and struck her ten times with a bayonet knife; four times on the back of the neck severing the muscles down to the vertebral column; once on the wrist, once on the face, and four times on the back. She will probably recover but will have a stiff neck. The soldiers left her for dead. She was found by another Japanese soldier who saw her condition and took her to some friends who brought her to the hospital.' (Actually she died of meningitis.)

'A 14-year-old girl who was not yet built for raping was raped with disastrous results that will require considerable surgical repair.'

By 10 January, a month after the fall of Nanjing, conservative western residents estimated that more than 10,000 unarmed Chinese had been killed, although the evidence which came in subsequently from burials indicated a figure which was nearer 40,000. An American wrote that 'able German colleagues put the cases of rape at 20,000'.

The American's letter continued: 'Girls as low as 11 and women as old as 53 have been raped on university property alone. In other groups of refugees are women of 72 and 76 years of age who were raped mercilessly. On the seminary compound, seventeen soldiers raped one woman successively in broad daylight. In fact, about one-third of these cases are in the daytime.'

These atrocities were not limited to the untutored ordinary ranks of the Japanese army. 'One motorized raid on the university at night was actually conducted by officers themselves, who pinned our watchman to the walls and raped three women refugees before carrying off one of them (another was a girl 12 years old).'

When the Japanese army first arrived, another western resident recalled:

'We thought order would soon be restored, and peace would come, and people would be able to get into normal life again. But the surprise of surprises came to us all. Robbery, looting, torture, murder, rape, burning – everything that can be imagined was carried out from the very beginning without any limit. Modern times have nothing to surpass it.

'Nanjing has almost been a living hell. There has been nothing or no one safe. Soldiers have taken anything they wanted, destroyed what they did not want, raped women and girls openly and publicly by the scores and hundreds. Those who opposed them were bayoneted or shot on the spot. Women who have opposed being raped have been bayoneted. Children who have interfered have also been bayoneted.

'One woman who was being raped on Fran's place – there have been about 150 people staying at his house – had her four- or five-months-old baby near her, and it cried, so the soldier raping her smothered it to death.... Finally we got Japanese guards stationed at the gates of the compound, but they often themselves go in and rape women.'

The holocaust continued after the New Year. At the end of January, a Chinese woman came into the university hospital for treatment by the western doctors with a virulent form of all three types of venereal disease – syphilis, gonorrhoea and chancroid. She had been taken by Japanese soldiers to their quarters and raped every day from seven to ten times for the preceding six weeks.

One old woman of sixty-two complained that soldiers came to her home at night wanting to rape her, and when she said she was too old they rammed a stick up her instead. On 30 January four soldiers raped a girl just over ten years old, one by one. A few days later some Japanese soldiers forced a man to kneel in the road, and when he refused to fetch a girl for them one of them drove the butt of his rifle down on to his legs, breaking both bones.

On 5 February a Japanese soldier came to a house at Te Chung bridge and asked for a girl. 'As there was no girl he pulled away a young man of about 17 or 18 years old and committed sodomy.' On the same day an old woman of 60 was raped at San Pai Lou: 'One of the soldiers asked her to clean the penis by her mouth', the official complaint read. 'Her grandson was stabbed twice for crying.'

This was the famous new era of civilization which the Japanese proclaimed they intended to introduce into China. In fact the civilian authorities, such as they were, had no power over these units which had spearheaded what seemed at the time the final Japanese victory against the forces of the Chinese Republic. Like Alexander's men at Persepolis, they had to be given – or could not be denied, perhaps, even by their senior officers – a completely free rein. At best the Japanese authorities could only regulate the needs of their soldiers. Eventually numerous posters were to be seen in Nanjing and other cities, of which the following is a fair specimen:

'Designated by the base camp authorities, House of Restful

Consolation Chinese Beauties. Number 4 hall for friendly relations between Japan and China, 600 metres along the bank of the stream from here.'

Much has been written about the reasons for the rape of Nanjing. The Japanese did not, by any means, have a monopoly on cruelty in this war, and indeed some of them professed, possibly with some justification, to be shocked by the extent of casual cruelty to be seen in Chinese life, especially Chinese rural life (and the cities accounted for less than a tenth of China's population).

In defence of what their own people did in Nanjing, some Japanese have cited cases where Chinese tortured Japanese soldiers or impaled Japanese women on sticks. The Chinese sometimes cut off the ears or noses of Japanese dead on the battlefield, to deprive their souls of a resting place. The Tongxian massacre (described on pages 21–2) was one case where this kind of behaviour was authenticated on some scale.

But on the Chinese side the violence was either isolated or else, in the case of Tongxian, provoked. What is indicted against the Japanese military command in the China war is not a series of incidental disorders of the kind to be expected in an invasion, but rather a regulated army procedure of mass execution and terrorization of civilian populace attested by surviving witnesses. There is evidence that the Japanese army sought systematically to habituate its men into taking the torture of Chinese as a matter of course. This can be seen in some of the Japanese diaries. That kept by Corporal Nakamura is particularly instructive. After an unwilling conscription and months of killing, looting and raping in China, he wrote of a village which his unit was ordered to take: 'We tried to capture this most interesting girl. The chase lasted for two hours. Niura shot one to death because it was her first time and she was ugly and despised by the rest of us.'

Once his unit caught a group of civilians and tortured them to death. Some of the new Japanese recruits watched with horror, and Nakamura commented patronizingly in his diary: 'All new recruits are like this, but soon they will be doing the same things themselves.'

The Japanese who had to answer international opinion about all this made several points in self-defence. A baseball player called Ito who was captured by the Chinese army told a visiting war correspondent, 'It's because uneducated coolies became officers! Now our government has given orders that no coolie can be an officer!' Another argument was that the soldiers who first entered Nanjing were third- or fourth-class reservists, middle-aged men 'more likely to get out of hand with women' than the youngsters! None of these so-called explanations is very convincing. More plausible was the reply of Matsumoto Shigei, the respected correspondent in Shanghai in the early part of the war, who told his western friends: 'It is the army. You can't know what they are like. You didn't meet those poor peasants who have been brutalized after years in the army. They are permitted to do this. It is worse than that; they are encouraged. It is their reward for taking a town; the officers promise them three days to do what they like, when a town is captured. They always do.... It is because Nanjing is so important that you Americans hear about it this time, but it has always been true. It is a universal shame.'

A western newsman who was in Tokyo at the time commented: 'The Japanese excesses in Nanjing were horrible but calculated. Men under discipline must have a little relaxation now and again.'

During the Russo-Japanese War at the turn of the century, the Japanese army had been universally admired for its high standards of discipline and its scrupulous treatment of civilians and prisoners. Yet by the 1930s that same Japanese army had become notoriously badly behaved. In the earlier war the Japanese officers came from *Samurai* families with high traditional values, whereas the much larger Japanese army deployed in China in 1937 was officered by men lacking these élite social traditions.

In any case, by the 1930s priority was given to solidarity, so that although many influential Japanese, up to and including the Emperor, did not like the way the adventurists and fanatics behaved, they were not willing to take a real stand against them in case it would discredit the good name of the army as a whole.

There was also a question of motive. The Japanese soldiers in 1904 could feel with justification that they were fighting to free Asia from western imperialism. But the army's goals in 1937 were much less readily defensible: the high-sounding propaganda about a 'new order in East Asia' could not be compared with what the army was actually doing in the field without a loss of self-respect.

As those who survived on the Japanese side were ready to comment, during earlier wars the goal was to make the other powers accept Japan as an equal, and so behaviour of a very high order was insisted upon. By 1937 that point had already been made (and fatally ignored), and it was no longer necessary to keep up the special behaviour of the past.

Emily Hahn, the American writer who was in China at this time, came to the conclusion that calculated mass rape was, for the Japanese, 'the quickest, surest way to humiliate a community. I think that they rape almost as a religious duty, a sacrifice to the god of victory, a symbol of triumphant power.'

Very often a Chinese victim of Japanese torture died, sometimes by disembowelment or, if that was not effective, a final bullet. But many survived. One such survivor told afterwards how a group of Japanese took him and a group of others to stand by a ditch, whereupon they were shot at from one side and bayoneted from the other.

This man, whom we have to call lucky, fell into the ditch and managed to escape the bayonets of the Japanese who jumped into the grave afterwards to ensure they were all dead. 'I stayed there all day. No one came to cover up the grave, and the worse thing of all was the knowledge that people were moving in the grave near me, moving quietly, alive, but pretending to be dead. . . .'

A Japanese prisoner of war confessed to his captors: 'In July 1941 I was assigned to the Military Dog-Training Institute at Changxindian, southwest of Beijing. One day they brought about fifty Chinese civilians into a high-walled courtyard. Major Kato ordered us to take positions along the wall, and when we were settled he cried, "Sergeant Oisi, begin the attack!"

'A little door on the far side of the courtyard opened and a pack of sharp-toothed dogs came bounding out and made straight for the throats of the screaming Chinese, who tried to beat them off with their fists. The spouting blood only made the dogs more ferocious, and they literally tore their victims to pieces. Eventually all the Chinese lay dead of their mutilations, and the glutted dogs were led away.'

Naturally many Japanese soldiers resisted such behaviour. But their progressive brutalization was thus depicted by one Private Tajima: 'In May 1940 the Third Company of the Thirty-Ninth Battalion, Ninth Independent Mixed Brigade, was garrisoned in Shanxi Province. One day Second Lieutenant Ono said to us: "You have never killed anyone yet, so today we shall have some killing practice. You must not consider the Chinese as a human being, but only as something of rather less value than a dog or a cat. Be brave! Now, those who wish to volunteer for killing practice, step forward."

'No one moved. The lieutenant lost his temper.

'"You cowards!" he shouted. "Not one of you is fit to call himself a Japanese soldier. So no one will volunteer? Well then, I'll order you." And he began to call out names: "Otani – Furukawa – Ueno – Tajima!" (My God – *me* too!)

'I raised my bayoneted gun with trembling hands, and – directed by the lieutenant's almost hysterical cursing – I walked slowly towards the terror-stricken Chinese standing beside the pit – the grave he had helped to dig. In my heart I begged his pardon, and – with my eyes shut and the lieutenant's curses in my ears – I plunged the bayonet into the petrified Chinese. When I opened my eyes again, he had slumped down into the pit. "Murderer! Criminal!" I called myself.'

Japanese soldiers were taught by many of their officers to look on the Chinese as little more than animals. Ruth Benedict, the American anthropologist, wrote a celebrated interpretation of Japanese wartime behaviour in her book *The Chrysanthemum and the Sword*, which explained that moral obligations in Japanese society were particularized and local, not universal. Almost all the rules of Japanese life could safely be broken on foreign soil.

The many stories of experimental surgery on Chinese prisoners support such an analysis. A bizarre case where a doctor took a captured Chinese given to him by the commanding officer for 'treatment' and kept syringing water into his chest, withdrawing blood, provides one instance. Shusaku Endo's novel, *The Sea and Poison*, gives a fictional treatment of a case involving American prisoners. One of his characters recalls after the war: 'But we had our fun in China too. We did whatever we wanted with the women. Any bastard that made any complaints we tied to a tree and used for target practice.'

Later a medical officer tells a story: 'You know in China.... No joke. I heard in my outfit there was a bunch who opened up a chink and tried his liver.'

'They say,' another officer remarked, 'it goes down surprisingly well.'

In Shanghai in 1944 Chinese workers were forced to sit on hot iron sheets and burn their bottoms.

In Wuhu Japanese soldiers hacked off the ears and arms of people in the street 'for sport', and a reliable observer saw Japanese soldiers force a pipe down a woman's throat and pump water in until her bowels burst.

The Japanese command eventually prohibited rape after the reports had become too monotonous, but the soldiers themselves took no notice.

In 1942 a case was found of Chinese being stripped, bound, whipped, beaten and hosed by Japanese, before being left for dogs to eat. Civilian – not military – Japanese administrators were said to have scalped some of their victims in Shenyang in north China. In another instance about 200 Chinese were herded together in 1943 to be stripped, hosed, beaten all over and burned with metal.

Most of the evidence of the Nanjing atrocities comes inevitably from Chinese or neutral sources. But one Japanese writer went back to the scene decades later to check the stories for himself. He concluded that by the second day of the Japanese capture of the city about 200,000 Chinese had been killed, and the figure had risen to 300,000 by February. These figures included at least 2000 who had been buried alive, several who had been roasted on high wires over a fire, and others who had been liberally doused with industrial acid. This Japanese investigator even found a case of one Chinese resister whose heart and liver had been taken out and eaten by a Japanese.

These figures are from Chinese sources, though accepted by a Japanese writer, and it was in the Chinese interest to exaggerate them. One of the most honest Japanese correspondents in the Japanese army, who was on the scene, believed that the figure did not exceed 20,000, as is also suggested by some of the missionaries. The official Guomindang figure was only 100,000.

Atrocities did not end with death. It became a recreation of the 50,000 occupiers to throw grenades at piles of bodies. In one small village just outside Nanjing twelve Chinese men were tied up and then grenaded.

The foreign mission reports agreed that the Japanese officers were usually polite and amenable, but could not always control their own troops. Auden and Isherwood reported the consensus as follows: 'The common soldiers are all right if they are not drunk. The Japanese, in general, are very easily intoxicated, however, and then the trouble begins. The lives of the male inhabitants will probably be spared, but most of the women will almost certainly be raped, so it is the women who must be got into the mission-buildings. What drunken and really undisciplined troops can do when they find themselves deprived of girls is uncertain. In one well-authenticated instance the missionaries themselves were murdered.'

Sometimes these acts were committed by Korean soldiers, but since they were under Japanese command this does not alter the responsibility.

It goes without saying that the brutal actions of the Japanese invaders took place in a setting where brutality had become only too commonplace whenever soldiers were let loose, whether Chinese soldiers against fellow-Chinese or other foreign intruders. Pierre Loti, for instance, had reported in *Figaro* in 1900, while following the Allied expedition (including German, Japanese, British, French and other units) against the Boxer rebels, how he came to a house in Tongxian – the same town where Chinese soldiers wrought atrocities on the Japanese garrison in 1937 – to see the lower half of a woman's body stuck, legs upward, in a bucket, with her severed head under a chair next to a dead cat.

After the Nanjing orgy had finished, the Japanese command held a burial service for their dead, and General Matsui spoke to the 300 officers, regimental commanders and upwards, present on the parade ground. 'Never before,' a Japanese correspondent commented, 'had a superior given his officers such a scathing reprimand.'

General Matsui admitted to an American correspondent that 'the Japanese army is probably the most undisciplined army in the world today'. Another Japanese general apologized to a westerner for the rudeness of his sentries by saying: 'You must realize that most of these young soldiers are just wild beasts from the mountains.'

Matsui, a small thin man who spoke Chinese and was a good general, attacked his officers for their indiscipline and for the bad deeds which had dishonoured the name of Japan. The newspaper man who was present was shaken by Matsui's severity, particularly since one of the officers standing before him was a prince of the Imperial blood. For what it is worth, the prince of the Imperial House who had ordered the massacre was recalled to Tokyo, and the Emperor, his nephew by marriage, commanded – too late – that specially good treatment should be meted out to the city of Nanjing.

While the Japanese army was moving triumphantly into Nanjing, it was supported by a new policy of sinking 'all craft on the Yangzi River', regardless of nationality, in order to leave the river clear for Japanese operations. In the course of this strategy the *Panay*, an American gunboat, was stopped in the Yangzi and bombed and machine-gunned by Japanese planes on 12 December. The *Panay* sank. Admiral Mitsunami, asked by an American correspondent where the order to bomb the *Panay* had come from, blurted out: 'It was the Bad Boy of the army, and not the fault of the navy.' Farther upstream, the British gunboat *Ladybird* was machine-gunned and shelled, and a British sailor killed.

The orders for these attacks on western warships in fact came from Colonel Hashimoto Kingoro, a member of the extremist

Young Officers' Group, who had assassinated Premier Okada in 1936. Hashimoto was recalled from his command of the shore batteries on the Yangzi, but was not punished, and his fame as a man of action spread widely in Japan.

General Matsui's explanations for the attacks were not considered convincing, and President Roosevelt at first demanded an apology from the Emperor himself. But in the end he did not press his complaint at the highest level, and apologies from the Japanese Foreign Minister were unwisely accepted. If Roosevelt had been just a little more self-confident at this stage, he might conceivably have made a real difference to the war.

Within days of the Chinese evacuation of Nanjing, the Japanese government offered peace terms through the German ambassador, Herr Oskar Trautmann. The Japanese proposed that China turn pro-Japanese and anti-Communist, accept a Japanese-controlled regime for parts of China, join Japan and Manchukuo in an economic bloc and pay indemnities to Tokyo. It became a famous story in China how Madame Jiang Jieshi, to whom the unfortunate German presented himself, loudly changed the subject whenever he tried to relay the Japanese peace feeler, so that in the end he had to withdraw and report that China would not talk.

Another source claims that the Generalissimo submitted the Japanese terms to Stalin, but there was never any real doubt that they would be spurned. Jiang had already on 17 December, after the fall of Nanjing, pledged that China would fight on until the end.

Not long afterwards the Japanese high command reorganized the armies which had conquered Shanghai and Nanjing, establishing a new Central China Expeditionary Army under a new commander, General Hata Shunroku. General Matsui and his colleagues were ordered back to Japan and their headquarters disbanded. Matsui retired to build a temple and, acting as his own high priest, do penance for the sins of the army at Nanjing. But their recall was less for the sacking of Nanjing than for allowing their men to dally there so long for their own individual satisfaction.

The official Japanese philosophy at the beginning of the war was *Sokk-sen, sokk-katsu* – quick war, quick settlement. If they had struck on swiftly against the retreating Chinese, they might, given the disorganized state of China's defences, have forced the war to a quicker conclusion. As it was, the Generalissimo was given a respite in which to settle down and organize the defence of Wuhan.

Japan's failure to press forward to the almost undefended Wuhan after taking Nanjing was probably her biggest strategical error in the entire war. An opportunity was offered to disrupt China's war effort, but it was not taken and was never repeated.

True, the Japanese high command were hoping at this time that Hitler would negotiate for them a truce with China. The Japanese were in any case impressed by China's heroic stand in Shanghai and Nanjing, and were consequently fearful about over-extending their forces. The Japanese path westwards was blocked by the highly respected Chinese armies of General Li Zongren. Yet, despite all these grounds for hesitation, a decisive strike immediately after Nanjing might have won Japan the war.

5

Battle for Xuzhou

Masters of both the old and new capitals, Beijing in the north and Nanjing in central China, the Japanese now sought to occupy the land in between. Early in 1938 the sackers of Nanjing began to march north to unite with the heroes of Beijing as they thrust southwards.

The natural meeting point would be the city of Xuzhou, the strategic junction of the north–south Tianjin–Nanjing railway with the east–west Belgian-built Longhai railway connecting Xi'an to the coast.

The Japanese by now controlled the entire northern bank of the Yellow River and had even been able to cross it to Jinan, thanks to the prevarications of the Chinese governor of Shandong, who was afterwards executed for his treason. From here they pressed southwards to Xuzhou, delayed only by Chinese guerrillas tearing up the railway and harassing their lines of communications.

The Japanese GHQ planned a converging attack on Xuzhou from north and south with landings at the port of Qingdao to the northeast. 'It must be', a Japanese soldier hopefully wrote home to his father, 'the last battle.'

The nearest Chinese base was Zhengzhou, farther west along the Longhai railway where it intersected with the Beijing–Wuhan line. But from here the Chinese rear was side open to the west and south. A Chinese stand at Xuzhou was therefore risky, since the Japanese could cut off the lines of supply on the south bank of the Yellow River west of Xuzhou, and even west of Zhengzhou as well.

There was another reason why Xuzhou was so important to

both sides in the spring of 1938. For the Japanese, its capture would render credible a federation of the various puppet governments which had been installed in the occupied parts of China into a single 'central' government friendly to Japan. For precisely the same reason it was vital for the Chinese to hold the city.

In the result, the Chinese, in spite of their demoralizing defeat at Nanjing, offered an unexpectedly spirited resistance. For one thing, General Li Zongren, the celebrated Guangxi general, was put in command. The German military advisers were also given their head more than in earlier campaigns.

The troops under Li were not in good shape, being units from various provinces which had not yet been integrated into the central government forces. They lacked their full complements and their morale was low. 'Compared to the troops that had fought at Shanghai,' General Li himself commented afterwards, 'they could only be classified as third or fourth grade.' But some new divisions were brought up fresh from training in western China with some of the first patriotic volunteers, including students and intellectuals in their ranks, and sporting heavy artillery and other arms on an adequate scale.

China's tactics were hammered out at a critical Staff Officers' Conference in Wuhan at the end of January. A few days earlier, the Generalissimo himself had carried out an inspection of the northern fronts, conferring unprecedentedly at Luoyang with the two Communist generals Zhu De and Peng Dehuai of the Eighth Route Army. The need for co-ordination between the various Chinese forces was self-evident, and one of the most insistent themes of the Generalissimo at the Wuhan conference was that individual Chinese armies must obey the general staff.

In a lecture at this conference Jiang Jieshi catalogued four errors which China had made in the first phase of the war, and which the Japanese had been able to exploit. The first was the false assumption that the great powers would act against Japan, so that China could therefore limit herself to defensive tactics. It was wrong for China to try to hold a stationary line when the Japanese were so much better equipped and thus able to retain the initiative. In Shanghai, for example, the Chinese infantry

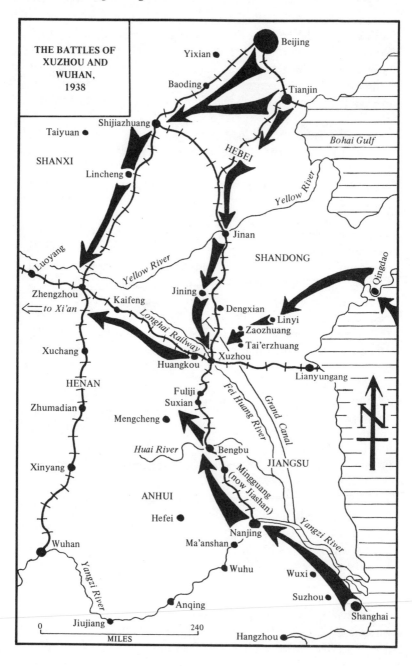

THE BATTLES OF
XUZHOU AND
WUHAN,
1938

Beijing

Yixian

Baoding

Tianjin

Shijiazhuang

Taiyuan

HEBEI

Bohai Gulf

SHANXI

Lincheng

Yellow River

Jinan

SHANDONG

Qingdao

Luoyang

Yellow River

Jining

Dengxian

Zhengzhou

Kaifeng

Linyi

to Xi'an

Longhai Railway

Zaozhuang

Tai'erzhuang

Xuchang

Huangkou

Xuzhou

HENAN

Fuliji

Lianyungang

Zhumadian

Suxian

Mengcheng

Fei Huang River

Grand Canal

Huai River

Bengbu

JIANGSU

Xinyang

Mingguang
(now Jiashan)

ANHUI

Hefei

Nanjing

Wuhan

Ma'anshan

Yangzi River

Wuhu

Wuxi

Suzhou

Yangzi River

Anqing

Shanghai

0   240

Jiujiang

MILES

Hangzhou

N

had remained passive, vainly waiting for the hand-to-hand fighting where it could shine, while the Japanese used their superior arms to the full.

The second Chinese mistake was lack of co-ordination. When the Japanese attacked at Shanghai, for example, the other fronts had remained quiet instead of counter-attacking to draw forces away from the city.

Thirdly, there was uncertainty about the line of command, not to speak of the treason of Governor Han Fuju in Shandong. Sound tactics had been misapplied. It was a good idea to lure the enemy deeply into Chinese territory in order to extend his lines and make him more vulnerable. But it was not enough simply to retreat; the Japanese advance had to be made costly by the defence of designated points along the line and massing forces on the Japanese flank for counter-attack.

Finally, Jiang explained, the Chinese army as a whole had failed to mobilize the strength and sympathy of the people, a comment which some observers read as a grudging compliment to the Red Army in Shanxi.

The basic Chinese strategy was partly one, in the words of General Chen Cheng, the Generalissimo's confidant, of 'trading space for time'. But it was also a sheer application of mathematics. 'The Japanese strength in north China is ten divisions,' argued Zhou Enlai, later the Premier of the People's Republic. 'If they could garrison each town with only one company of 100 men, they will have to use all their forces. But we can easily destroy such garrisons. If the Japanese put a battalion into each town, they will need thirty divisions.'

Specifically the Chinese now sought to entice the Japanese along the Tianjin–Nanjing railway and thus delay their westward advance along the Yangzi River to the citadels of western China. They also sought to impede the full-scale Japanese crossing of the Yellow River and delay the attack on Wuhan.

Instead of retiring with his beaten forces on to the Wuhan defence line, as he must have been tempted to do, Jiang sent them north to defend Xuzhou, following General von Falkenhausen's advice. If the Japanese had marched directly on from Shanghai and Nanjing to Wuhan, they might have taken it swiftly and divided the Chinese forces. Instead, following the Chinese army to Xuzhou, the Japanese not only withdrew forces from Shanxi which might otherwise have gone south towards Wuhan, but even diverted their Shanghai army northward instead of westward.

General Li Zongren, surveying his situation in Xuzhou as the Japanese advanced from both directions on his fewer than 80,000 weary men, wrote that he felt 'much like a praying mantis placing his body against a mighty engine'.

A useful delaying action was fought by the Chinese Thirty-First Army at Mingguang on the Nanjing–Tianjin railway. The Chinese held this city for more than forty days, giving time for the defences in southern Shandong to organize better. When the Thirty-First Army withdrew from Mingguang, the Japanese rushed through to Bengbu where the railway crossed the Huai River. But just as they were preparing to cross the river, the Chinese Fifty-First Army came to stand in its way, while the Thirty-First and Seventh Armies were ordered to attack the Japanese from their rear.

The taking up of positions for the battle of Xuzhou coincided with a noticeable heightening of morale in China. A Canadian Red Cross official who had lived in China for many years and knew the country well described the spirit of the Chinese up to the end of 1937 as depressed, almost desperate. The Japanese, he explained, was looked upon almost as a kind of superior being, unconquerable, courageous and in possession of inexhaustible supplies of murderous machines on land and sea and in the air, whereas the Chinese were mere humans. But in February and March 1938 the mood changed. People became more involved in the national war effort with the establishment of an effective information system, and the morale of the various guerrilla units improved.

At the same time China took heart from the successes at the beginning of 1938 of her reorganized air force, albeit with Russian and other foreign pilots. In January Chinese bombers raided and destroyed Japanese aircraft at Wuhu and Nanjing, and on 18 February a dozen of the eighteen Japanese bombers which raided Wuhan were shot down after a thrilling series of

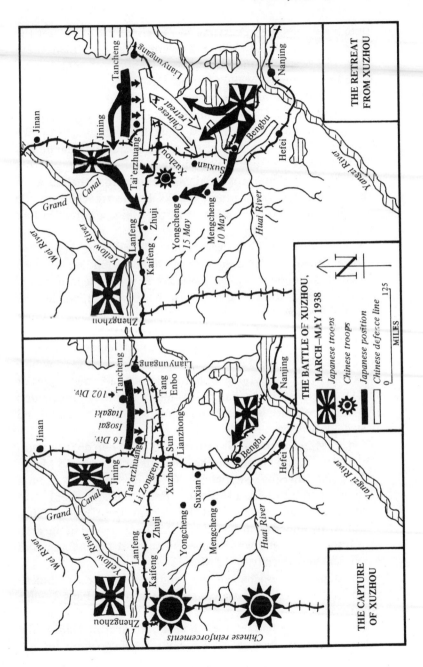

THE RETREAT FROM XUZHOU

Tancheng • Lianyungang Nanjing •
Jinan • Jining • Bengbu • Hefei
Tai'erzhuang Xuzhou Suxian
Chinese retreat
Grand Canal Yellow River Wei River
Lanfeng Zhuji Yongcheng 15 May Mengcheng 10 May
Kaifeng Huai River Yangzi River
Zhengzhou

THE BATTLE OF XUZHOU, MARCH–MAY 1938

Japanese troops
Chinese troops
Japanese position
Chinese defence line

0 — 125 MILES

N

THE CAPTURE OF XUZHOU

Tancheng • Lianyungang Nanjing •
Jinan • 102 Div. Tang Enbo
Isogai 16 Div. Iiagaki
Lianzhong Bengbu • Hefei
Jining Sun
Tai'erzhuang Xuzhou Suxian
Li Zongren
Grand Canal Yellow River Wei River
Lanfeng Zhuji Yongcheng Mengcheng Huai River Yangzi River
Kaifeng
Zhengzhou
Chinese reinforcements

dogfights watched by everyone in the city. Five days later the Chinese even raided Taiwan and destroyed a power plant there – and this was only the beginning of a new and more active phase of air support for the Chinese.

The first engagement in the complex battle for Xuzhou was at Linyi, where the Chinese gained an initial victory. General Nishio's Second Army attacked them from the north in two separate columns. The Japanese Tenth Division commanded by General Isogai Rensuke marched south along the railway from Jinan, the Shandong provincial capital, towards Xuzhou without meeting much resistance, thanks to the treachery of the local governor and the weakness of the Chinese forces in that sector.

Meanwhile the Fifth Division under General Itagaki Scishiro made a forced landing at the port of Qingdao. Finding the town militarily abandoned on 12 January, it proceeded to march southwestwards towards Linyi, with the idea of supporting the Isogai division as it came down the railway, and joining together with it at Taierzhuang.

These two crack Japanese divisions under Itagaki and Isogai were unusual in the Japanese army. They contained in their ranks many of the young militarists who had staged earlier incidents against the civilian government, and they represented the cream of the Japanese ambition to overrun China and destroy its army.

On 13 March General Nishio ordered these two divisions into the attack. Itagaki arrived on the outskirts of Linyi on 15 March with a full division, supplemented by an auxiliary cannon regiment and a brigade of cavalry. The Chinese had only five regiments to field against him, but luckily the Chinese Fifty-Ninth Army under General Zhang Zhizhong arrived in the area as reinforcement and was detailed to support the defenders of Linyi, reaching the city on 12 March.

The Japanese also had in the vanguard a force of Chinese puppet troops under a dissident general hostile to Jiang Jieshi's government.

General Zhang had led the Chinese retreat from Beijing the previous summer. Now, at the head of troops who wore, instead of the usual divisional insignia, armbands inscribed with the slogan 'Down with Japan', he so redeemed his reputation that Generalissimo Jiang hung his portrait conspicuously in his private study.

The Chinese defenders first let the Japanese into the town of Linyi and burnt the surrounding villages, then drove them out again. Since the Japanese had no place to rest, they attacked Linyi again, and the town changed hands three times in four days of bloody fighting between the 20,000 soldiers on each side.

Finally, having lost 4000 men including three regimental commanders, Itagaki withdrew to the next town. Even here the Chinese pursued and ejected his men, immobilizing the Japanese left flank in the Xuzhou campaign for almost two months. General Zhang was now officially pardoned for his role in the surrender of Beijing.

At Linyi the Chinese demonstrated for the first time that they could not only attack but could also pursue their enemy. The victory was owed both to the spirit and leadership of the troops on the field and to the staff work which led to fierce fighting and harassment on other Japanese fronts and lines of communication, as a result of which reinforcements could not be brought up.

General Li, commanding the Chinese campaign from Xuzhou, now sent the Chinese Forty-First Army (hailing from Sichuan) to southern Shandong to restrain the advance of the Isogai division. It undertook a bloody defence of Dengxian, which was bombarded with Japanese heavy guns and tanks for three days, falling on 17 March. The whole of one Chinese division, the 122nd, including its commanding general, was lost in this action to delay the Japanese southward thrust.

When these men of the Chinese Forty-First Army had first been offered to General Li Zongren, rather apologetically, because the Chinese GHQ regarded their fighting capacity as below standard, General Li had barked down the telephone: 'Zhu Geliang* put up scarecrows to scare away the enemy.

*Hero of the medieval classic *The Romance of the Three Kingdoms.*

Surely they are better than scarecrows. Please get them here quickly.'

In the event they proved their worth.

The Isogai division was now marching south along the railway with its cavalry brigade, cannon regiment, heavy artillery company and 100 armoured cars and tanks.

It was at this point that Generalissimo Jiang decided to reinforce Xuzhou with General Tang Enbo's Twentieth Army Corps and General Sun Lianzhong's Second Group Army. Tang's force comprised five divisions including a heavy artillery battalion armed with German 15 cm guns, while Sun had three divisions at full combat strength.

The first units of General Tang's Twentieth Army Corps were immediately sent north by train to help stall the Japanese southward advance, reaching the front line a day too late to save Dengxian.

General Li ordered General Sun to proceed to Taierzhuang to prepare defence works in the hope that the Japanese could be tempted to penetrate the Chinese lines along the railway and expose themselves to Chinese attack.

'I was certain,' General Li afterwards recalled, 'that a man as proud as General Isogai would not wait until the Japanese armies marching forwards from Bengbu had come within supporting distance but would fall on Taierzhuang immediately, in the hope of taking Xuzhou with a single stroke and gaining the honour of being the first to clear the Tianjin–Nanjing railway line.

'My intention was to lay a trap for the enemy when he did so. As soon as our defenders at Taierzhuang were fully prepared, I would order Tang's army to come south secretly, attacking the enemy from behind, encircling him and finally annihilating him.'

General Li's scenario was more or less followed. Isogai did indeed send his men southwards in very large numbers from Dengxian, only to meet with weak resistance from General Tang's crack units, which fell back in the hills as ordered. Tang's heavy artillery battalion was transferred to the south bank of the Grand Canal at Taierzhuang.

Isogai left Tang's army alone in the hills and forged ahead along the railway line in the direction of Taierzhuang. This Japanese force now consisted of 40,000 men, with numerous big and small tanks, field guns, heavy artillery and large numbers of machine-guns of various sizes. Isogai was supported by a large squadron of aircraft which bombed Xuzhou city and all the bridges and stations along the railway into rubble.

On 20 March General Sun Lianzhong, a six-foot northerner, took up his headquarters in an old temple near Taierzhuang. He worked, according to a visitor, 'in a sunny courtyard in which a peasant woman drove a blindfolded donkey round and round to operate a primitive wheat-mill, composed of one flat stone rotating against another'.

General Sun of the Second Group Army enjoyed explaining the Chinese plan to VIPs visiting the front. Here the Chinese could 'make a strong stand while other divisions of my army closed in on the flanks of the enemy, thus bringing him into a salient. I depended largely upon the rashness and over-confidence of the Japanese leaders, who are contemptuous of our military strength.'

Isogai bit at the Chinese bait, seeing Taierzhuang on the Grand Canal as an ideal place of operations against Xuzhou. His tanks reached the north wall of Taierzhuang on 23 March, and his field guns began to batter the Chinese defence works. By the Chinese account the rain of shells reached a maximum of 6000 a day at the height of the battle. The shells were followed by tanks, and then by the Japanese infantry, who pressed into Taierzhuang step by step.

When the Japanese tanks came to within a few hundred yards of the perimeter, the Chinese sent an armoured car with an anti-tank gun across their path, firing at each one. And when the tanks reached the Chinese trenches, the Chinese soldiers jumped out to throw bundles of hand grenades under their wheels and into the ports. But once the Japanese had infiltrated behind the rock walls characteristic of Taierzhuang's houses, the Chinese could no longer counter-attack, lacking more anti-tank guns or any tanks of their own.

The battle from the Chinese side was controlled by General

Li Zongren from Xuzhou. He was interviewed there by a foreign correspondent who had to push his way through a herd of large black pigs donated by a local peasant. General Li, a 'short, square-shouldered, round-faced, twinkling-eyed farmer's son', was middle-aged. 'His short, bristly hair is shot with grey but he is as full of energy as a steel spring.' At Taierzhuang, Li declared, the Japanese were surrounded. 'More than a division of them are cut off and they are fighting like tigers in a cage.... They can't break out.'

After three days of intense fighting on the outskirts, Isogai's men entered the city itself and there was now bitter street fighting.

'Thus far,' General Sun told an American officer visiting the front at Taierzhuang, 'the plan has worked beautifully. We hold a line along the Grand Canal, and we hold the western two-thirds of the walled city of Taierzhuang. The Japanese are in a salient twenty-five miles deep and fifteen miles across. We are now endeavouring to cut their lines of communication to the north....'

The Japanese now found themselves in a confusing and dangerous situation. The renowned Seya detachment, comprising five infantry and four artillery battalions, split up on 23 March, one part to go to Taierzhuang and the other towards Linyi. Two days later, however, the latter was encircled by a superior Chinese force and General Seya had to divert some of his main strength, earlier intended for Taierzhuang, to rescue it.

Even those of his men who were fighting at Taierzhuang, occupying one corner of the city, could make no progress against the Chinese numbers and fortifications. 'The enemy,' a Japanese report of this battle noted with dismay, 'used 15 cm howitzers for the first time.' The Japanese now deployed almost 100 field guns, and the Chinese about half as many, although they claimed that almost one in three of the Japanese shells were duds. The Chinese Twenty-Seventh Division drew enemy fire by sticking windlasses from the village pumps into the ground in groups of four to look like field guns.

By the end of March the Japanese controlled two-thirds of the city. On the night of 1 April the same Chinese Twenty-

Seventh Division raided a Japanese regimental headquarters north of the town, killing the commander and capturing many documents including a poem written by one of the officers:

> Four hours we fought and took Tianjin;
> Within six hours, Jinan was ours.
> This tiny village, Taierzhuang,
> Why does it take so long to fall?

A diary kept by one of the Japanese soldiers exclaimed: 'Why do we fight? The Chinese people are facing the devil's own tortures. We also are constantly suffering and dying. Heaven alone knows where our bones shall whiten and who shall gather them.'

Meanwhile there was a fatal misunderstanding between two of Japan's crack units, the so-called Sakamoto detachment and the Seya detachment, which resulted in their unnecessary withdrawal from the Taierzhuang battlefield.

At several moments the Japanese seemed on the point of winning in Taierzhuang. On 2 April they used tear gas and sneezing gas and by the end of that day were holding four-fifths of the town, in spite of the efforts of the depleted Chinese Thirty-First Division.

On the same day a press party arrived in Taierzhuang on the Chinese night train, to see 'a sheet of flame ... angry on the horizon'. A Chinese officer grimly explained: 'That is Taierzhuang. It has been burning for three hours.'

The journalists spoke to General Sun, 'tall, thickset, hoarse-voiced and red-eyed with fatigue'. He explained to them the importance of Taierzhuang. The Japanese 'needed it as a base from which they can attack and to which they can return if their attack fails. We too cannot afford to lose Taierzhuang. We need it to frustrate Japanese attacks on Xuzhou.... The key to the possession of Taierzhuang lies in the surrounding villages.

'So long as we hold these villages, the Japanese in the city will feel as cramped and restless as a clumsy man who can find no place to put his hands and feet.' But with the Japanese deploying over sixty field guns and almost forty tanks, the pressure on the Chinese lines was intense.

On 5 April Chinese planes came to bomb the Japanese positions and munitions dump at Taierzhuang, and Yunnanese reinforcements arrived on the Chinese side: the Chinese HQ was jubilant. 'Eight hundred Japanese in the northeast corner of Taierzhuang,' a Chinese adjutant boasted, 'are entirely surrounded. We shall wipe them out tonight.'

The Japanese were aghast at the Chinese air attacks. A Japanese war correspondent captured the mood when he reported for the *Asahi Shimbun*:

The Chinese mountain guns must have worked round behind the Japanese lines. We now hear machine-gun fire as well, and the rattle of rifles. A considerable Chinese force must be in the neighbourhood. It must be the Chinese tactics to swing round in the rear of the Japanese whenever the opportunity offers. It is like chasing flies. On Monday twenty-one Chinese fighters attacked the Japanese trenches. Their raid was very irritating. The breeze is warm and pleasant with the scent of flowers, wheat and tea, but hard fighting rages around us.

But General Li's plan to squeeze Isogai unexpectedly from behind was frustrated by the tardiness of General Tang Enbo, who was ordered at the end of March to come rapidly to attack the Japanese at Taierzhuang from the other side. In the end his men reached the field only when the heroic defenders of Taierzhuang had already expelled the Japanese by themselves in spite of their cruel losses. During these first weeks of April General Sun in Taierzhuang repeatedly pleaded with his commander-in-chief to be allowed to withdraw.

'The Second Group Army,' General Sun told his superior, 'has lost 70 per cent of its men. Enemy fire is too strong and their attack too fierce, although we have succeeded in exhausting them. May I ask permission to withdraw to the south bank of the Grand Canal temporarily? Let the Second Group Army have some men left alive. It would be a great and magnanimous act on the part of the commanding officer.'

But Li firmly expected that Tang's army from the north would reach the scene by noon the next day. If Sun and his men abandoned Taierzhuang now, all their efforts would be frustrated at the last minute. He ordered them to continue defending until morning or else face the penalties of martial law.

General Li went even further and ordered the city's defenders actually to raid the Japanese that night in order to frustrate their plan for an early dawn attack and facilitate the nutcracker operation which he planned in the afternoon following Tang's arrival. When General Sun still tried to plead off, Li brought out another card from his sleeve.

'I offer a reward of $100,000,' he said. 'You get together every man who can carry a rifle – carriers, cooks and whatever – and have them join the men at the front to form a dare-to-die corps for the incursion. The reward will be divided among them. With such a high sum at stake, there must be men of courage. Do your best. Victory or defeat hangs on this last act.'

When General Zhi of the Thirty-First Division came yet again to seek permission to withdraw, General Sun told him: 'If the men are all finished, you yourself go to fill their place. After you, I shall be the next. Whoever dares to cross the Grand Canal will be executed.'

It was in this context that the survivors of Sun's army organized a dare-to-die corps of several hundred men to attack the Japanese lines, some of them wielding their long swords.

Captain Carlson of the US armed forces was there on the night when the Japanese were driven out of Taierzhuang. Chinese commanders explained the events to him: 'Last night General Zhi, who commands the Thirty-First Division, reported that the Japanese were using tear gas. We decided that this indicated their situation was desperate. General Sun ordered him to assault.

'At four o'clock this morning about 400 of the enemy broke out of the northeast gate of the city and joined those outside in a general retreat towards Yixian. The remaining 200 barricaded themselves in a building in the southeast corner. We tried to get them to surrender, but they wouldn't. So we set fire to the building and smoked them out. All were slain.' This was on 7 April.

Next day General Zhi himself confirmed this account. 'Then I ordered a reserve regiment to move in and assault. We used hand grenades and big swords. The fighting was hot, but the Japanese gave ground. . . .'

The Chinese were said to have fielded 800,000 men for the battle of Taierzhuang. Their patrolling and reconnaissance were weak, and the artillery was still poor. But 20,000 Japanese were killed or wounded in the worst defeat ever suffered by the Japanese army.

A Chinese general told Carlson that Japan's big mistake was over-confidence. They still depended upon artillery fire and air bombardment to prepare a path for their infantry. But the Chinese countered by digging shelters, so they could come out and meet the Japanese infantry with heavy machine-gun fire.

'The Japanese infantry fights by the drill-book. When the drill-book instructions don't work, they are lost. . . . Our attacks are conducted at night when the Japanese cannot use their aviation, and we are too close in for them to use their artillery. We direct these assaults so as to bring our troops into hand-to-hand conflict with the enemy infantry, for our men are superior in big sword fighting.'

For Sven Hedin and some other military observers, Taierzhuang was the spiritual turning point in the whole war. Hedin commented, 'The Japanese learned that strength and warrior spirit lay dormant in the armies of young China, which properly directed could be roused to accomplish respectable feats.'

But von Falkenhausen, the German adviser, complained that the Chinese did not follow up their famous victory. 'I told the Generalissimo,' he confided to an American observer, 'to advance, to exploit his success, but nothing is done. Soon the Japanese will have eight, ten divisions before Xuzhou. Then it will be too late. Now they can destroy this small Japanese force, for the morale is low. . . .'

The most influential Chinese generals continued to talk defensively. General Bai Chongxi, for example, told the German advisers that China would win by outlasting the Japanese. 'We can afford to lose four men,' he argued, 'if the Japanese lose one.' Vinegar Joe Stilwell, who was present, commented afterwards that the Chinese 'cannot get the idea of the offensive into their heads'.

The reaction in Tokyo was indignant. General Sugiyama, then Minister of War in the Konoye cabinet, flew to Beijing to make a full tour of all the fronts. He concluded that the guerrilla activity in the rear areas was so dangerous that further Japanese advances into China should be postponed until a thorough consolidation had been made. But his colleagues in Tokyo would not accept his logic. Taierzhuang had to be avenged, since the army's blood was up. Sugiyama was sacked, and the taciturn, fanatical General Itagaki was summoned from the front line to take his place in the cabinet.

The virtual annihilation of two of Japan's best divisions, and the subsequent retreat along a wide front, did, however, convince the Japanese command that there could be no 'quick victory' in China. More troops, and troops of quality, were therefore needed in central China and the only source of reinforcement was in north China.

So far the war had been fought by second-line reserves from Japan, with only a few picked mobile units from the Japanese army in Manchuria assisting. In the minds of the latter élite officers the highest priority was still to be ready for an attack on the Soviet Union. The consolidation of Japanese military supremacy in north China and Inner Mongolia was only a stepping stone to this ultimate aim.

But now much greater numbers were needed in central China and they could only come from those 300,000 troops in Japan's élite army within the borders of Manchukuo, the finest offensive force Japan could muster.

On 7 April Imperial GHQ briefed the field commanders in Tokyo on their new orders 'to destroy the enemy forces in the vicinity of Xuzhou'. Such importance was attached to this operation that Imperial GHQ sent Major-General Hashimoto Gun to head an Imperial GHQ liaison team in the field for the forthcoming six weeks.

The more detailed plans of the Japanese field commander envisaged that 'a great enemy force will be drawn into the Xuzhou area and into the area east of the Tianjin–Nanjing railway. First, the route of retreat of this force will be cut by an enveloping movement west and southwest of Xuzhou, and later it will be destroyed and Xuzhou will be occupied.'

One division of Japan's First Army was to cross the Yellow River in order to defend the Longhai railway to the east of Lanfeng and co-operate with the Second Army. But although a show of strength would be offered on the north bank of the Yellow River, no effort was to be made to establish a foothold on the south bank, because of lack of numbers.

On 12 April the Second Army was given the green light for the Xuzhou operation. It had a new royal commander in Lieutenant-General Prince Higashikuni Naruhiko, another indication of the importance attached to the operation by Tokyo. Reinforcements were rushed from Tianjin as well as Nanjing, so quickly that they left parts of Japanese-occupied China without adequate garrisons (a fact of which the Chinese guerrillas were able to take good advantage, for example by sneaking up to the very walls of Nanjing itself).

After two weeks of Chinese ascendancy, the Japanese now seized the initiative once more. Afterwards they claimed that they had intended all along to display a certain weakness during the Taierzhuang battle in order to decoy as many Chinese divisions as possible into Xuzhou before encircling them.

By now Japan, which had started out to conquer China with fifteen divisions, was fielding no fewer than thirty-one. Of the 1.1 million Japanese troops who had landed in China since the war broke out, almost a quarter had been killed or wounded.

By contrast, General Bai Chongxi told foreign correspondents that China could put 15 million soldiers into the field if necessary to defend herself. In the battle of Xuzhou which was now unfolding the Chinese had 600,000 men against Japan's 400,000.

Japan's supply problems were becoming acute. They were accidentally revealed in an order intended for the Japanese Twentieth Division at Linfen, which was dropped by aeroplane on the Chinese lines by mistake. 'In future', it read, 'we will send you ammunition once a week by plane. You must economize. Decide yourselves where and when to engage the enemy. Reinforcements are out of the question at the present time.'

Events in the Xuzhou area, where four provinces meet, now

moved towards a classical *démarche*. The two armies were deadlocked. The Japanese armies above and below Xuzhou could not unite, but were striving to combine by moving up from the Huai River in the south and down from the Grand Canal in the north so that they could join together, capture the city and consolidate the Tianjin–Nanjing railway.

A junior Japanese lieutenant described the first of the battles which his unit had to fight after crossing the Huai River, leaving it with about a hundred dead and several hundred wounded. The heavy overnight rain transformed the red soil into mud, through which they had to advance 'virtually by swimming', and their light machine-guns and rifles became so mud-caked as to be useless. The red soil on their uniforms became a badge of honour.

A Japanese diarist wrote to his father: 'It will be my first experience under fire for a long time. I am sure that I will never be hit by a Chinese bullet, so do not worry about me.'

In a letter to a friend at home, the same writer was less cheerful. He wrote his friend a patriotic poem:

> Resolved to bury my life,
> I go to the front.
> My way shines brilliant.

But he held his poem back from the mail to Japan. 'The sense of approaching death which I felt then is completely different from the feeling which going to the front gives me now.' Unless the poem were 'discovered after my death, it would seem empty rhetoric'.

This campaign probably represented the peak of Japanese military skill and success. Their commanders revealed remarkable co-ordination and organization, an acute sense of timing, and, above all, daring and imagination beyond what they had shown earlier in the invasion of China.

It began with a tactical retreat, by the independent regiment of the Fourteenth Division from Lincheng. Meanwhile the Japanese Seventh Division closed in on Jining, on the Grand Canal, and the Sixteenth and Tenth Divisions also moved north to the same vicinity. Air reconnaisance might have warned the Chinese commander of the Japanese plan to encircle the lakes and his left flank, and he might then have been able to break through the holding forces of the Japanese around Taierzhuang and attack the invaders from the east of Jining. But increased pressure from the Huai River area compelled the Chinese to withdraw from the east side of the Tianjin–Nanjing railway.

On 9 May the stage was set and the Japanese Ninth Division coming up from the south captured Mengcheng, in spite of rains which prevented Prince Chichibu from visiting the front. The Japanese here were alarmed to find that the chemical composition of the local soil made their shit red and their saliva yellow.

On 12 May, based on Yongcheng, the Japanese forces coming from the south split into two columns. One headed northwest towards Zhuji on the Longhai railway, the other directly for Xuzhou in a northeasterly direction. The Japanese troops concentrated at Bengbu on the Huai River simultaneously pushed northwards along the railway to Suxian, just south of Xuzhou.

Meanwhile the Japanese Sixteenth and Seventeenth Divisions struck southwards from Jining, having gained control of virtually the whole of southwest Shandong. On the coast there were large-scale Japanese landings at Lianyungang, the terminus of the Longhai railway. The chastened remains of the Itagaki and Isogai divisions joined together at Zaozhuang to await reinforcements.

By now the Chinese were ready to bow to the inevitable. General Li Zongren and his Chief of Staff, General Bai Chongxi, at their Xuzhou headquarters, learned that a Japanese tank unit, far out in front of the main Japanese body, had at last cut the Longhai railway bridge at Huangkou, twenty miles to the west, depriving the Chinese of their only railway supply line. Meanwhile 180,000 Japanese soldiers were marching from both directions to reinforce this forward action.

The Japanese had thrown up to the west of Xuzhou a great barrier extending from Shandong province to the north across the Longhai railway into Anhui province to the south. The Chinese were shut in between this barrier and the sea, their supply lines intercepted and their retreat apparently cut off. General Li had no choice. Although three broad rivers lay in his line of march, and he was bound to be attacked in the rear with all his baggage at his heels, he had to retreat. On his escape from the Japanese pincer depended the fate of one-third of the organized Chinese army and probably of the Chinese Republic itself.

Using Xuzhou and the Grand Canal as a pivot, General Li now ordered his men to the east of Xuzhou to swing south and west while he remained in the city holding the line and directing the retreat. Chinese troops poured through the city in the execution of the first step of this manoeuvre, first the infantry, then the artillery and vehicles, with the wounded at the rear.

By 17 May Xuzhou was a dead city. The Chinese generals had moved their headquarters to a garden in the suburbs to follow the retreat by radio. During the morning Japanese guns were dragged up Tyrant King Hill overlooking Xuzhou and unlimbered, and shells began to descend on the city.

On one occasion the Chinese commander-in-chief sent a messenger with an urgent instruction, but a shell dropped, hitting the messenger. 'When I went over to help him,' General Li later recalled, 'I found that he was badly injured with a big piece of his backside torn off.'

The Japanese plan to annihilate this huge Chinese force seemed to be on the point of success. Itagaki, Isogai, Terauchi, Doihara and Hata had baited the trap brilliantly. The enemy was caged and could surely not escape. The news bulletins were already going out to Japan: '300,000 Chinese trapped.'

One articulate and sensitive Japanese soldier expressed the mood of the Japanese army as it set out to capture this huge Chinese force. He wrote in his diary on 19 May: 'As I stood dreaming on the hill of pomegranate trees, the order to depart must have been given. Soldiers got up from under the willow trees, yawned and stretched themselves. Soldiers who had been in houses, on the mountain or in the rye fields gathered in straight lines and taking up their guns soon began the eastward march.

'I watched them from my hill. Far to the right a unit was

advancing through the calm sea of rye fields along the foot of the mountain. To the left too marching soldiers stretched as far as the eye could see. Even down the centre of the rye fields they formed a long line.

'Burnt by brilliant sun and enveloped in yellow dust, they advanced to the new battlefield in the east. For me this was a sight of supreme beauty. The advancing army gave me an impression of steadily increasing power. The regular pulsation of this power overwhelmed me, enveloping me up in its sublime waves.

'When I first came to the vast plain of the northern Huai River, I was overcome by the tremendous fields of rye. I was impressed by the vitality which this ground called forth, its unmovable strength. Looking at the troops as they advanced with steady steps far across the rye fields, I felt struck to the very core of my being by an overpowering sense of overwhelming vitality.'

But General Li did have an escape plan. He had already shortened his line, by abandoning the sector east of the Grand Canal, and evacuated Xuzhou in order to avoid unnecessary casualties from air bombing. He now ordered his men to move southwards and westwards across the Tianjin–Nanjing railway, and then to head westwards in four large groups to break through the Japanese encircling line.

The orders for this had gone out to all units on 15 May. The Chinese generals who had held their lines inviolate for so long, delaying significantly the Japanese assault on China, had to accept the humiliation of retreat. General Tang Enbo is said to have wept when the order came.

But now the Chinese had a stroke of luck. Everything depended on the central column under General Tang Enbo, whose Thirty-Second Army was ordered down from the banks of the Grand Canal and sent marching southwest. To give the other remnants of the Chinese armies the start which they needed to conceal the direction of their flight and prevent the massing of the Japanese on their line of retreat, the Thirty-Second Army had secretly to march thirty-three miles with all its wounded and supplies and armour and then to get off the road and hide from the Japanese before daylight.

In fact it was still on the march at eight in the morning on 18 May when the Japanese air force began its daily reconnaissance. But a merciful thick fog appeared to drown the retreating Chinese in a snowy mist, hiding them from sight. The Chinese were able to reach their destination and disguise themselves, assisted in the afternoon by a sand storm, which covered the ground with an impenetrable haze of silica so that the Japanese planes could not fly low.

Thanks to these freak weather conditions, Japanese intelligence did not know of the concentration of Chinese forces at Fuliji on the Tianjin–Nanjing railway, so that the three groups of the main Chinese force were able to join and plan the next stage of their retreat.

A British journalist was on one of the retreat columns from Xuzhou as it left Kaifeng towards Zhengzhou. He described the procession: 'Dainty Chinese girls in silken semi-modern dress and slippers, older women hobbling along surprisingly quickly on their bound feet with the aid of long poles on which they balanced; occasional old men; rich wives of merchants in rickshaws; peasant girls plodding stolidly; tiny children wet to the skin but impassive in the long-suffering Chinese way; whole families on heavy oxcarts with solid wooden wheels, drawn by inconceivable combinations of domestic animals, their small household goods all mixed up with the equipment of the soldiers trotting beside them; babies in boxes on tiny wheels or strapped to the back of tottering older children, occasionally sturdy farmers lifting the handles of gigantic loaded wheelbarrows, their remaining donkey or wife or children pulling in front; these were inextricably mixed with the retreating Chinese army.

'There were almost no motor vehicles, and the few were piled to the sky with women and goods.... An occasional horseman trotted by; a few officers and officials pedalled along on bicycles. But except for occasional groups on the oxcarts, most of the soldiers, like most of the refugees, simply walked.... Soldiers in every shade of khaki, from dust yellow to pale green and blue, peasants in everything under the sun, all were mingled in one endless procession. . . .

'Never have I seen such wounded. They were few enough, the bulk having simply been left behind, somewhere. But those who could walked. Helped by comrades or limping alone, Chinese soldiers with bandaged arm, shoulder or leg, staggered forward along that endless rain-swept highway. Many were able to keep erect only thanks to long poles, like those of the deformed old women. Their faces pale to almost occidental pallor or drawn into knots with the pain, they stubbornly went on.

'A bareheaded boy staggered forward, his steel helmet pressed to his belly and in his helmet a section of his intestines. Not an ambulance in sight, not a doctor. . . . The army had next to no equipment, the southern soldiers never had had shoes; there was hardly a coat in the long defile, steel helmets were the exception. Bayonets were anything but universal. On the other hand, umbrellas were plentiful.

'I saw a few machine-guns, one small thing that looked like a trench mortar, one anti-aircraft gun. In the course of two days on the road with troops, I hardly noticed more than half a dozen batteries of field guns. During a week, not a single Chinese airplane flew over us while Jap planes were everywhere. . . .'

So confused were the conditions of the Chinese retreat and Japanese chase that some units got mixed up. One Japanese soldier, Umemoto, described such an encounter to a colleague: 'It happened after the sun had set when it was so dark that they could not even see the noses in front of their faces.' As they marched he was startled to hear gun shots going off in the darkness nearby, and was told that a survivor had been shot.

'A soldier leading a horse had begun to talk to another soldier marching near by. Being exhausted, he had kept silent up till then, but something made him suddenly anxious to talk. At first the soldier to whom he talked did not answer, but when he talked to him again, he answered in Chinese.

'Thinking this strange, the first soldier captured the second, who turned out to be Chinese. The Japanese soldiers were amazed and shouted out that Chinese survivors had got mixed up in their ranks. At this others tried to escape. Several were seized and discovered to be Chinese survivors. . . .

'Confused by the darkness, the Chinese had felt sure that they had met a friendly unit in retreat and gladly joined the march. Exhausted troops do not talk, and even if they had heard voices, the Chinese survivors might not have realized that it was the Japanese army.

'Chinese soldiers had come to Xuzhou from all over China and there were probably many from distant provinces who could not understand each other. Even when the Japanese soldiers began talking, the Chinese must have thought that they were comrades from some far-off district. . . .

'Presumably through lack of food and drink, they were in a feeble condition and could offer hardly any resistance. When a short break was ordered, the exhausted soldiers went to sleep on their backs. When the order to depart was given, they all got up except for one, who did not get up at all. A Japanese shook him awake with the words, "Get up quickly. You'll be left behind," only to discover that it was a Chinese. This sort of thing happened to Umemoto twice.'

The Japanese next hoped to catch the Chinese army at the Fei River, where once before, in the fourth century AD, a Chinese army had defeated northern barbarians trying to conquer China. General Li Zongren and his legions arrived on the historic banks of this river on 21 May, having survived what could have been a fatal error on the part of the Chinese engineer corps.

The commander-in-chief's train from Xuzhou was supposed to steam down to Suxian, but the line was blown up by the Chinese sappers ahead of General Li's train in the mistaken belief that it had already passed. The whole party of more than a thousand people had to walk the remainder of the journey, only to find that the Japanese had already taken Suxian anyway. General Li's group had then to make a detour around Suxian, evading bomb attacks and once almost running into several hundred Japanese cavalrymen. Luckily for them, most of the Japanese had already rushed to the north, expecting to take the Chinese army there. If they had waited, instead of hurrying to close the pincers, they would have caught the Chinese.

On discovering this, General Li split his men into three

columns, and in order to protect the flank of his main force over the rivers he sent two divisions to retake several strong points on the Mengcheng–Yongcheng highway. The Japanese infantry in this area drew back, and its transport, taken by surprise, was ambushed.

'The soldiers', one correspondent reported in a poignant aside, 'going through the pockets of the dead enemy and finding fountain pens, handkerchiefs, toothbrushes and toothpaste – all things which they never owned before but only wistfully hoped for – helped themselves.'

The peasants were told not to cut the wheat, so that the Chinese main force, following behind, could use it to hide from the Japanese aeroplanes.

With these precautions completed, General Li, at the head of four divisions of foot soldiers and an anti-tank gun regiment, came out on to the north shore of the Fei River and poured across the rude bridge of timbers, stones and mortar which the Chinese engineers had hastily assembled. Only two and a half miles upriver the Japanese were camped by two well-built bridges, with a complement of tanks and armoured cars, vainly waiting for the Chinese to appear.

At last two Japanese planes spotted the Chinese crossing. When all but two regiments had crossed, the Japanese infantry attacked. But they were now inferior in numbers and soon had to fall back. Incidentally, some of their porters, middle-aged Chinese farmers, were captured and solemnly told the Chinese army in a bizarre flight of fancy or wishful thinking that 'a flock of women, both Chinese and Japanese, was with the Japanese army, dressed in uniforms and with hair cut short like men. So as to make their force look greater than it was, the Japanese often paraded them about ostentatiously....'

Li's divisions crossed the next river and on 21 May he was able to radio to the Generalissimo in Wuhan that the withdrawal from Xuzhou had been successfully completed.

Meanwhile the Japanese entered Xuzhou in triumph, and General Hata Shunroku, commander-in-chief of the Japanese forces in central China, boasted: 'We intend to end the China incident.' But the *Japan Times* was 'greatly surprised to learn that when our forces neared the city walls of Xuzhou, there were but a thousand Chinese soldiers to offer resistance'. As one official Japanese account of the battle conceded, the Japanese attack was 'spread too thinly and many of the enemy escaped to the west'. The Chinese high command claimed that Japan had not captured a single Chinese officer in this battle over the rank of captain.

For five months between the fall of Nanjing and the fall of Xuzhou the Chinese army gave the rear areas time to prepare for the next stage of the war, the great battle for Wuhan. But General Li remembered that he and his colleagues at Xuzhou felt like 'marooned men fighting a desperate war'.

There is a neutral description of the Japanese occupation of Xuzhou, horrifying in its detail, convincing in its explanations: 'Appropriation of houses begins, officers and soldiers alike breaking from one house into the next to choose a place of shelter to their taste. A certain sense of power seems to sweep over them, of power unopposed to break the bonds of civilized restraint. In this orgy of emotional release, they think not even of their own comfort. Here fire for the evening rice is lighted in the centre of a reception hall; here, the choicest bedrooms of a stately ancient house become latrines; here the very walls are befilthed and daubed....

'Two children and an ancient man are roped in a bundle; amid shouts and laughter they are drenched with kerosene; flame is applied. An officer appears, and with the light of human torches he directs his men in drill. The Chinese, mostly men and children – women have other uses – are forced into a line. Bayonet practice begins; clumsy thrusts, the officer insists, must be repeated. Transfixed by terror and paralyzed by fear, the Chinese stand still and empty-eyed. None of them attempts to bolt; each dazedly awaits the thrust about to disembowel him....

'A screaming woman is dragged into the streets and raped. Carried away by a surge of reckless power, a soldier slices at her with a knife and jumps on her body. Other soldiers in the group grow angry; they have been deprived of sport; why should this one be selfish? And a quarrel breaks out in hoarse and shouted curses.

'An officer runs up and reproves the man for impoliteness, argues that everyone should take his turn, and promises to lead the soldiers on to further prey. A soldier kicks at the breast of the murdered woman and laughs as blood spurts forth. Peace restored, the soldiers move shouting down the street.'

The day after Xuzhou fell, General Hata claimed that a quarter of a million Chinese, belonging to forty divisions, had been surrounded. But four days later the number of prisoners was put at only 30,000. Once again the Chinese showed their amazing capacity to steal away during the retreat, either evading the encirclement altogether or else disappearing into the ground, arms and all, to come into action later after the Japanese had moved forward.

Generalissimo Jiang Jieshi himself had gone to Zhengzhou in the middle of May to take overall command of the Xuzhou operation. He was able temporarily to recover some of the towns on the Longhai railway and save a number of trains and rolling stock, and to buy precious time, but he could not stop the retreat.

Xuzhou was almost a textbook victory for the Japanese, won by superb generalship in difficult circumstances. But once again the fruits of the Japanese victory were stolen before they could be enjoyed, and the bulk of the Chinese army, its spirits raised rather as those of the British were to be at Dunkirk, survived to fight another day.

It was at this stage that the German advisers, now numbering over a hundred, were recalled. Hitler had at last won control of the German army from its anti-Japanese leaders. The Führer forced von Falkenhausen home by threatening reprisals against his family. Unlike the Italians, however, whose detailed aerial surveys of China were profitably sold to Japan, the German advisers took great care not to divulge Chinese secrets to Tokyo.

The Japanese boasted that the Chinese army had lost a quarter of its fighting strength as a result of the German exodus. But a few Germans did stay. Captain Walther Stennes, having once been so prominent in Hitler's entourage, decided to remain in Jiang Jieshi's, and a handful of others, Jewish or leftist, stayed on in China. They included Dr Baerensprung, a police adviser who had voted against Hitler in 1933, and Frank Hoebich, a young fortifications engineer. For fundamental military strategy, however, China was henceforth on its own.

The role of the Europeans in the Chinese defence was a fascinating one. The Germans were certainly the closest to the Chinese: the Generalissimo's younger son actually marched into Czechoslovakia as an NCO with the German army.

Most foreign observers praised the German influence on Chinese defence strategy, particularly for having laid out the Zhabei–Liuhe defence line which had held the Japanese in Shanghai for two months. But the 'Hindenburg line' was more controversial. The former Chinese Foreign Minister, Eugene Chen, said after the battle of Shanghai: 'The German advisers erred concerning the fortifications.... Their theory of a Hindenburg line of fortifications which could not be broken was useless in a country so vast as China. They were good drill sergeants but this is not what we wanted, and their conceptions and tactics were unsuitable in China.'

But Stennes put it differently. 'The French', he told a British correspondent in the early months of the war, 'are too arrogant and impatient to be of any use as military advisers in China. They tell the Chinese command what it should do and then shrug their shoulders when it doesn't get done. The British are too lazy; only the Germans have the necessary patience. You should have seen the tact and patience with which von Falkenhausen got his view adopted. He would never say, "I think this ought to be done." He would say, "I think the best strategy would be that plan you suggested a week or two ago," and then proceed to outline his own plan.'

The Russians, too, were helpful though less prominent. Zhukov, the Second World War hero, had been Jiang's adviser just before the war.

6

Wuhan Captured

Even before Xuzhou fell, the Japanese had despatched a vanguard for the breakthrough southwards across the Yellow River, choosing for this glamorous role the Fourteenth Division under the former Colonel, now General, Doihara Kenji. Doihara was probably the most hated man in China, the incarnation of all that was worst in Japanese imperialism. 'Doihara is my particular enemy,' General Xue Yue once declared. 'We ... are fighting a duel together.'

For seven years he had been the most powerful man in Manchuria, in the intelligence service of the Japanese occupation army, a Chinese-speaker and a self-professed expert on Chinese affairs. Short, ugly and arrogant, he was a man of brilliance but also of controversy, earning for himself the title of the 'Lawrence of Manchuria'.

It was Doihara, when a mere colonel, who had spirited away the former Chinese boy emperor Pu Yi from Tianjin on a Japanese destroyer in 1931, an exploit which made him a household name in both countries. The only time he had come second best to a Chinese leader was in 1935 when General Song Zheyuan and Generalissimo Jiang Jieshi between them sat out his threat to impose a Japanese military occupation in north China.

Just before the war an American correspondent described Doihara as 'a short, rotund man, with a smile and an off-hand manner of answering questions. He struck me as a none-too-prosperous shopkeeper rather than a man who did so much under-cover work for his country.'

Doihara's brief was to cross the Yellow River above Lanfeng

on the Longhai railway, about 170 miles west of Xuzhou, disperse the retreating Chinese and advance quickly on China's new wartime capital at Wuhan.

Facing Doihara on the opposite side of the Yellow River was the Chinese Thirty-Second Army, which learnt through spies late in April 1938 that Doihara's Fourteenth Division was indeed on the move in Henan province. Its Twenty-Third Division under General Li Bifan was ordered up to the Yellow River bank, to anticipate Doihara's arrival.

On 9 May information came that a raiding Japanese force of Doihara's men was approaching this Chinese forward unit on the south bank of the river from the east. General Li Bifan assumed that it could only be a small force, perhaps a battalion. He took it lightly, not bothering to warn all his officers. On the morning of 10 May, however, the Japanese, having marched all night, suddenly appeared in front of one of these Chinese regiments, taking it completely by surprise.

The Japanese then pushed on in motor trucks to take a second regiment, again by surprise, and wiped it out. Now the Japanese raiding party, planting the Rising Sun flag on the south bank of the Yellow River, signalled to Doihara on the other bank that the Chinese garrisons had been eliminated and he could cross. Doihara's main force immediately threw pontoons over the waters. At first the Chinese air force bombed the makeshift bridges, but eventually 500 trucks and motorized artillery rapidly crossed the river.

General Li Bifan, left behind in the walled town of Heze with the one surviving regiment of his original three, blocked all the gates. But within forty-eight hours the Japanese smashed through the walls and destroyed the entire garrison. General Li's inexcusable carelessness gave Doihara the opportunity of accomplishing what had seemed an almost impossible feat.

General Li, anticipating the verdict which the Chinese high command would pronounce upon him, shot his brains out. His was not the only example of indifferent leadership on the Chinese side. Another general, a favourite of both the Generalissimo and his German advisers, was so indignant at being given command of new recruits, quite raw and inexperi-

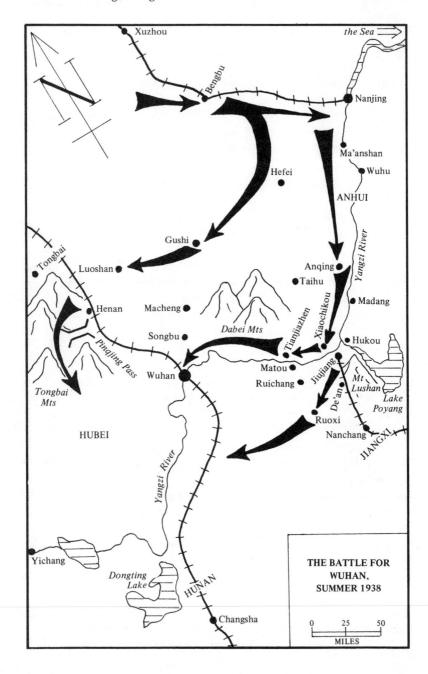

Xuzhou

the Sea

N

Bengbu

Nanjing

Ma'anshan

Wuhu

Hefei

ANHUI

Gushi

Luoshan

Tongbai

Henan

Macheng

Anqing

Taihu

Yangzi River

Madang

Dabei Mts

Tianjiazhen

Xiaochikou

Hukou

Songbu

Pinqjing Pass

Wuhan

Matou

Ruichang

Jiujiang

Mt Lushan

De'an

Lake Poyang

Tongbai Mts

Ruoxi

Nanchang

JIANGXI

HUBEI

Yangzi River

Yichang

Dongting Lake

HUNAN

Changsha

THE BATTLE FOR WUHAN, SUMMER 1938

0   25   50

MILES

enced in battle, that he refused to go out at their head and sulked in his tent instead, pretending to be ill.

Cut off by Doihara's unexpected crossing of the Yellow River, the Chinese General Gui Yongqing tried to resist the Japanese breakthrough with scratch divisions south of the Longhai railway. In the third week of May he received from his HQ seventeen old Vickers tanks and a few precious 155mm guns, and was able to launch a modest but in the end useless attack. The Japanese then moved southwards, as if in flight. The Chinese HQ was delighted. 'Doihara,' boasted General Gui, 'has no place to go. He is running away wildly. . . .'

But next morning artillery bursts were heard from the south and west, and the Chinese realized that Doihara had been going even faster than they imagined and was in fact encircling them. In the afternoon came news that the Japanese cavalry had seized Luowang railway station to the northwest, so the Chinese were surrounded.

At a council of war, General Gui asked General Long Mu'an to take his Eighty-Eighth Division to attack Doihara at Luowang. 'If we don't open the railway tomorrow,' General Gui explained, 'he'll come in behind us and cut us off. If we stay here day after day, we'll be wiped out bit by bit. We have no food, only these two wells for water and not much ammunition. . . .'

But General Long was reluctant and General Gui complained to an American correspondent who was with them: 'He has no business being a division commander.' He never did attack, and was later executed for insubordination.

All this time the disastrous Chinese retreat from the Yellow River was still in train. Jack Belden, who was there, described it: 'There were a few big Krupp-made guns, pulled by motor trucks, mountain guns packed on long-eared mules and bird rifles from the nineteenth century. There were fragile Vickers tanks, and high-wheeled carts loaded with bric-a-brac creaking noisily in the night. There were high-backed mules and low-backed gaily caparisoned donkeys, and small, fleet Mongolian ponies. There were dull, brutish peasants, bent low under loads as heavy as those any beast of burden carried. There were soldiers in tattered, stained rags, with bare feet or feet in rope sandals, with caps or rags above their heads and only one or two with helmets. There were Henanese and Cantonese and Sichuanese, Shanghailanders and Pekingites, each speaking to his brothers in a different village tongue. . . .'

Now the story took another unexpected turn. At Yanggu, the town where the Chinese reassembled, a grinning Chinese tank commander told a visitor; 'The enemy have gone back to the Yellow River. They have no ammunition. Doihara has been defeated this time.'

General Gui's comment was: 'I knew I should have attacked westwards. The enemy would have been badly defeated then. Oh, this is too bad.' Abruptly he turned to the American correspondent: 'You were there when I said we should have attacked westward, weren't you? You heard me say so? Sonofabitch, we would have had a big victory.'

His chief of staff added sardonically: 'Have you ever seen anything like this before? Two armies retreating at once?'

But when General Gui and the American correspondent went into some of the nearby villages they saw what the Japanese had left. In one ruined house the American made out a 'broken, half-burned bed and the charred bodies of a man and a woman. Their flesh was black and corrupt. With my hair rising, I crept on tiptoe inside the room. The man's body had no head. I saw it over against the mud wall. A pulpy mass, sightless, with the lips stretched in a tight grimace.'

Doihara had run short of supplies, and it was this that had brought him back to the banks of the Yellow River, only to be closed in on three sides by Chinese troops. With his back to the river, the Japanese Lawrence of Manchuria faced fourteen Chinese divisions out for his blood.

But help was at hand in the form of the Japanese Sixteenth Division, now moving westward from captured Xuzhou. Also, General Gui relied on the Chinese Eighth Army to make a stand at Zhuji on the Longhai railway, so as to give him enough time to deal with Doihara. Instead, the Eighth Army retired after only two hours of fighting.

The Chinese commander-in-chief now had to draw off some

of the forces encircling Doihara in order to check the unexpectedly fast Japanese advance towards Suxian on the north–south
railway leading to Nanjing. Only nine divisions were left to
press Doihara into the river.

General Gui with his five divisions reached Suxian before the
Japanese and formed defence lines through the area. But Jiang
Jieshi chose this moment to order, for secret reasons which
were to become apparent, a general retreat over the whole
front, including Suxian and the Doihara trap. The dreams of
revenge on Doihara dissipated, and the frustrated Chinese field
commanders had to forgo any hopes of a consolation victory on
the Yellow River plain.

As the men who had pinned Doihara down, together with the
· vast army of General Li Zongren escaping from Xuzhou,
swarmed in full retreat across the Yellow River plains, the
Japanese careering in hot pursuit towards the city of Zhengzhou
where Jiang Jieshi had been directing the Chinese movements,
the Generalissimo desperately sought time to prevent the
Japanese from taking advantage of their victory.

From Zhengzhou, junction of the two vital Longhai and
Beijing–Wuhan railways, the Japanese could sweep to the west
against the Chinese guerrillas, and also south towards the
wartime capital of Wuhan which was China's industrial heart.
Jiang needed to dismantle his factories and ship them with his
government almost a thousand miles up the gorges of the
Yangzi to Chongqing in Sichuan province if he was to establish
a new and final base of resistance in China's far west.

One of the foreign correspondents covering the war spotted
an armoured train at Zhongmou, halfway between Zhengzhou
and Kaifeng. He assumed that it was covering the Chinese
retreat, but one of the Chinese railway workers confided that it
was actually protecting the Chinese who were working on the
Yellow River dykes to the north of the town.

'Funny moment to be building up the dykes. . . .' the journalist wondered aloud.

The Chinese winked. 'Who said anything about building
them up? You know the river is higher than the plain.'

'Yes.'

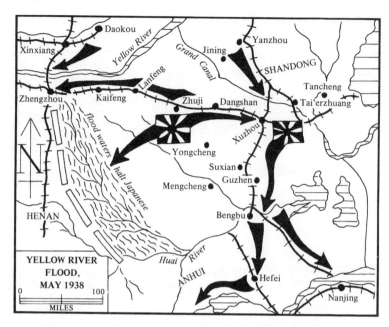

'Well, the Chinese are planting dynamite in the dykes at two places not far from Zhongmou.'

A few days later the Chinese high command issued a statement that stray Japanese bombs had hit the dykes of the Yellow River, and flood waters were pouring south in front of the advancing Japanese columns.

'Very providential of the Japanese,' was the knowledgeable Chinese railway official's comment.

It was, of course, the Chinese themselves who had pressed into service their oldest friend and enemy in this region, 'China's sorrow', the Yellow River itself.

After its long course through deep ravines from the barren Mongolian mountains, the Yellow River comes out just west of Zhengzhou into an immense alluvial plain covered with fine loess dust. Over the millennia of Chinese history the river has constantly overflowed and changed course, and now runs between protective embankments which the precipitation of sediment has caused to rise higher and higher. It flows not so much through a bed as along an aqueduct, a river on stilts.

Around Zhengzhou in 1938 the bed of the river stood anything between 23 and 29 feet higher than the surrounding plain.

The secret Chinese plan to break the Yellow River dykes was almost thwarted by the low spring waters at this particular time. In most years the Yellow River was a dangerous flood menace to Chinese farmers, but in this year of military crisis for the entire country it could not easily be turned into a flood just when it was needed. Eventually, however, the Chinese engineers found a place where the ground was sufficiently low for a flood which would impede the progress of the Japanese, where the Huayuan River entered the Yellow River, just north of Zhengzhou – the same place where the river had broken its banks of its own accord seventy-five years earlier and changed course.

General Shang Zhen was given the job of blowing up the dyke. For several days in succession Jiang Jieshi anxiously telephoned him to find out whether or not he had done it. But he held his hand until the right moment, and when his own men were safe. This came on 11 May when a small Japanese force burst into the area which the Chinese engineers planned to flood, with the Chinese army retreating just in front of them.

General Shang pressed the button, the dykes exploded and a breach some 200 yards wide was driven into the earthen banks at Huayuankou. The water hesitated maddeningly, but at last spilled over with a roar and swarmed onto the Japanese, drowning their advance guard by the thousand, miring their tanks and guns into the ground and throwing an impassable wall of water between the Japanese and Zhengzhou.

The Yellow River waters thus rolled down the Lulu and Huai river beds to the south, eventually to merge with the Yangzi near Shanghai. For several weeks these rivers, thus widened, interposed a barrier between the two armies. The Chinese gained the vital respite they needed, while the Japanese plans had to be scrapped.

Eleven cities and 4000 villages were flooded by this action, crops and farms across three provinces were devastated, and 2 million people were made homeless. One can only guess at the price which the Chinese government had later to pay for that involuntary contribution to the war effort.

After the fall of Xuzhou the Japanese held a more or less unbroken line from Hangzhou Bay to Inner Mongolia, with a foothold on every single Chinese railway north of the Yangzi. The way to Wuhan seemed to lie open from three directions – along the Longhai railway westwards from Kaifeng, by road from Hefei in Anhui province over the Dabie mountains to Xinyang on the Beijing–Wuhan railway, and directly upriver from Nanjing along the Yangzi itself. But the Yellow River flood made the first of those three routes a cul-de-sac, and the main theatre of the drive on Wuhan now shifted from the Yellow River area to the valley of the Yangzi.

On 3 June a cabinet reshuffle in Tokyo saw General Itagaki, the defeated 'hero' of the Pingxing pass and Taierzhuang, installed as the Minister for War. A notorious fire-eater, and identified with the Japanese continental adventure in China ever since its inauguration in 1931, he entered a cabinet dedicated to drive vigorously and swiftly on Wuhan.

Not all the new Japanese arrivals on the front shared the official optimism. One captain in the Japanese 113th Division wrote in his diary after sailing to Shanghai to join the war on 7 June: 'Landed feeling the cruelty of war, although we must win the victory without any discrimination as to means. Why and for whom am I perpetrating this cruelty – I only know it in my heart, for I dare not speak it with my lips.'

The new Chinese recruits were even more to be pitied. A correspondent watched a division of Sichuanese troops marching through Wuhan on their way to the battlefield 150 miles to the east, having already been on the road for several months:

Young men and boys, not too well armed, coolies carrying officers' baggage and cooking cauldrons, junior officers, little to be distinguished from the rank and file. No one in the streets paid any attention to them as they marched past. These soldiers had no bands or drums to cheer them, no girls to throw them flowers or give them cigarettes. All the pageantry of war familiar in the west was absent in China. At night the Bund was crowded with the soldiers sleeping side by side sprawled out on the scanty grass or the hard pavement, their rifles stacked at intervals and watched over by a sentry. The gay life of the city to defend which they were going to give their lives was unknown to these peasant boys, or to the junior officers who slept alongside them. . . .

Japanese bombers had already, of course, been softening up Wuhan. Auden and Isherwood were there on the Japanese Emperor's birthday, when 500 civilians were killed and thirty planes destroyed – nine Chinese and twenty-one Japanese.

Over by the other gate lie five civilian victims on stretchers, waiting for their coffins to arrive. They were terribly mutilated and very dirty, for the force of the explosion had tattooed their flesh with gravel and sand. Beside one corpse was a brand-new, undamaged straw hat. All the bodies looked very small, very poor and very dead, but, as we stood beside an old woman, whose brains were soaking obscenely through a little towel, I saw the blood-caked mouth open and shut, and the hand beneath the sack-covering clench and unclench. Such were the Emperor's birthday presents.

Another foreign visitor investigating the damage of the day's raid 'almost stumbled over the body of a man lying by the waterside, his entrails exposed. He was still breathing. No one had time to attend to him, apparently, or he was regarded as a hopeless case. Perhaps he was unconscious and could feel no pain, as my companions assured me, but as we passed one gruesome sight after another, I wished above all things that there had been morphia for the wounded.'

But this time the Chinese fighter interception was much more effective, boosted by Russian pilots. Lieutenant Kobayashi Saburo confided to his diary before being shot down in the air battle over Wuhan: 'The terrible thought that it is impossible to conquer China has gripped our army and air force.'

The battle to take Wuhan was different from the earlier campaigns of the war. Now the Chinese were in their own milieu, while the Japanese lines were badly stretched. The Chinese spirit of resistance was higher than it had been at Shanghai or Xuzhou. 'We will defend Wuhan,' said a Chinese general, 'as the Spanish did Madrid.'

The Chinese were established in field fortifications which had been dug in advance, notably at Madang on the Yangzi to guard the entrance to Lake Poyang. They were able to deploy along the Yangzi mobile artillery detachments equipped with small-calibre guns and anti-tank guns; with infantry and engineering support they effectively interfered with Japanese water transport and troop movements.

To compensate for all this, the Japanese deployed every defensive resource they had, including many small naval vessels operating on inland waters. But their infantry was beginning to tire, just as the Chinese war apparatus was getting into working order. The joke was spread that whereas the Japanese had won the gold medal for the marathon in the Berlin Olympics two years earlier, it now took them six months to cover the ground from Nanjing to Wuhan.

A fleet which included twenty transports and aircraft carriers with 150 planes now steamed upriver to Shanghai for the great Wuhan offensive. The Japanese planned a co-ordinated action by their navy with ten infantry divisions pushing along the north bank of the Yangzi River, with landing parties ready to go ashore at various strategic points on the south bank.

Of the three prongs in the Japanese attack on Wuhan, the right-hand one was immobilized by floods, the central one had the great Dabie mountain range to cross, and so the left-hand prong now assumed the greatest responsibility. It was the strongest equipped and also the least impeded by natural obstacles.

Generalissimo Jiang Jieshi disposed his Chinese forces along the lower slopes of the Dabie mountains and along both banks of the Yangzi River. His southern units were commanded by General Chen Cheng, and included the Cantonese armies of General Xue Yue and the troops of General Zhang Fakui.

North of the Yangzi the commander was General Li Zong-ren, newly recuperated from a relapse of a bullet wound in his cheek inflicted in a minor civil war in 1916, with the same men who had fought on the Tianjin–Nanjing railway – the crack Guangxi divisions, the Generalissimo's own units under General Tang Enbo and General Sun Lianzhong's Second Army Group which had won the victory at Taierzhuang.

General Tang was a strict disciplinarian who was said once to have shot dead with his own hand a soldier who stole a bucket of water from a woman. He felt optimistic about the Wuhan campaign, claiming to a foreign visitor that in the first stage of the war:

The Japanese fought like lions; in the second stage they were still a fresh, hard-driving force but they had just begun to flag a little; today they are war-weary and have lost their heart for the war.

Our men, on the other hand, are beginning to learn to stand up to modern armaments and we are better equipped.... On these hills the Japanese cannot use their heavy artillery and when it comes to pitting infantry against infantry our soldiers are superior to the Japanese. The Chinese can climb hills faster and stand more hardship.

The greatest danger to our defence of Wuhan is gas. We haven't yet got gas-masks and the Japanese are now using gas constantly. Even when it is only tear or mustard gas it lays our men out for long enough to enable the enemy to come and bayonet them as they lie gasping for breath. A few days ago two whole battalions of my troops were wiped out in a gas attack.... Malaria is also a serious problem, for we are short of quinine.

The Japanese were not only well equipped with artillery and fully supported by their navy and air force, but also boasted chemical-warfare units enabling them to make frequent use of gas. The Chinese had limited artillery, an air force that was still far too small, and none of the more sophisticated instruments of war of that day.

The Japanese objective in this campaign, as before in Xuzhou, was not just to take the target city, but more importantly to draw the Chinese into battle and destroy their main force in order to bring the war to a decisive end. The Chinese, by contrast, assumed that Wuhan would be lost, but that the war would continue and would eventually be won by new and better-equipped Chinese armies, so that their intention was to preserve the core of their army intact, ready for the final counter-offensive. They would not risk their main strength in tactically unfavourable circumstances.

The Japanese armada took Anqing on the river Yangzi on

12 June, and soon afterwards the first fighting in the Wuhan campaign broke out around Taihu on the north bank of the Yangzi. On 23 June, however, floods stopped the fighting, and for a time it looked as if China's two great rivers would between them frustrate the Japanese high command.

But the high water on the Yangzi, unusual for that time of year, also helped the Japanese to move heavy ships farther upriver. It was now the Japanese navy which took the initiative, therefore, beginning a general assault on the Madang boom, just below Jiujiang, at the mouth of Lake Poyang. A large force of infantry was landed on the south bank to attack the boom's defences.

This was the so-called Hata detachment, a small element of which recovered the initiative after a day when the Chinese air force successfully bombed Japanese ships in the Yangzi and forced them to scatter. When the Hata detachment attacked the Madang fortress a piece of Chinese slackness characteristic of the old warlord days gave the Japanese their opportunity.

The Chinese commander, instead of being at his post, was feasting in another town. There was no one to give orders when the sudden assault came, and so the forts were reduced within a matter of hours, with the help of phosgene and chlorine gas. The commander was later shot by the Chinese authorities, but one of their strong points in the Yangzi defence system had been lost.

On 29 June the Japanese fleet steamed through the Madang boom, which turned out to be surprisingly flimsy. Fifty ships, three of them loaded with stones, had been sunk off Madang at the expense of the local provincial government, and the forts there had been built under German supervision as models of modern fortified construction. The Chinese expectations were expressed by the general who boasted to a group of Russian visitors that 'Madang should hold up the Japanese for a month, and we are thinking of defending Wuhan for a year'. Meanwhile the main force of the Hata detachment pressed up the Yangzi on a mission to clear the water route as far as Hukou. In fact it chose to land earlier and advance overland to Hukou, which it captured on 4 July.

The Japanese forces landing south of the Yangzi reached Jiujiang, after fierce fighting and with heavy casualties, and advanced along the railway southwards towards De'an. Luckily for China, the air force maintained its record during this campaign and during the first days of July put out of action almost a dozen Japanese naval craft, including a small aircraft carrier.

The Japanese now needed reinforcements but found, to their anger, that they not only could not bring in units from the territories they had already occupied but were actually obliged to move soldiers away from the main theatre of war to deal with the spreading guerrilla activity at their rear.

By mid July the Chinese Fifth and Ninth War Zone Armies had more than sixty divisions in the field around Wuhan, while China's troops in the Third War Zone Army south of the Yangzi were seriously threatening the Japanese lines of communication.

The river harbour of Jiujiang was captured on 26 July, but there was then a month of relative idleness on the part of the Japanese due to the intense heat and the combined ravages of dysentery, cholera and malaria.

It was 22 August before Japan's assault on Wuhan finally got under way. On that day Imperial GHQ issued an army order signed by Prince Kotohito, Chief of the General Staff, that the Japanese Central China Expeditionary Army together with the navy should 'invade and occupy key points in the vicinity of Wuhan', destroying as many of the enemy as possible, while the Japanese North China Army would take diversionary action.

The Japanese Central China Expeditionary Army commander prepared first to gain and then to extend a foothold in the northern hills of the Dabie mountains and along the north bank of the Yangzi, and then planned to concentrate forces at Xiaochikou, on the Yangzi opposite Jiujiang, cut the Beijing–Wuhan railway and capture Wuhan.

It was the central Japanese column going westwards from Anhui towards the Beijing–Wuhan railway which was ultimately to decide the fate of Wuhan. But the Japanese also sought a breakthrough on the south bank of the Yangzi, and September saw epic battles for the towns of De'an and Ruichang. Gas was used in them, and in one engagement a complete regiment of Cantonese troops fell victim to it. But the Chinese lines managed to hold, and on 2 September, in the battle of Ruichang, there were thousands of casualties on both sides.

In early August there was a scare in Wuhan when Japanese bombs blew out the wall of the Generalissimo's dugout. Jiang Jieshi and his wife escaped by a miracle and the incident was never publicized.

On 4 August a Japanese captain wrote in his diary: 'I am weary unto death and so thin that my body is no more than skin and bone to commit cruel deeds. In my conscience I dare not face my parents. The Chinese soldier has the sacrificial spirit and modern armaments, and they have a geographical advantage over us. They watch us very carefully. They are not so tired as the Imperial Army and we are having great difficulties in transporting supplies. There seems little hope of our winning the war....' He was killed next day. Defeatism was, however, rare in the Japanese ranks.

Matou, a south-bank fortress crucial to the Wuhan defence system, fell on 15 September and the corresponding point on the north bank, Tianjiazhen, two weeks later. Tens of thousands of casualties were suffered during the course of these battles, roughly in the proportion of one Japanese to every two Chinese.

In the Dabie mountains the Japanese Second Army found the going very difficult. The plan had been to use the Thirteenth Division alone in the Macheng sector, but because it suffered heavy casualties in attacking a 'stubbornly resisting enemy' on a river bank, and again during a night attack on 2 September while crossing the river, as well as suffering from a heavy toll of malaria after the Xuzhou operation, the Sixteenth Division had to be added. The Japanese right flank finally reached the north–south railway by the end of September.

The other major area of fighting was around Ruichang and De'an in northern Jiangxi between Lake Poyang and the Hubei border. Foreign observers saw with disappointment the natural

Above The Chinese bombing of the Great World Amusement Park in Shanghai, August 1937
Below Japanese advance patrols enter Guangzhou, October 1938

Above Generalissimo Jiang Jieshi (right) and Madame Jiang with Dr Kung, the Finance Minister, 1937

Below The Fall of Nanjing: General Matsui enters the capital of China in December 1938

Fighting back: the Eighth Route Army defending the Pingxing Pass,
September 1937

Left Chinese guerillas
operating at night to destroy
the railways
Below left Chinese troops
with Japanese battle trophies
from their successful defence
of Chongqing, China's
wartime capital
Right Generals Zhu De (left)
and Peng Dehuai of the
Communist Eighth Route
Army
Below Generalissimo Jiang
addresses cadets of the
US-run Infantry Training
Centre in Jiangxi in 1944

Left The Gimo (right) and his deputy chief of staff Bai Chongxi, with General Thomas Arms at the Infantr Training Centre

Right Major-General Claire Chennault, the 'Flying Tiger', with his dog Joe

'Vinegar Joe' Stilwell with Sun Liren in North Burma

Right General
Hata Shunroku

Left (from top to bottom) Generals Itagaki
Seishiro, Doihara Kenji and Matsui Iwane, all
hanged as war criminals

mountain defences which the Chinese had in this area being abandoned one after the other. The American military attaché, Colonel Joseph Stilwell, commented at the end of September: 'The Chinese are continually abandoning positions which they ought to be able to defend with a few thousand men, and then making a heroic stand for weeks or even months, in a theoretically indefensible position. They *will* fight this war their own way, and it's no good getting upset about it.'

The Japanese Twenty-Seventh Division concentrated on the east of Mount Lushan on 10 September, ready to link up with the Ninth Division and drive westwards to Ruoxi. They swung as far as the Guangzhou–Wuhan railway which was cut in two places on 27 September.

The Japanese Eleventh Army was meanwhile trying to evict the Chinese from De'an, in the shadow of Mount Lushan. The 106th Division was assigned to break through the Chinese positions at Wutailing and attack De'an from the side and rear, beginning on 25 September. But this Japanese unit complained of bad roads, bad maps, bad communications and inferior personnel – most of them being reservists with little training, even the officers.

After a fortnight this division was surrounded by superior Chinese forces at Leimingguliu and suffered heavy casualties, losing provisions and ammunition as well. The Japanese commander had to order the Twenty-Seventh Division, which was preparing to attack westwards from Ruoxi, to turn round instead and attack the Chinese rear at Kanmukuan. Jiang Jingguo, the Generalissimo's son and present-day President of the Republic of China in Taiwan, was one of the high level advisors involved in winning brilliant victories at De'an, trapping the Japanese in between the hills and annihilating them before that town was captured on 27 October.

To the north of Wuhan, the Japanese Tenth, Thirteenth and Sixteenth Divisions pushed westwards along the northern foot of the Dabie mountains. They took Gushi early in September, and then Fuchinshan, forcing the Chinese back to prepared defences. Here the Chinese were able to hold the Japanese up for more than a month, but on the northern foot of the

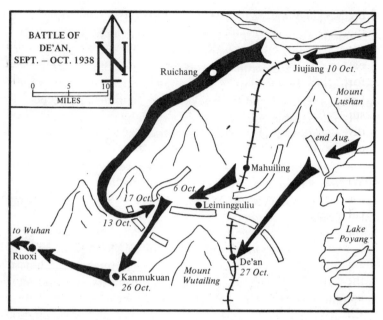

BATTLE OF
DE'AN,
SEPT. – OCT. 1938

0   5   10
MILES

Ruichang

Jiujiang *10 Oct.*

*Mount
Lushan*

end Aug.

Mahuiling

6 Oct.

17 Oct.

Leimingguliu

13 Oct.

to Wuhan

*Lake
Poyang*

Ruoxi

Kanmukuan
26 Oct.

*Mount
Wutailing*

De'an
27 Oct.

mountains the Japanese were able to drive westwards to occupy
Luoshan.

What the official Chinese report called 'sanguinary fighting'
then broke out in the Xinyang area, on the Beijing–Wuhan
railway. Xinyang itself was evacuated on 12 October, whereupon the Chinese took new positions in the hills of Tongbai to
the west of Xinyang.

Just before the loss of Xinyang, Generalissimo Jiang had
come to the Chinese headquarters of this sector to stay the
night. The commander-in-chief, General Li Zongren, had his
HQ in a temple outside the market of the small town of Songbu.
Jiang took the general's bed, while Li slept on a door placed
over the table in the central hall.

Despite the mosquito net, the Generalissimo was harassed by
these insects and repeatedly called to aides to come and drive
them away. But the more they worked, the more the mos-
quitoes came, and neither the Generalissimo nor General Li got
any sleep that night.

General Li ordered General Hu Zongnan, who was defending Xinyang on the railway, to withdraw to the south and hold the Pingjing pass through the Tongbai mountains in order to cover the large Chinese forces withdrawing westwards from eastern Hubei. General Hu was a bachelor with a short, massive forehead like Napoleon's. He had a direct line to the Generalissimo and was often inclined to disobey his immediate superior in the field. On this occasion he calmly took his seven divisions directly west to Nanyang, instead of south, leaving the central section of the Beijing–Wuhan railway wide open.

These various operations, all designed to ensure the fall of Wuhan, constituted the greatest undertaking which the Japanese armed forces had ever up to that time mounted. It was calculated that 2 million soldiers took part, 400,000 on the Japanese side.

The numerical superiority of the Chinese prevented the Japanese from forcing a conclusion to the war in spite of all their encircling operations. Their powerful mechanization enabled them again and again to break irresistibly through China's defensive lines without ever fully reaping the fruits of victory.

Wuhan fell on 25 October. But during the ten months between the fall of Nanjing in December 1937 and the fall of Wuhan in October 1938 the Chinese leaders had been able to make preparations for industrial defence facilities to be withdrawn to the western provinces. Arsenals were sent to Sichuan, new strategic roads and railways were built. The capacity of coal mines was expanded, and in all these ways China was able to ensure her survival in the interior.

The retreat of personnel and equipment up the Yangzi gorges in the last days of the Wuhan campaign was something of a 'Dunkirk' for China. The industrial skeleton of the country, its entire government apparatus, the museums and libraries and a great part of the educational force were concentrated at Yichang, ready to go up the gorges to the safe interior.

After the fall of Wuhan there were still 30,000 people and 90,000 tonnes of material waiting to be transported at the bottleneck. Everything had to go on the ships of the Minsheng Steamship Company, but so many government and army authorities tried to direct operations that total confusion resulted.

Eventually the capable chairman of the Minsheng Steamship Company told the officials to end their piecemeal negotiations and useless formalities and allow his staff time to do their real job of running the ships. There were forty days of safety left for the bigger steamers to sail up the gorges and the maximum tonnage which could be shipped in that time should, he argued, be rationed out to the different organizations. His plan was agreed, and in forty days the mountain of goods and machinery had vanished and the 30,000 men had gone inland.

General Chen Cheng, sometimes known as the Crown Prince because of his devotion to Jiang Jieshi, had been put in charge of the defence of Wuhan, with the Guangxi generals, including Bai Chongxi, under him. Many believed that General Chen, who was no great general but was wholly loyal to the Generalissimo, had been given the reponsibility because Jiang feared that the Guangxi generals might threaten his own political supremacy if they were given overall command of the armies.

General Bai in particular might have saved Wuhan, and the Cantonese might have put up a much tougher resistance in Guangdong and prevented the fall of Guangzhou itself if all their best troops had not been deployed 500 miles away on the Yangzi when the Japanese attacked in the south.

The attack on Guangdong province followed Chamberlain's appeasement at Munich and the consequent drop in prestige not only of Britain but also of the pro-western politicians in Japan.

General Yu Hanmou, in command in Guangzhou, was notoriously inefficient and careless, and he never dreamed that the Japanese would provoke the British in Hong Kong by attacking nearby Guangzhou. Yet four-fifths of China's supplies from the outside came in through the port, and Guangzhou was an obvious target at this stage of the war.

A Japanese seaborne armada assembled off the Pescadores and landed at Daya Wan (Bias Bay) on 12 October. Amidst rumours that a deal had been done between the Japanese and

Chinese commanders, the Japanese force quickly established a beach-head. Within nine days it was in the great city of Guangzhou, whose population of more than a million people was depleted to only 10,000 for the occasion.

As usual, the city had been subjected to massive bombing attacks, which Ambassador Yoshida in London publicly admitted were for the purpose of demoralizing the civilian population. The usual horrific reports came out of the city from foreign observers:

Close to a wall a woman, in a last feeble effort, was trying to draw back to herself her poured-out entrails. A ricksha stood intact, the coolie between the shafts; but his head was gone, his torso putty-grey and naked. Nearby lay a dead mother mangled and torn, the body of her baby crushed into her own....

The principle of scorched earth had been grimly adopted by the Chinese. When the Japanese took over the city they found the power station, waterworks, radio station and numerous factories irreparably damaged. On the following night the ammunition dumps blew up, and the Chinese made sure that Japan gained virtually nothing from the city's capture.

Alas, these measures were not always successfully timed. The city of Changsha, capital of Hunan province and the place where Mao Zedong had gone to school, was burned to the ground by misguided Chinese officials when the Japanese were still a hundred miles away – and without warning to the population, many of whom, including wounded soldiers, died in the flames. Generalissimo Jiang Jieshi rushed to the stricken city and ordered the immediate execution of the men responsible, despite the fact that several of them had been his close followers. But the damage had been done.

7

The Partisans

When the Chinese partisans began to operate behind the Japanese lines in the early part of the war, some Japanese had never heard of the term 'guerrilla', and the official news agency, Domei, once protested to the world that the despicable Chinese were training certain kinds of apes to wreck railways and throw hand-grenades. The Chinese sometimes called this kind of activity 'sparrow warfare', because it usually meant surprising an enemy with only a small force.

During and after the battles for Wuhan, neither side was in any doubt about the importance of guerrilla operations behind the Japanese lines. Their extent by 1938 was extraordinary, and not believed at the time. In the early weeks of that year Captain Evans F. Carlson of the US navy intelligence department made a long tour of the partisan areas in north China and was astonished at what he saw.

He came to within 150 miles of Beijing and yet remained in Chinese-controlled territory, and crossed railway lines supposedly controlled by Japan. He visited schools, factories, hospitals and radio stations which were in regular communication with the Chinese government far to the south. Some of the guerrilla areas even had their own administration, with elections and economic planning.

'The Japanese,' he told the foreign correspondents afterwards, 'cannot conquer such a people. They are like men trying to plough the ocean.'

Haldore Hanson of the Associated Press came back from the partisan areas of Hebei with similar reports. He described physics and chemistry professors sitting in guerrilla headquarters devising techniques for the partisans to destroy Japanese planes. Shortage of dynamite was their biggest problem, so the engineering specialists told the partisans to pull out certain rail-spikes at places where the lines curved. When a heavy train passed, the tracks would spread and the train fall over the embankment.

Once the Japanese tumbled to this, they began to send light trains ahead of the loaded ones in order to look for missing spikes, so the partisans replaced the iron spikes which they had taken out with wooden pegs painted to look like the original. These pegs were supposed to stand the weight of the light trains, but break when the heavies came along. Thirty trains, Hanson reported, were derailed on the Beijing–Wuhan railway in the course of three months.

Small wonder that the Generalissimo eventually set up a school of guerrilla tactics to which all Chinese army officers were to be withdrawn in rotation for three months' training in partisan warfare, under the direction of General Ye Jianying, former chief of staff of the Red Army and later the key figure in the post-Mao rise to power of Deng Xiaoping. It was reliably reported that a Chinese translation of T. E. Lawrence's *Seven Pillars of Wisdom* was used as a textbook by the railway guerrillas.

One of the most successful practitioners of this kind of warfare, General Peng Dehuai, the Communist of whom Mao came to develop such an excessive jealousy, described it to an American visitor: 'For individual battles we have the principle of the short decisive attack. We attack one point and demolish it in a short period. The advantage is the enemy cannot use new equipment advantageously. Airplanes are of little use, poison gas of no use, and tanks of little value. By the time the planes arrive the battle is over – they can only bomb the dead....

'With the enemy in our country, we have the advantage that the people support us, so that we can know the enemy's every move and they have no information whatsoever. The terrain is always fully known to us....'

For Peng, the introduction of democratic politics to the Chinese villages was the most important prerequisite for parti-

san victories over Japan. The Japanese themselves fanned
Chinese anger and patriotism by their own actions.

One group of Chinese volunteering for partisan duties
explained how on their way to the partisan HQ they had seen
many dead bodies of slaughtered Chinese youths. 'In many
places the Japanese had taken one, two or three men from each
family and killed them; they had sometimes killed all the young
men of a village. They roped them together and then split their
heads open with swords, on the general theory that living
Chinese – particularly youths – are "dangerous".'

One famous partisan general, the Manchurian General Ma
Zhanshan, introduced an American visitor to a young hero
called Liu, who had been moved to form a small partisan group
after his son had been killed and his daughter raped by the
Japanese.

Another partisan explained how once he was attacking a
railway station and climbed up on a roof and saw inside ten or
fifteen Japanese 'devils' as he called them – 'and they had
Chinese girls with no clothes on. We were sorry for the girls, but
we couldn't help it. We set fire to the building and hurled
hand-grenades through the windows.'

The morale of some Japanese was wavering slightly. Captain
Ishiguro Yeichi wrote in his diary on 23 October 1938: 'As a
result of the fierce barrage laid by the enemy this morning, only
forty members of this company are left, while over half of our
Sixty-Eighth Company are either killed or wounded. Every
time I see a funeral pyre, my heart feels acute pain. After each
battle a fire is made with wood or charcoal, and the bodies of
our dead comrades burned. Their ashes will be sent back to
Japan. Why is it all necessary?'

The guerrillas did not underestimate the Japanese. General
Zhu De, commander of the Eighth Route Army, told a foreign
correspondent that the Japanese were well trained and better
armed than the Chinese. 'They use their mechanical arms –
tanks, armoured cars and planes – to great advantage when they
get the opportunity. They are good at taking cover, shoot well
and keep their arms in good condition.

'But,' he went on, 'they have very definite weaknesses. One

weak point is their infantry. The Japanese infantry, we have found, are not very good at independent action. They depend entirely on mechanical means of transport for communications and supplies. If these are cut off, they are at a real disadvantage. They cannot use animal transport or human labour, as our armies can. They cannot take advantage of the hill country, but must follow the easiest and most level route.

'When we fight the Japanese, we try to avoid their strong points, and select their weak points for attack. So we always fight in the hills, and not in open country. And we have the assistance of the people, whom we organize and train into partisan units, to harass the enemy lines of communication. . . .'

General Zhu pointed out the respective positions in Shanxi and neighbouring provinces on the map. 'Outside of their main lines of advance,' he said, 'the Japanese hold nothing. Our troops are deep in their rear, and – in co-operation with the volunteer mobile units in Hebei, and the partisans – occupy practically the whole of the territory through which they have advanced.

'*We* have no rear to worry about, for we are fighting in our own country, and everywhere the people support us, give us food and asisstance. If necessary, we can rely on the Japanese themselves for ammunition, for their cartridges fit our rifles. So you see there are very good prospects for continuing the war in north China.'

Political work was thus given high priority in these guerrilla units. The Political Commissar of one of the Eighth Route Army divisions was that consummate politician Deng Xiaoping, later to become famous throughout the world as the man who presided, in the late 1970s and early 1980s, over the debunking of Mao Zedong.

It was General Zhu who had issued in November 1937 the following stern orders to his partisan units: 'It is essential . . . that the people must know how to help our troops. You must know how to destroy roads and railways, armoured cars, trucks and tanks. You must know how to destroy completely all roads over which the Japanese can move their mobilized columns. These roads must be turned into wheat and corn fields. No road must remain for the use of the enemy. . . .'

In the better-disciplined villages the sternest measures were taken against anybody helping the Japanese. One day in northern Henan a troop of Japanese marched through the main street of a small village. A small boy selling peanuts remained at his post, perhaps because he did not see them in time or did not realize the risk he was running.

The Japanese stopped, took some peanuts, and tossed the boy a few coppers. But hardly had the dust of their tramping boots settled on the road again when a rifle appeared from a nearby shrubbery and the boy was shot through the head. There was no trading with the enemy, and there were no exceptions.

The worst lack of the Chinese guerrillas was medicine. Dr Richard Brown, a Canadian missionary doctor, sent this despatch on 6 June 1938 from one of the Eighth Route Army divisional headquarters at Lanxian in northwest Shanxi: 'Many of the wounded have had no attention at all, and some have been on their dirty beds for months. In one place many soldiers were absolutely naked, verminous all of them, half-starved and slowly dying of sepsis. The other day we came across a poor wretch with half of his face shot away, also two-thirds of his tongue. He cannot swallow and is slowly dying of starvation. . . .'

Brown quickly exhausted the few medical supplies he had brought with him, and was then operating without antiseptic or sterilizers or even gloves. He performed what he called 'wet surgery', boiling gauze for two hours in a pot of water and bichloride. This was a poor area, and the Japanese in the spring had burnt the growing crops, so that food was desperately short.

Brown was by no means the only foreigner to become involved in helping the Chinese guerrillas. Another book could well be written about Dr Norman Bethune, the Canadian doctor who lost his life of septicaemia after countless operations behind the lines in the same appalling circumstances; Dr Kotnis, an Indian doctor who similarly offered his skills, and Michael Lindsay, the son of the Master of Balliol College at Oxford University who ran one of the most important partisan radio stations, were two more foreign volunteers. There were many others.

As for military equipment, the partisans had to devise their own. The Eighth Route Army had no artillery or guns to be effective against tanks, so they buried shells, attached to detonators, in the roadway. Several tanks were exploded by this means.

But then the Japanese forced Chinese farmers and peasants to ride in front of their columns in heavy ox carts to test the road, as a result of which several innocent victims died.

The Chinese guerrillas next changed their tactics to burying large bombs beneath the road which could be exploded by a lanyard from a concealed position off the road. The Japanese then used bandit-suppression tactics, sending out columns through the Chinese villages to browbeat them into no longer supporting the partisans.

A Chinese brigade leader described one operation where his men built what looked like heavy fortifications halfway up a mountain: 'The Japanese scouting planes noticed this, and for several days bombed the mountain very heavily. We left a few troops nearby, with orders to scatter as if in flight; no doubt the Japanese airmen reported that the "Chinese defences" had been destroyed, and our troops routed! So the enemy sent a large cavalry force to come and clean up the remnants.

'Meantime, our forces had been waiting in ambush at the foot of the hills – very much nearer the Japanese than the latter suspected. We surprised their cavalry when they advanced, attacking from short range with machine-guns and hand-grenades; and inflicted very heavy losses on them before they retreated.'

In response to this kind of tactic the Japanese tended to resort to the desperate measure of burning all the neighbouring villages within reach. But this only advertised their own impotence and further alienated the population.

One of the villages which suffered most from the policy of vengeance and example which the Japanese eventually adopted was in eastern Hebei near Fengrun. Here on the eve of the Chinese New Year the Japanese troops surrounded the village before dawn.

The entire family of the village head was killed, and then the rest of the inhabitants were driven to a large empty basin at the end of the village where they were executed *en masse* by machine-guns, and their buildings set on fire with grenades. In this incident the Japanese killed 1035 people, the great majority of them women and children. The purpose was to prove the invincibility of the Imperial Army and to cow anti-Japanese feeling among the peasants. In fact the Chinese government was able to gain much political support from publicizing this case.

A Japanese writer has documented a horrifying revenge on another village in north China which had been helping the Eighth Route Army. On the night of 24 January 1940 some 3000 Japanese troops together with 2000 'good Chinese' puppets surrounded this village secretly by night. The 1500 villagers woke up to gunfire on a freezing morning to face systematic slaughter. This lesson in good behaviour ended with the survivors being herded on to oil-soaked rags and burnt alive.

General Peng Dehuai of the Eighth Route Army once gave a melancholy catalogue of heroes: 'Liu Chanfang, treasurer of the Hou Chai Cheng village ... died without telling the enemy the location of the government stores even when his whole body was burnt by boiling water; Wang Muyong, of the Shang Nan Hui village, died without disclosing the hiding-place of the co-workers or the whereabouts of the government stores, even when pins were driven beneath his fingernails, his eyes gouged out and his head smashed. . . .'

There was a complaint among the people of one part of Shanxi, which had frequently changed hands not only between the Japanese and Chinese, but also between the Chinese Nationalists and the Chinese Communists: 'Japanese, too many killed; Guomindang, too many taxes; Communists, too many meetings.'

By all these means and bravery, many things could be accomplished. A Guomindang general operating in occupied Hebei wanted to publish a newspaper for his men. With the help of the commander of the puppet Chinese militia in the nearest town, he succeeded in buying printing presses and paper from Tianjin and shipped them over Japanese-controlled railways. All this was smuggled across country to the guerrillas, and the newpaper flourished.

In Hebei province tunnel warfare became a specialized military art. The Chinese villagers dug cellars to hide in when the Japanese came, and connected them to make a village warren, and then connected each village's tunnel system with the next. These networks of tunnels presented a challenge to the Japanese as well as an easy means of entrapment. They tried all kinds of devices to force the Chinese out, such as tying a cylinder of gas to a pig's tail, pouring kerosene on its back, setting fire to it and sending it down the ramp of a tunnel – whereupon the partisans built water traps across the tunnel floor to drown the pig and neutralize the gas.

Later an imaginative Japanese officer brought a gramophone to play the sound effects of trucks passing, to keep the villagers underground in the hope of starving them out. But after a few days the Chinese realized that the sounds were coming without the vibrations which should have been felt in the ground, and so they came up and exposed the trick.

The columns of Japanese which drove up and down north Shanxi and western Hebei hunting partisans during the winter of 1937–8 sometimes embraced as many as 3000 men, with tanks and air cover and artillery.

At the beginning of 1938 the Chinese central government took in about 5000 remnants of Communist units in southern Jiangxi and reorganized them as a New Fourth Army, to conduct guerrilla operations south of the Yangzi from a base in southern Anhui. General Ye Ting, its commander, was interviewed by an American correspondent soon after his appointment at his Wuhan HQ in a former Japanese residence complete with tatami floor matting and a charcoal brazier.

'A smooth-faced, vivacious, thickset Cantonese, noted for his spectacular personal courage', General Ye had as his theatre of war a long narrow belt between fifty and seventy miles deep along the southern bank of the lower Yangzi valley. By the autumn the New Fourth Army had fought 231 battles, captured mountains of weapons and equipment, destroyed 200 Japanese trucks and railway waggons, and had put thirteen miles of railway, ninety-five bridges and thirteen miles of electric power lines out of operation.

The Japanese dropped handbills by air along the south bank of the Yangzi to deter those collaborating with the Chinese partisans. One of them was a cartoon in four pictures. The first shows the dark figures of partisans destroying a bridge by night, while a little Chinese boy watches from a distance; the next two show the boy running to the Japanese HQ to betray his countrymen; and the last shows the child's laughing face as he waves a banknote in the air.

One of the sad features of this war was the extent of mutual betrayal. The Japanese were able to find Chinese agents to work for them in great numbers. Once when Chinese aircraft were returning to their base after a successful bombing raid on Japanese positions, a hand-grenade was thrown which wrecked one plane and seriously injured two airmen. The bomb was thrown by a Chinese, who answered for it with his life. Such Chinese were bound by threats made by the Japanese to kill members of their families if they did not obey Japanese orders.

Sometimes when they came unexpectedly to a village, the partisans would be met by village elders bowing in welcome and waving Japanese flags in their hands. To be mistaken for Japanese and received in this way was a mortifying experience for the partisans, one of whom wrote in his notebook: 'Our work among the people is too inadequate.... There are so many traitors.... But they are driven by hunger and they are so ignorant....'

The Chinese puppet militia working for Japan often kept contact with the Chinese guerrillas beyond the limits of the towns in which they were working, seeing this as a way of serving China better. At least some Chinese units would be fed, clothed and armed by the Japanese, after all. And they could warn the guerrillas whenever there was a plan to attack them. 'If we are forced to join in,' they would say, 'we can pretend to fight but fire our rifles into the air. Thereupon we retreat, leaving our guns and ammunition for you.'

Sometimes the two kinds of Chinese troops met face to face in the open battlefield. A Chinese commander described how he was leading his company up a hillside one night to storm a Japanese position when he heard a Chinese voice above them saying.

'*Lao Xiang* [countrymen], come no farther! We have orders to use poison gas!'

'Traitors!' the captain indignantly exclaimed.

'There is no other way,' explained the anonymous voice apologetically.

The captain led his men back down the hill and then around it, with the idea of attacking from the rear, only to be surrounded by a whole battalion of Manchurian Chinese puppet troops. The puppet commander wanted the company to retire with their guns, promising that his men would fire high in the air.

'You are traitors!' the captain repeated, to which the puppet leader answered that when they had been conscripted by the Japanese in Manchuria their families had also been registered. If they deserted or refused to fight, their families would be killed.

The Chinese captain argued that loyal Chinese in his own army also had families in Japanese-occupied territory and that all Chinese were men without homes. In the end the Manchurian told the captain how to escape: 'Don't go in that direction; there are machine-gun nests there and the gunners are Japanese....'

On the other side, there was a very small number of Japanese prisoners who defected to the Chinese side, sometimes for ideological reasons and sometimes out of hatred for the government which had launched Japan into its Chinese venture. One of these was Aoyama, who used to hail his compatriots on the other side of the battleground through a loudspeaker above the noises of battle.

On one occasion the firing stopped as Aoyama was doing this, and everybody listened as this young Japanese appealed emotionally to his fellow-countrymen to stop killing their brothers, the Chinese, and to turn their guns against the capitalists who had made 10 million yen out of the war. Suddenly the Japanese were reinforced, and the fresh troops made an unexpected rush on the radio unit and the unfortunate Aoyama was captured.

Over wide areas of northern China these partisan methods now began to pay off. In Shandong, where the famous guerrilla commander Liu Zhendong died in the defence of Laixi in January 1938, the Japanese eventually had to evacuate the road between Yantai and Weifang, so that a large area of the province was made available for Chinese guerrilla activities. Even Jinan and Yantai were retaken. By the middle of May guerrilla actions were in full spate in southern Shandong, northern Jiangsu and eastern Anhui.

Meanwhile other important operations were launched in Hangzhou, Xuancheng, Nanjing, Wuhu and Guichi. At one point the Chinese partisans penetrated Hangzhou and in mid March they forced the Japanese to launch a five-pronged attack on the Jiangsu–Zhejiang–Anhui border area. It had to be called off a month later without having achieved very much.

Sometimes the results of partisan attack were spectacular, as on 28 October 1938 when a Japanese brigade near Guangling was claimed to have been wiped out, together with its commanding general. After the Japanese capture of Kaifeng, Chinese soldiers broke into a meeting of the puppet government there and shot them all, in the middle of a large city occupied by Japanese troops.

In fact many villages maintained two separate heads, one to deal with Chinese officials and one to deal with the Japanese. Each would keep the other informed of developments. An American missionary travelling in the guerrilla areas commented that the old men of the village would go out at night to break up the motorable roads, coming back to sleep in the daytime when, at the command of the Japanese, the younger men would go out to repair them again.

One of the most famous guerrilla bands was that of Zhao Tong, which began with a single family in the north. Zhao's mother was in charge initially of purchasing weapons and managing the commissariat for this partisan group.

Its most daring exploit was a raid on a Beijing prison in which forty partisans released 570 prisoners from under the noses of the Japanese. It was Zhao Tong's group also which once claimed the credit for downing a Japanese aeroplane near Beijing with a lucky rifle shot.

The Chinese partisans fell back on the mythology of their own ancestors, the Chinese equivalent of Robin Hood. One of the cavalry guerrillas from the northwest reminisced: 'In summer, we moved through the fields among the thick, tall crops, or during cold winter nights we often left a village or town abruptly at an order and swiftly moved thirty or sixty miles, to suddenly appear in another "pacified" area [i.e. enemy-held territory]. When we dashed past a fortification held by the Japanese or puppet troops, the enemy could do nothing but crouch under the battlements and watch us. We bivouacked in sand dunes, on earth mounds or hollows in the ground. . . .'

Some of the Chinese learnt their lesson hard. Not untypical was the experience of one warlord general who, astonished by the might and modern equipment of the Japanese when they first arrived, simply dropped his arms and ran for the hills, where he and his men stumbled one afternoon on a Chinese guerrilla detachment.

'Where are you going in such a hurry?' the guerrilla commander asked.

The warlord general explained that the entire Japanese army was at his heels. The guerrillas detained him for the evening and at the end of a long discussion the warlord general went back to his men with a plan. He told them to form a thin circle around the Japanese troops and then to make all the noise they could. His soldiers obliged, shooting off all their ammunition, banging kettles, shouting at the tops of their voices and building fires.

The effect on the Japanese commander was just as the guerrillas intended. He inferred that a new situation had presented itself after the successes of the previous days. So he called for reinforcements of men and munitions against an obviously larger surrounding force.

A long caravan of trucks duly wound along the supply road soon afterwards, preceded by protecting troops. But at the top of a narrow pass between two mountains, just after the last truckload of soldiers had passed, the road exploded and there were the sounds of an attacking force. The soldiers rushed ahead after the enemy, failing in their excitement to hear behind them the sounds of the other half of the warlord general's army systematically stripping the unguarded supply trucks.

When the Japanese troops came back they found their supply trucks empty. The Japanese commander decided to catch the retreating Chinese before they could escape, but whenever he advanced he found there was nobody to fight. He had no option eventually but to return to headquarters, but on the way he again encountered the warlord general, who had placed his men along a mountainous stretch of road which he had also been sensible enough to mine. The Japanese commander got back with only a small fraction of his original strength, having lost virtually all of his arms and supplies.

The most spectacular feat of the Chinese resistance movement in the occupied parts of China was the assassination of the collaborationist Mayor of Shanghai, Fu Xiao'en, in the autumn of 1940.

Constantly guarded by Japanese soldiers, Fu evaded several attempts on his life by underground gunmen. The guerrillas decided to change their tactics. They discovered that the mayor's personal valet had just married a young girl who had come out of her school intensely patriotic. He was persuaded, with the help of a cash payment, to emulate her convictions.

At four o'clock one morning the valet climbed the stairs to his master's room with a meat cleaver up his sleeve. He stopped before the two Japanese sentries before the door and bowed reverentially.

'Work for my master,' he murmured.

The young Chinese entered the room and, with the Japanese soldiers only a few feet away, hit his master across the head, across the abdomen and across the neck – the traditional Chinese treatment for traitors. Then he slipped away unsuspected, walked down to the kitchen, took his bicycle and pedalled away beyond the city limits to safe guerrilla country.

8

China Wins at Changsha

The Japanese regarded the capture in October 1938 of Wuhan, the largest interior city of central China, as something approaching victory in the war, especially when one of China's senior politicians and a rival to Jiang Jieshi for national leadership, Wang Jingwei, succumbed to the temptation to capitulate and make the best possible deal with Japanese militarism. In the middle of that 1938–9 winter Wang went to see the Generalissimo to urge upon him the peace terms offered by Prince Konoye at this point. But he was thrown out after five minutes.

Wang then flew to Yunnan and tried to organize the defection of the southern provinces, including Sichuan, from the war. But he was rebuffed, and fled to Hanoi. His failure to split the Chinese united front against Japan was one of the factors which prompted Premier Konoye to resign. A new cabinet was formed in Tokyo under Baron Hiranuma, fully committed to the army's case for a military solution in China.

One of the Baron's early pearls of wisdom, in a speech to the parliament, was: 'As for those Chinese who fail to understand to the end, and persist hereafter in their opposition to Japan, we have no alternative but to exterminate them.'

Wang represented only a small minority of Chinese political opinion, which was by now surprisingly and unprecedentedly united against the Japanese menace. Jiang Jieshi made a statement on Boxing Day of 1938 expressing China's defiance:

If China could now consent to Japanese troops being stationed in north China, and allow Inner Mongolia to be set aside as a special area, as

Japan now demands, China would not have begun the armed resistance on 7 July 1937. . . .

What Japan still lacks is a China which can be deceived or threatened into surrender. The situation being as it is, if we hoped to live under a tiger's chin, and to secure independence and equality for our nation through peace and compromise, we shall not be different from a lunatic talking in his dreams.

The Generalissimo was described by a foreign adviser at this time as wearing a 'khaki uniform without insignia but with a white tab with characters above the upper left pocket'. Slightly stooping, he would gaze inquisitively at his visitors. 'Although he was only 51 he carried himself like an old man. He was a frail figure, with dry hands and shifty eyes, garbed in a deliberately plain uniform.' The uniform which he wore throughout the war is still displayed in his memorial hall in Taibei, distinguished only by its eleven brass buttons.

At the Nanyue Military Conference in November Jiang had reviewed China's defence strategy with his generals. The assessment of the Chinese high command was that the mountainous and rugged terrain of western China, especially the rocky gorges of the Yangzi which commence above Yichang, would prevent the Japanese in the future from being able to concentrate any large military and naval forces for a combined attack on the Chinese army. The war would henceforth be conducted at arm's length.

Jiang divided his army into three parts. One was assigned to mobile warfare in the provinces already invaded by Japan, acting somewhat along the lines of guerrilla forces but on a larger scale and under the control by radio of central military headquarters in Chongqing.

Another part of the army would remain in central China to meet any Japanese advance, although this threat was believed to be small. Finally, a third portion was to undergo training in western China free from the threat of bombing.

Actually Chinese military planning was not always as thorough as it should have been. 'The Chinese army,' a staff officer complained to the Generalissimo, 'is not a European army, it does not carry out orders precisely, and therefore whatever plan is drawn up will go to pot.'

To which Jiang Jieshi, stuttering as usual, replied, 'There has to be a plan, even if it's a poor one. One must make one's will known.'

The Japanese high command claimed that the Chinese army of 2 million men at the beginning of the war had now been halved as a result of its great losses in successive battles, especially the battle of Wuhan. At the beginning of 1939 Japanese intelligence put China's actual strength at 'about 210 divisions, totalling 900,000 men with gradually deteriorating equipment'. The Chinese themselves claimed 240 divisions with 2½ million men under arms, but most of these were new and untrained recruits. It was admitted that their greatest problem was the training of new officers.

The high command in Chongqing worked out that whereas the Japanese army had advanced at about ten miles a day in the Xuzhou campaign, the rate of advance had been slowed to only about one mile a day during the battle for Wuhan. Similarly the ratio of Chinese to Japanese losses had been five to one in the Shanghai and Nanjing fighting, whereas at Wuhan the losses were about equal. Besides, the retreat from Wuhan had been an organized one, with the maximum salvage of men and weapons.

The Chinese plan was to wear down Japan and outlast her, by sending small units to attack her lines of communication and her concentrations of troops and thus render it impossible for the Japanese to hold the territory they already claimed to occupy.

By 1939 the Chinese soldiers were becoming truly anti-Japanese. 'The soldiers' hatred towards the Japanese,' said one Chinese general, 'is enormous. It is impossible to have a prisoner delivered to headquarters although we pay from 50 to 100 yuan on delivery, and there are severe punishments for not doing so. The soldiers say that the prisoners die along the way.'

Japan had at this point about a million men in China, of which just over half were combat troops. These were disposed in more than twenty-three divisions and supported by more than 500 aeroplanes.

The Japanese had captured Wuhan only after extremely heavy losses, and their commanders now, in 1939, faced the prospect of even wider battlefields, more scattered units and longer lines of communication. An average divisional front for the Japanese Expeditionary Army was now a hundred miles! The Japanese therefore turned their attention to countering Chinese attrition, holding their line at its present location and blockading the ports in order to prevent supplies from reaching the Chinese army. For this second phase of the war the slogan was *Gen-chi Ho-kyu*, fight the war with local Chinese resources – self-help warfare.

What it amounted to was that Japan was able to have the major cities of eastern China, together with strips about six miles wide along the lines of communication, and this entirely occupied the twenty-five divisions which she deployed. As a foreign observer put it, the Japanese occupation of China was like 'stretching a few clotheslines across a yard'. Even Prince Konoye lost his optimism. 'The present war,' he told correspondents, 'cannot be completed as quickly as was the case with the preceding Sino-Japanese war. At this moment one cannot even think about the end of the war.'

The Japanese still had fourteen divisions and two air groups in Manchuria and Korea. But these were, in the minds of the Japanese military leadership, committed against the Soviet Union, which remained the major threat and eventual prime target on the Asian mainland.

Another seven divisions were engaged in garrisoning Taiwan and Japan itself. Although Japan mobilized more divisions to fight America at the end of 1941, she did not substantially reinforce her troops in China in 1939–41. From then onwards Japan could take only a handful of new Chinese cities, and those were acquired at a tragically high cost.

The Japanese army was compared by one foreign observer to a fly caught on flypaper, desperately trying to free one leg after the other but always sinking deeper into the glue.

'China,' Mao Zedong explained to the American military attaché, 'is like a gallon jug which Japan is trying to fill with half a pint of liquid. When her troops move into one section, we move to another. And when they pursue us, we move back again.

'Japan hasn't sufficient troops to occupy all of China. A drive is made here, and another there. Instead of throwing a large force in at the beginning, reinforcements have been brought in piecemeal. But her greatest mistake has been in the attitude of the army towards the Chinese people. By burning, raping and slaughtering they have enraged the populace and cemented the will to resist.'

The foreign correspondent Nym Wales described in a memorable passage the archaism of the invader:

The Japanese army and its samurai officer caste has shown itself to be the vestigial remains of feudalism – one of those anachronisms which history inexorably destroys. It is rapidly committing *hara-kiri* in China by its own hands. It is not even a modern unified force bringing true imperialism to China. It is not a colonizing force, but a looting and raping expedition in the traditions of the Huns and Spanish conquistadores. Already it has demonstrated that it is trying to establish, not a true imperialist colony, but groups of feudal Shogunates, all quarrelling for power among themselves.

The Japanese, in their new military circumstances, assigned an enhanced role to their air force, which hitherto had been merely supporting ground operations, bombing enemy supply lines and combat units and dropping food and ammunition for Japanese forces when they were cut off. Only now was the first major strategic bombing attack launched. Bombing raids from Wuhan against the areas surrounding Chongqing began on 26 December 1938, the day of Jiang Jieshi's Churchillian announcement of defiance.

Japan now had about twenty-four squadrons in China, of which nine were reconnaissance and six fighters. But Baron Tokugawa continued to complain that he was not getting his lost equipment replaced fast enough, so that the efficiency of his planes, especially his long-range bombers, was falling.

The communications equipment for night flying and navigation was faulty. Daylight bombing was proving less and less fruitful, yet central Chinese airfields were unsuitable for night use by heavy bombers and there was a shortage of pilots trained to fly at night: the headquarters reconnaissance squadron, for example, had only two or three such pilots.

The Chinese air force now had about 400 planes, and was receiving around seventy new ones every month from Russia. Not everyone admired the Generalissimo's appointment of his own wife as the head of the Chinese air force. 'She had good intentions,' said Eugene Chen, a former foreign minister, 'but she was just a well-meaning girl who knew nothing about the subject.' The air force was now, however, beginning to get into gear.

The new Russian planes which the Chinese were receiving were regarded by the Japanese as superior to their own Type 95 aircraft. The newer Type 97 bombers and fighters were better, but the factories in Japan could not produce enough of them. They therefore bought for the new strategic bombing role seventy-seven Fiat BR-20s from Italy.

The Japanese succeeded only too well in the area surrounding Chongqing, but they did less well at Lanzhou, the key airfield on the Chinese supply route to Russia, which normally harboured about 100 planes, mostly Russian, of the E-15 and E-16 type. Even the Russians themselves took part in air combat from this airfield.

The Japanese attacked Lanzhou during February 1939 with about thirty aircraft and claimed to have damaged 100 enemy planes. But the Japanese commander commented afterwards: 'It appears as though the morale of the enemy air force is high, and air battles were often carried on for a long period of time.' The casualties were so heavy that the attacks were suspended.

Another major bombing of Lanzhou was launched later in the year. The navy air force had been bombing Chengdu and Lanzhou, usually at night, but found it difficult to locate targets and judge results.

A joint daylight attack was therefore planned using a combined air force with about 100 planes – thirty-six Type 97 bombers and sixty-four medium attack planes from the navy. The Japanese claimed to have bagged about twenty Chinese planes, 'but', a Japanese account bitterly complained, 'the enemy air force retreated and frustrated ... efforts to destroy it'.

It was the bombing of Chongqing, the new Chinese capital, where Jiang Jieshi lived in a house called, like Hitler's at Berchtesgaden, 'Eagle's Nest', which had the most political significance. Chongqing soon became the most bombed city in China. Only the fact that heavy fog every winter kept the Japanese bombers away for half the year prevented it from being smashed out of existence. Its houses were mostly made of wood and plaster, and the city was full of fire traps as well as being hemmed in by a high wall.

Chongqing is, however, built upon rock, and the population quickly built caves and dugouts where they could gain safety from the Japanese bombs. From May until October it was bombed almost daily by swarms of a hundred planes, sometimes releasing a thousand bombs in a few seconds, coming over in waves every twenty minutes with about thirty planes in each wave.

An American YMCA leader who was there explained that because Chongqing is a very compact city, unable to expand sideways and obliged to build upwards instead, often with inflammable materials, its bombing 'is nothing but mass murder'. He witnessed two raids 'both by three squadrons of bombers, twenty-seven planes, each manned by a crew of six who were bent on the destruction of an open city and the cold-blooded slaughter of as many innocent human beings as possible.

'To achieve their ends they dropped their bombs on the most densely populated sections of the city. The only military objectives in this area ... are the airfield and a small arsenal, and both of these they have left untouched on all five of their raids. The last raid ... was only a few days after Cordell Hull announced to the world that the Japanese had given assurances that they would endeavour not to bomb civilian populations....'

But the Chinese spirit was not destroyed. A Chinese economics professor, a graduate of Harvard, tried to show that, according to the law of diminishing returns, China was winning.

Four-fifths of the city might already have gone, but this meant that every time the Japanese came over they dropped four-fifths of their bombs on parts of the city they had already destroyed.

'It has cost us less to rebuild Chongqing in the suburbs,' he boasted in conclusion, 'than it cost the Japanese to destroy so much of the city. You can't even compare Japan's costs with ours, and we have practically a whole new city in the bargain. And today, Japan is wasting money right and left. Let them bomb Chongqing. We are safe. And they soon will be poor.' Such childlike bravado was common.

Meanwhile, on the ground, the lower Yangzi valley writhed in agony as Japan drove wedges southwards from the river and localized fighting continued into the new year of 1939.

Up to now the war had been a series of dramatic set-pieces – the ambush at Pingxingguan, the bloody clash at Taierzhuang, the grabbing of Shanghai and Nanjing. But from 1939 onwards the story-line gets lost amid innumerable battles of lower pitch and lesser importance, often happening simultaneously at various points on the great map of China and merging into a continuous mutual irritation leaving neither side victorious.

The Japanese had originally intended to take Nanchang, the provincial capital of Jiangxi, which controlled the river communications around the Poyang Lake up to Jiujiang on the Yangzi, as part of the battle for Wuhan. The capture of Nanchang would also cut the railway between Jiangxi and Hangzhou on the coast, and thus interrupt the Chinese lines of communication. The Japanese now carried out a separate campaign for it at the beginning of 1939.

They massed five divisions to confront the eighteen Chinese divisions which were scattered along the right bank of the Yangzi below Lake Poyang, and another twelve divisions around Nanchang in positions constructed in depth along the banks of the River Xiu. They took Wucheng on 24 March and Nanchang itself three days later.

The Chinese tried to counter-attack at the end of April and reached the outskirts of Nanchang, but had to retreat after a week of severe fighting in which they suffered repeated gas attacks from Japanese aeroplanes.

Meanwhile the Japanese navy seized the island of Hainan in February and took the Spratley Islands in the following month. From Hainan the Japanese air force was then better able to cut Chinese supplies coming from Indochina and Burma. The Chinese GHQ could do little about it.

The first major battle of this new slow-tempo phase of the war came in May, after General Tang Enbo, whom the Japanese themselves acknowledged as 'one of Jiang's most competent ... generals' (he had trained at Japan's Military Academy in 1924–5), led his Thirty-First Army Group northwards across the Yangzi to the Zaoyang region near the Hubei–Henan border.

Finding the Chinese troop concentrations north of Wuhan a threat to their hold on the city, the Japanese launched an attack with four divisions, together with a cavalry brigade, totalling more than 100,000 men backed by 200 light and heavy guns and hundreds of war vehicles. They advanced towards the Henan–Hubei border in the area of Xiangyang, Zaoyang and Tongbai, with three columns.

Their left wing came up the Han River from Zhongxiang, a central column marched up the road from Huayuan on the Beijing–Wuhan railway towards Zaoyang, while a right-wing column set out from Hsinyang farther up the Beijing–Wuhan railway, aiming for Tongbai at the foot of the mountains. The aim was to encircle the Chinese in the Tongbai and Dahong mountains and thus ensure the security of Wuhan.

General Li Zongren, commanding the Chinese defence in this region, assigned the Thirty-Third Group Army of General Zhang Zhizhong to protect the southern slopes of the Dahong mountains, and the Second Group Army of General Sun Lianzhong to defend the northern slopes of the Tongbai mountains, while other Chinese units were assigned intervening and fringe sectors.

General Li received intelligence from Shanghai outlining the Japanese strategy just before the battle commenced. On the basis of these reports he laid a trap for the Japanese on the Xiangyang–Huayuan road.

General Tang Enbo's five divisions stationed themselves on

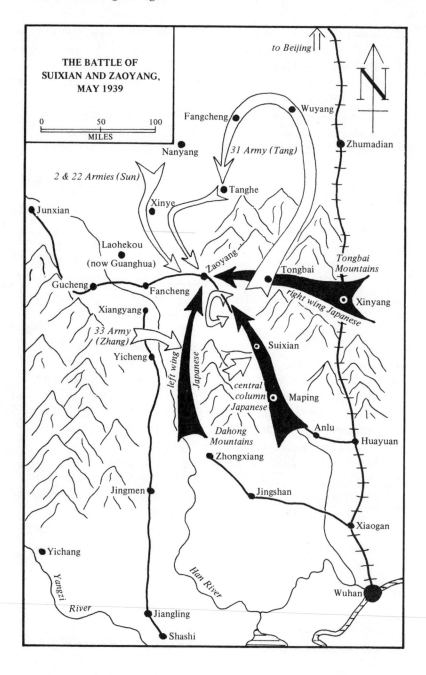

THE BATTLE OF
SUIXIAN AND ZAOYANG,
MAY 1939

0   50   100
MILES

to Beijing

Fangcheng

Wuyang

Zhumadian

31 Army (Tang)

Nanyang

2 & 22 Armies (Sun)

Tanghe

Xinye

Junxian

Laohekou
(now Guanghua)

Zaoyang

Tongbai

Tongbai
Mountains

Gucheng

Fancheng

right wing Japanese

Xinyang

Xiangyang

33 Army
(Zhang)

Suixian

Yicheng

central
column
Japanese

Maping

Dahong
Mountains

Anlu

Huayuan

Zhongxiang

Jingmen

Jingshan

Xiaogan

Yichang

Han River

Yangzi
River

Wuhan

Jiangling

Shashi

the southern slopes of the Tongbai mountains. Assyrian-like, they were to come down like 'the wolf on the fold' to savage the Japanese once they had fallen into the trap. Li reasoned that the Japanese would use mainly cavalry and tanks in a bid for a quick victory.

According to Li, when General Tang called at his head-quarters on his way from Chongqing to rejoin his army at the front there was a confrontation. Told of General Li's plan, Tang burst out: 'No! No! You cannot sacrifice my troops so easily!'

Li explained that his men's role in the Tongbai mountains would be at the rear, where there was little danger. But Tang stalked out of his office in a rage.

The campaign was launched on May Day. The left and right Japanese columns almost locked the Chinese into a horseshoe. Meanwhile the central column came into a large plain where it was able to use its mechanization to great effect. Japanese tanks roamed freely around this terrain and the Chinese, without anti-tank guns, could not resist them.

Outside this flat zone, however, around Suixian and in the mountains themselves, the Chinese were able to hold the Japanese at bay for more than ten days, fighting numerous small engagements without sacrificing their central line of defence.

General Li ordered General Tang's forces now to come down, like the Assyrian, from the Tongbai mountains, and attack the Japanese flank, allowing the Chinese to surround the Japanese forces and repeat the victory of Taierzhuang. But Tang did not wish to see his force eroded, and instead of joining in the battle he turned about to the north and retreated to Wuyang in Henan. The Japanese were then able to capture Suixian.

The Chinese had rushed reinforcements to Nanyang, just north of the Japanese-held points, and these now advanced south to repel the Japanese columns. Other Chinese forces along the Han River and in the Dahong mountains attacked the Japanese flank in order to block the line of retreat.

They had come prepared for a three-month campaign against the Chinese guerrilla bases, but after three weeks of bitter fighting they left in disorder, having lost more than 5000 dead.

Meanwhile, in the north a Japanese thrust towards Xi'an ran out of steam, and for the most part the Japanese contented themselves with trying to 'mop up' the partisan and scattered regular Chinese troops behind their own lines. In the summer of 1939, for example, the Japanese First Army launched such an operation in the Wutai mountains in northern Shanxi.

Because of the difficult terrain and the lack of roads (which meant that the Japanese would have had to bring in supplies on pack-horses), and also because the villagers had become indoctrinated by the guerrillas with strongly anti-Japanese feelings, the Japanese had not garrisoned this area.

But when at the beginning of 1939 Communist forces assembled in the Wutai mountains for a series of attacks against the Beijing–Tianjin region, the First Army decided to try to clear the area.

One of the Japanese wrote on the wall of the building which his unit had used as a barracks the words:

Fighting and death everywhere and now I am also wounded. China is limitless and we are like drops of water in an ocean. There is no purpose in this war and I shall never see my home again.

But the Chinese, especially the Communists, were undeterred from harassing Japanese lines near Beijing and Tianjin, and one of the most famous Red generals, General He Long, was gassed in central Hebei in the summer of 1939 while commanding a detachment in flooded areas during the rainy season.

The summer of 1939 also saw activity along the southern third of China's coastline. The Goto detachment of the Japanese Twenty-First Army, with naval support, captured Shantou (Swatow), the key port in northern Guangdong, on 21 June and went on to take towns in southern Fujian.

Most of China's southern ports had some kind of western interest, but the Japanese now for the first time began to show signs of overcoming their inhibitions about acting against the international settlements at Xiamen (Amoy).

When the British, French and Americans sent warships there,

however, and landed troops, the Japanese found it prudent to withdraw most of their forces from what they had perhaps intended as a test case for Shanghai. The continued, nevertheless, to blockade foreign trade and shipping, and this was stepped up in the middle of 1939.

Japanese soldiers tried to land at Fuzhou and Wenzhou on the coast, and twenty-six men-of-war lay off Fuzhou for several weeks, bombarding the town. The Japanese demanded that Britain and the US withdraw their ships from Fuzhou, but this ultimatum was rejected and the consuls of the two countries remained at their posts. The British landed thirty-six marines to protect their subjects and property, whereupon the Japanese landed a much larger force near Fuzhou which began to attack western-owned buildings.

This blockade of the western parts of southern Chinese ports had an impact on the north, where the Japanese were in outright control of cities like Tianjin while still technically respecting the international settlements. In Tianjin itself there was an extraordinary, almost farcical campaign of undressing Europeans, as part of the pressure against the foreign settlements.

The Japanese accused the British and French in June of harbouring in their Tianjin concessions the suspected murderers of a Chinese collaborator. They blockaded the concessions, with the real objective of gaining control of the silver bullion which the British held as collateral for the Chinese currency, which the Japanese intended to drive out of circulation. Foreigners going in and out of the concessions were searched by Japanese soldiers, and made to strip in public in order to prove they were not smuggling.

This degradation of westerners in front of Chinese had a profound moral impact. It was a crude but vivid way of deflating the prestige of westerners in East Asia, and in Chinese eyes it raised the Japanese to a role as self-appointed deliverers of Asia from European oppression.

'It was a new expression of contempt,' a European observer commented, "never before heard of, to tear the clothes from white men and women to leave them naked to be viewed by

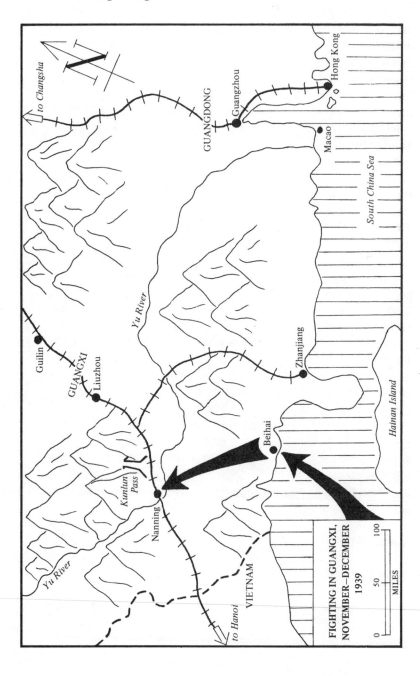

to Changsha

Hong Kong

Guangzhou

GUANGDONG

Macao

South China Sea

Yu River

Guilin

GUANGXI

Liuzhou

Zhanjiang

Hainan Island

Beihai

Kunlun Pass

Nanning

Yu River

VIETNAM

to Hanoi

FIGHTING IN GUANGXI, NOVEMBER–DECEMBER 1939

100

50

MILES

0

people of a different race. The real symbolic ulterior motive no
doubt was that just as these respectable men and women were
undressed by the brutal sentries guarding the barricades, so will
in time the white robe [of western imperialism] be torn from
Japan as well as the rest of Asia.' But Britain still refused to
surrender the silver.

In May 1939 the Chinese defector Wang Jingwei arrived in
Shanghai under Japanese auspices to prepare the launching of a
new puppet 'central' Chinese government. The Europeans were
fully preoccupied by their crisis with Hitler, and in September a
Japan–Soviet cease-fire took the pressure off the Manchurian–Mongolian frontier, where there had been fighting.
The Japanese military HQ decided to take advantage of this to
try to end the war once and for all by capturing Changsha, the
capital of Hunan province.

General Nishio Toshizo was made commander-in-chief of the
newly designated Japanese Expeditionary Forces to China, with
Lieutenant-General Itagaki Seishiro as his chief of staff and a
HQ in Nanjing. Two Japanese divisions, the 101st and 106th,
were massed on the western bank of the Gan River in northern
Jiangxi, while another four, numbering 100,000 men in all,
assembled in northern Hunan. The Japanese navy gathered
along the Yangzi River in northern Hunan ready to invade
Changsha.

On 14 September the Japanese 106th Division advanced to
Fukuan in the first step of the intended destruction of what the
Japanese HQ called China's 'highly trained and well-equipped
central government army'. The Chinese directed their attention
first to the Japanese column striking from Jiangxi. Once this
was stretched out westwards, Chinese troops attacked its flank
from both north and south, compelling it to retreat before it had
reached the Hunan border.

Meanwhile on 19 September the main Japanese force attacking from the north engaged Chinese positions along the Xinqiang River, just east of the Dongting Lake, using large
quantities of gas.

On 23 September three separate Japanese columns began
a co-ordinated march towards Changsha. The Thirty-Third

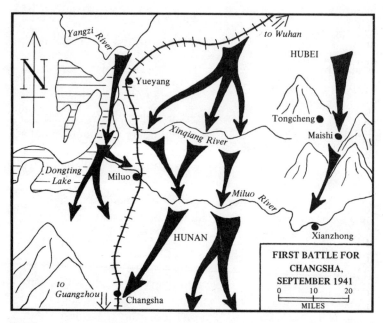

FIRST BATTLE FOR
CHANGSHA,
SEPTEMBER 1941

Division on the left came from Tongcheng in southern Hubei,
and although it was intercepted below Maishi, it made an eastward detour and then came towards Xianzhong on the Miluo
River. The Japanese central column, including the Sixth and
Thirteenth Divisions, crossed the Xinqiang River under heavy
artillery cover, and advanced towards the Chinese fortifications
along the Miluo River immediately south. On the right wing
waterborne Japanese forces sailed over the Dongting Lake to
try to land on its southern shores in order to attack the Chinese
flank and rear. The fighting was fierce in all of these sectors
during the last week of September, the Chinese retiring step
by step but preventing the Japanese from winning an easy
victory.

By 29 September the Japanese had reached the outskirts of
Changsha, but three days later a Chinese counter-attack forced
the Japanese to retreat when they found their supply lines
cut. By 6 October the Chinese had regained all their original
positions.

This first battle for Changsha was costly for China, but

inspiring to her people. In one of the Japanese accounts it was claimed that heavy casualties had been inflicted on the Chinese army, 'however, it was felt that the objective of breaking the enemy's will to fight was still far from achieved'.

More could not have been expected, however, from these four divisions involved – a rare admission in the Japanese records of the inadequacy of the Japanese numbers in China. The other four divisions in the Japanese Eleventh Army were on guard duty in the north or at the rear. Changsha was proof that the Japanese had reached the limit of their capacity.

The only time that Japan considerably extended her occupation of China was at the end of the year when a large assault force was landed at Beihai in southern Guangxi, penetrating northwards for about a hundred miles to capture Nanning, a strategic crossroads for transportation to Indochina. This operation was undertaken by the Fifth Division and a brigade from Taiwan specially trained for landing operations. The landing took place on 15 November, and Nanning fell on the 24th; then the Japanese tried to thrust farther northwards and to the northeast.

To thwart this Japanese interruption of his southwest communications system, Generalissimo Jiang massed twenty-five divisions early in December, totalling 150,000 men, and from a headquarters in Guilin he counter-attacked on 16 December.

The strategic Kunlun pass was recaptured within a few days, and a brigade of Japanese destroyed. The Chinese had three mountain guns and fifteen tanks deployed for this battle, and although the Japanese Twenty-First Infantry Regiment tried to relieve the Kunlun pass garrison, it was unable to break through. At the end of the battle, according to Lieutenant-Colonel Ishiwari Heizo, they buried their field artillery and other guns deep underground to keep them out of Chinese hands.

Now the Japanese counter-attacked and took back the bloody Kunlun pass, only to lose it again to the Chinese on New Year's Eve.

Meanwhile, on the south of the You River, Chinese units struck eastwards on 17 December to threaten the Japanese line of communication. The Japanese response was to concentrate part of the Imperial Guards Division and the Eighteenth and Twenty-Eighth Divisions in a northwards attack in January to encircle Chinese troops in the Kunlun pass, and this forced the Chinese garrison to retreat yet again from the pass.

Eventually the Chinese did regain the pass and the Japanese decided to evacuate the southern part of Guangxi province, leaving only a small garrison to hold Nanning and Longzhou.

This was a time for China of systematic evacuation, not only of weapons but also of machinery and even cultural relics. Jiang Jieshi even arranged for the ashes of Genghis Khan to be taken from their resting place behind the Great Wall near Yan'an to a wartime sanctuary in the far western interior, where Japanese invaders could never reach. They were not returned until the 1950s. In the midst of being invaded by one enemy, China found time to secure the remains of another, older conqueror.

9

The Hundred Regiments

The military impasse continued during 1940, although in the new circumstances of fixed Japanese positions the Chinese were able to carry out effective propaganda. Volunteers used to throw leaflets, sometimes using bows and arrows to shoot them, into Japanese positions. Where Chinese and Japanese trenches were close together they would sing anti-war songs or deliver lectures in Japanese through megaphones.

One of these Japanese-speaking volunteers once delivered speeches to Japanese soldiers for two nights in succession. On the third night an officer stuck his head up above the Japanese trenches and fiercely asked him who he was. The Chinese volunteer gave a Japanese name and address.

'I chose a very stylish address in Tokyo,' he explained to his own side. 'I told the officer that he lied to his troops in saying that Chinese tortured Japanese captives to death, and I said that bullets used against China were the sweat and blood of the Japanese people.'

'You are a traitor,' the Japanese officer retorted, 'and a disgrace to the great Imperial army! We will tear you limb from limb! Japan grows stronger and richer by the war!'

The Japanese played tit-for-tat on this kind of propaganda, however. One Japanese colonel in Hubei sent a letter to a Chinese guerrilla detachment on 23 January urging it to mutiny:

I am a Japanese colonel and I feel very sorry about the war between China and Japan. I am a man of East Asia; you are men of East Asia. Why, now, do we men of the same race wage war? My empire is now building a happy world in which Japan, Manchuria and China will go forward together.... Open your eyes and look at the condition of the world. Russia, France, England and America are all occupied with their own affairs and are at odds. They have no time to think of China. Why does your army not realize this? Look at the condition of the Chinese armies that come over to us. They are very happy. Hand in hand with the Japanese army they are rebuilding East Asia....

Leaflets dropped over Chengdu showed Konoye's picture dominating Hitler's and Mussolini's on either side. The text explained how Japan, Germany and Italy were dividing the world: Germany had already conquered Europe, Italy held Africa and Asia must soon be Japanese.

The Chinese guerrillas' military pressure on the Japanese also intensified. An official Japanese account described how 'the destruction of railway and communication lines was the most annoying part of guerrilla activities. Besides cutting railway and communication lines with tools and instruments, the guerrillas frequently blew them up and, as they became more and more skilful in the use of explosives, many trains were blown up by landmines.'

These more sophisticated tactics forced the Japanese to improve their own protective measures. Observation patrols were no longer enough. Along the Beijing–Wuhan railway, for example, the Japanese 110th Division, according to the same official account, 'made efforts to mop up the occupied areas by searching every private house for guerrillas'.

At the end of 1939 and the beginning of 1940 the Chinese forces behind the Japanese lines undertook a winter offensive. The non-Communist units were commanded by General Zhang Zhizhong, who had just overcome his addiction to opium. They included the brigade which had first challenged the Japanese at the Marco Polo bridge. General Zhang and his lieutenants were in no doubt as to the fighting capacity of the Japanese. When a foreign correspondent spoke to his chief of staff about the failings of the Japanese infantry, he replied: 'Don't let anyone tell you that the Japanese still fight by book-rules. They have practised on us for nearly three years and learnt much. They can make every kind of assault – frontal, flank or even guerrilla. What is far worse, they have studied our military, political and social weaknesses and use them against us.'

Most Japanese soldiers, after all, were literate and educated, and their conscription system as well as their physical and cultural standards remained higher than those of the Chinese. General Zhang conceded that China's conscription methods were haphazard. Even young boys were taken, and new conscripts were still sometimes led away tied with ropes, as in the old feudal days. The political training which such soldiers needed was almost non-existent, except in the Communist armies.

The winter offensive raged up and down the entire country. Bridges and railway stations were sabotaged on all the main railway lines. The station at Luowang was captured, the Japanese garrison in Kaifeng was captured, and the town of Xinyang fell to the Chinese.

At dawn on 10 December there was a general Chinese attack on southern and eastern Shanxi to destroy Japanese troops in that area. It was claimed that the Japanese were 'largely' driven out by mid January. In western Shanxi, however, the Guomindang complained of Communist interference in military food supplies, and said that insubordination by Bo Yibo and other Communists in the Eighteenth Army Group was hindering Chinese success.

In mid December the Chinese Third War Zone forces attacked in succession the cities of Hangzhou, Fuyang and Linping. But the Japanese were reinforced in this area and took the city of Xiaoshan. Chinese soldiers in mufti came up the Gan River to damage Japanese installations in Nanchang.

In Guangdong province in the far south the Japanese sought to extend their territory under air cover, taking Wengyuan, Yingde and Qingyan. But the Chinese were able to send more men to the area and launched a counter-attack, while the Japanese returned to Guangzhou to relieve the front at Nanning which was more important to them. All the original positions were reoccupied by the Chinese by mid January.

In western Anhui, northern Hebei and southern Henan the

Chinese Fifth and Ninth War Zone Armies also went to the offensive in mid December. In northern Hebei they were successful in Huayuan and Guangshui, but by late January the Japanese were still holding their strong points in most of this area and refusing to come out and fight in the open. They lost serveral thousand men, all the same, together with a number of minor positions.

In the northwest the Chinese troops of General Fu Zuoyi attacked Baotou in the Mongolian border region, but were repelled. He equivocated in his reports to the central government, but Jiang Jieshi, learning of the failure, told him to make another attack.

He was supported in the new year of 1940 by 10,000 Chinese troops marching from the west along the Yellow River by way of Xamba and Wuyuan, while other armies tried to cut the railway line between Suiyuan and Baotou. Another 30,000 Chinese troops were operating north of the Yellow River – at this time of year frozen with ice thick enough for troops to march over – and west of Baotou.

The Japanese garrison army came out to deal with the threat and occupied Wuyuan on 3 February. The Chinese local commander went back to General Fu Zuoyi's headquarters and ordered him to reorganize and counter-attack; he promised to do so the moment it thawed. On 21 March the Chinese attacked Wuyuan before dawn and recaptured the inner castle after stubborn fighting.

The Japanese rushed in reinforcements which, in spite of having to cross the River Wujia under Chinese fire, reached Wuyuan on the 26th. But the Chinese, following earlier precedents, broke the banks of the River Wujia and created a flood which stopped the Japanese in their tracks. They had to leave Wuyuan on 1 April and return to their original positions.

Meanwhile in Shanxi the Japanese were in a remarkable position to observe the results of Chinese Communist–Guomindang squabbling. Large areas of southern Shanxi, especially around the Dahong and Zhongtiao mountains, were held by the Chinese Guomindang to form the largest base for Chinese guerrilla operations in the whole of northern China.

But the nearby mountainous area north of Changzhi was the home of General Zhu De's Communists, competing with their Guomindang allies for the control of the Changzhi plain. In the southwestern part of Shanxi the regular provincial army under General Yan Xishan was strongly entrenched, but suffered from internal quarrelling. Generalissimo Jiang Jieshi therefore sent General Li Wen into the Xiangning area with men from the central government army in order to stiffen the unity of the Shanxi troops and keep an eye on their behaviour.

Even the Japanese admitted that the fighting spirit of the Guomindang army in southern Shanxi was high, and in mid March about thirty non-Communist Chinese divisions suddenly advanced from the south banks of the Yellow River to Gaoping, forcing the Chinese Communists in the Changzhi plain to retire northwards.

In January 1940 the Japanese attempted to surround the Chinese forces of Generals Sun Lianzhong and Tang Enbo at Yangcheng, first attacking Sun and then, taking advantage of his retreat, turning on Tang. But the Chinese merely retreated into the mountains.

On the south bank of the Yangzi, in northern Jiangxi, Hubei and Hunan, the Chinese made diversionary attacks and sabotaged railways, rendering the Nanchang–Jiujiang railway useless, for example. One key sector of the Guangzhou–Wuhan railway was working for only a brief period.

The Chinese Third War Zone troops occupied the area from the Poyang Lake eastwards along the southern bank of the Yangzi, and its men on the right bank of the Qiantang River near Hangzhou were now disrupting Shanghai and threatening to take receipt of supplies and ammunition by sea.

The Japanese planned to set up the new puppet government under Wang Jingwei in Shanghai in March, and did not want any distractions from the guerrillas only a short distance away. The Japanese Thirteenth Army therefore sent a division across the Qiantang River to take Xiaoshan, opposite Hangzhou, on 22 January. The Chinese route to Shanghai was thus cut. Early in February the Chinese Tenth Army Group tried to recapture Xiaoshan, but was repulsed by the Japanese.

Meanwhile the Chinese Twenty-Third Army Group began special training in Anhui in order to prepare for the interception of Japanese shipping along the Yangzi River during the spring, especially around the time when the new puppet government was going to be established. But the Japanese Thirteenth Army tried to forestall the plan, sending on 22 April two divisions to attack at Miaoqian.

The Chinese claimed that during their winter offensive covering this wide area from December 1939 to the end of March 1940 they killed more than 77,000 Japanese, a high figure which some neutral observers doubted.

On 29 April, the Emperor's birthday, the Japanese air force began its fourth large-scale operation of the war, with a new regime of sustained bombing of Chongqing, Chengdu and their surrounding areas. The army aeroplanes struck from Anyi in northern China and the naval aircraft from the sea, in what was code-named by the Japanese HQ Operation 100. The bombings were suspended only on 10 September, when the air force was diverted to support the Japanese invasion of Indochina.

But the Japanese continued to be troubled by Chinese guerrilla attacks in the Shanxi–Hebei area so vital to their communications. When General Tada Toshi took over from Sugiyama in this sector at the end of 1939, he invented a new system of defences called the 'cage policy'.

He made his men dig deep moats and high walls along the sides of the railways to screen them from the guerrillas, and he borrowed from Jiang Jieshi himself the policy which the Generalissimo had taken from his German advisers of building concrete blockades and pill-boxes to deter the guerrillas.

But this was not enough, and in April the Japanese First Army issued orders to 'destroy enemy forces throughout southern Shanxi province and paralyse their activities at their sources, thus crippling Jiang's government and, at the same time, extending the Japanese-occupied area in order to expedite the creation of a peaceful and orderly north China'. In the last hours of darkness on the morning of 17 April, following these orders, the Japanese troops attacked the north bank of the

Yellow River at Monan. They were fiercely resisted, and did not capture Jincheng until 25 April.

Meanwhile the Shanxi army was rallied into the Fenhe plain to take advantage of the depleted strength of the Japanese garrisons there. By the time the Japanese had organized an operation against Xiangning, in May, they found that the Chinese had regrouped elsewhere and begun a second counter-offensive. Because of this Xiangning operation the Japanese troops in southern Shanxi were in turn reduced, allowing the local Chinese commander to launch a co-ordinated counter-offensive throughout southern Shanxi at midnight on 20 May.

It happened that the Japanese commander at Linfen in southern Shanxi had years before been a classmate of Marshal Yan Xishan, the long-time governor of Shanxi, at the Tokyo Military Academy. He sent a student of Yan's in the middle of May with a message saying: 'It is really unfortunate for us Asiatic people to kill one another. What effective means do you have in mind for restoring peace and good relations between us?'

To which Yan replied grimly: 'Since Japan has been fighting purely for her own necessities, she has not gained sympathy from the other peoples of Asia. If Japan were to fight for the necessities of the Asiatic peoples as a whole, it would surely be easy to restore peace and good relations.'

But now the centre of interest switched southwards to the upper reaches of the Yangzi River. The Chinese believed that their winter offensive had severely damaged the Japanese army, and they widely publicized their victories in order to get more help from abroad as well as to raise their own morale at home. At the same time they began their third reorganization and training programme in preparation for the next military counter-attack.

The Chinese now had 260 divisions, according to the Japanese estimate, with about 2 million men – though one may doubt if they were all in good shape. During the summer of 1940 the Japanese GHQ expected that China would raise an additional eighty divisions by reorganization and training.

After the lull following the winter offensive, Chinese preparations for new activity in the Yangzi River sector became visible. General Tang Enbo's Thirty-First Army Group was deployed around Nanyang, while other Chinese crack units were stationed on either side of the Han River running north-west from Wuhan. The Japanese, for their part, recognized that the Chinese winter offensive had 'shown the Japanese army the defects in its defences', and they now made every effort to strengthen their fortifications and communications.

Although the Japanese had driven the Chinese back during the winter fighting, both sides had suffered heavy casualties. Japanese units had been spread over a wide area, throwing some of the front-line units into disorder. 'This,' a Japanese account conceded, 'gave the enemy a sense of victory and strengthened their morale, whereas it had an adverse effect on the Japanese army.'

To counteract this, the Japanese Eleventh Army drew up plans to strike against the Chinese Fifth War Zone before the rainy season began. Not only were these plans approved by Imperial GHQ, but the Japanese commander was even allowed temporarily to extend operations beyond his permitted theatre for May and June for the purpose.

Two detachments of the Thirteenth Army were ordered into the campaign, along with a brigade from the Third Air Group. The plan was to strike early in May to destroy the main strength of the Chinese Fifth War Zone north of the railway line between Suixian and Xiangyang, and then destroy it on the right bank of the Han River after cornering it at Yichang. A command post was established by the Japanese Eleventh Army for this campaign at Yingshan and, to secure the rear, a feint was carried out south of the Yangzi in late April.

The main Japanese offensive in what became the battle for Yichang began in May as planned. But it was learned that General Tang Enbo's Thirty-First Army Group had begun to march south simultaneously with the Japanese action, and was threatening the right flank and rear of the Japanese Third Division.

This division captured some Chinese troops, but the main force escaped in the direction of Nanyang and Dengxian.

Meanwhile several divisions of the Chinese Thirty-Third Army Group crossed the Han River and advanced north towards Yingcheng. After engaging with the Japanese they reached Tongbaishan on 13 May, cutting the Yingshan–Zaoyang road, the main Japanese line of communication, for several days.

By 10 May the encircling movement envisaged by the Japanese had been completed, with three columns, having started out from the line Xinyang–Suixian–Zhongxiang, converging on the Bai River. But the Chinese had already extricated themselves from the trap, moving to the Japanese flanks and rear to counter-encircle them, as in the Japanese game of *go*.

The main force of the Chinese Thirty-Third Army Group was in fact encircled by the Japanese, however, in the northern foothills of the Dahong mountains, and its famous commander, General Zhang Zhizhong, was killed. He and his two regiments fought for eight hours on 16 May before the general was hit by machine-gun fire.

In the entire history of the Sino-Japanese War Zhang was the only army commander to sacrifice his life on the field while directing the battle. His aides and even his Russian adviser urged him to retreat once his impossible situation had become clear, but he had evidently made up his mind to fight to the death.

In spite of this blow against the Chinese southern wing, the Japanese Third Division was then encircled in its turn and attacked by a superior Chinese force at Luyeni. But Zaoyang, which the Chinese had briefly retaken, was back in Japanese hands again within hours.

The Chinese now thought that the Japanese were returning home to their original bases, and since the Chinese were massed on a comparatively narrow front in pursuit of the Japanese, the Japanese commander decided on a counter-attack instead of the planned crossing of the Han River. There were fierce clashes along the front on 19 May, and the Chinese were forced to retreat westwards and northeastwards.

After a short breathing space a second phase of the battle of Yichang opened up. The Japanese sought to mop up the remaining Chinese in the Dahong mountains, take Yichang

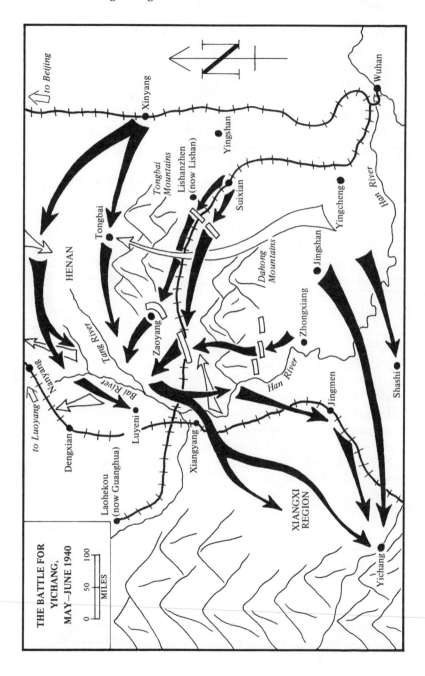

to Beijing

Wuhan

Xinyang

Yingshan

Han River

Tongbai
Mountains

Lishanzhen
(now Lishan)

Suixian

Yingcheng

Tongbai

HENAN

Jingshan

Dahong
Mountains

Zhongxiang

Zaoyang

Tang River

Bai River

Nanyang

Han River

Jingmen

Luyeni

Xiangyang

Shashi

to Luoyang

Dengxian

Laohekou
(now Guanghua)

XIANGXI
REGION

Yichang

THE BATTLE FOR
YICHANG,
MAY–JUNE 1940

0   50   100

MILES

itself and secure Xiangxi.

The Japanese HQ believed that the Forty-Fourth and Ninety-Second Chinese armies, hidden in the Dahong and Dabie mountains respectively, together with the Forty-Fifth Army which had crossed the Han River, planned to cut Japanese lines of communication at Lishanzhen and advance to Zaoyang again. To prevent this it was necessary to smash the Chinese in the Dahong mountains.

Defending the Yichang area on the right bank of the Han River were no fewer than six Chinese armies. On midnight of 31 May the Japanese Eleventh Army nevertheless sent two of its divisions to make surprise crossings over the Han River and march to Yichang.

In fact the Japanese Thirty-Ninth Division disobeyed orders by bombarding the Chinese the previous evening and conducting a forced river crossing, thus losing the element of surprise. But the two divisions were successful in driving southwards in parallel lines, causing the Chinese to lose contact with each other and making them engage with the Japanese separately, as a result of which they were defeated and retreated to the mountains in the west.

The Generalissimo hastily sent Chen Cheng, commander-in-chief of the Fifth War Zone Army, from Chongqing to stiffen morale and unity. But now the Japanese sent other units to follow the Third and Thirty-Ninth Divisions across the Han River. By 6 June they had occupied Jingmen and then there was a race to Yichang among the Japanese themselves.

Each division was told to rush three battalions to Yichang so that they could take the city in unison on 12 June. It was a morale-boosting habit of the Japanese artificially to share such military glories in this way.

Meanwhile the Fortieth Division was trying to clear the Chinese from the Dahong mountains but found the terrain difficult. Only with additional help, including heavy field and anti-aircraft artillery, did it break through to Jingshan on 20 May, with its commander wounded in the fighting.

Yichang, described as a 'perilous and man-draining outpost', of strategic value only in the event of a Chinese attack on

Wuhan, controlled the water-transportation system of Sichuan, Hubei and Hunan. Only 240 miles from Chongqing as the crow flies, it also provided a useful air base for bombing the Chinese capital.

Once the town had fallen, the main strength of the Chinese Thirty-Third Army Group fled north into the mountains. The Japanese high command in Tokyo decided that it would be necessary to continue occupying Yichang not merely as a base for bombing, but also for the propaganda effect on foreign countries.

The Japanese Thirteenth Division was told therefore to secure Yichang; in a messy postscript to the battle, a radio breakdown meant that it never received the order. In the meantime its men had begun to withdraw so that they now had to turn back from outside the town, re-expelling the Chinese who had begun to re-enter.

The Japanese estimated that China had thrown eighty-one divisions into the battle for Yichang, with 350,000 soldiers of whom 60,000 became casualties. The Japanese claimed to have captured large amounts of artillery and weapons, with their own losses claimed at only 2700 killed and 7800 wounded.

The occupation of Yichang strengthened Japanese pressure against Sichuan in the interior, and cut off communications between the Chinese Fifth and Ninth War Zone Armies. It also dealt a blow to Chinese morale and fighting capacity, and no large-scale Chinese offensive was ever mounted again.

In order to fight the battle for Yichang, however, units from other Japanese armies had been sent to help, and this enabled the Chinese Communist guerrillas to intensify their activity in those depleted areas. This was especially true in the area bounded by the three waterways – the Grand Canal, and the Yellow and Yangzi rivers – where the Japanese Thirteenth Army could do little in reply.

After the Yichang battle had ended, the Japanese Thirteenth Army sent soldiers to Jingxian, in the centre of southern Anhui, near the south bank of the Yangzi, where they were surrounded by the powerful Chinese Twenty-Third and New Fourth Armies, only disengaging after two days of severe fighting. Other units were sent to other areas of guerrilla activity, and there was stubborn Chinese resistance in the mountains.

Although one operation had been conceived on a 'grand scale,' a Japanese report complained, 'and it appeared as though the Japanese troops had surrounded and destroyed the enemy, the results were far from satisfactory, as the Thirteenth Army had been forced to carry out its operations over a vast area with an extremely small force. In fact, the Chinese claimed that they contained the Japanese Fifteenth Division in the vicinity of Jingxian and destroyed it.'

Meanwhile the Communists in central Shanxi were preparing their most famous offensive of the war against General Tada, author of the 'cage policy'. General Zhu De's Eighth Route Army concentrated a force of 100 regiments for a surprise attack on all the important railways in northern China on the night of 20 August.

The attack not only put out of commission the railways controlled by the Japanese, but also, according to General Peng Dehuai, the Red Chinese commander, 'smashed their blockade-houses, destroyed their walls and ditches, burnt their stations and depots and blew up their railways and bridges'. In particular the Jingxing coal mine was destroyed, at great cost to the Japanese. The cutting of roads and railways prevented numerous Japanese garrisons which had been attacked by the Chinese Communist forces from being rescued.

Two separate operations against the Communists in central Shanxi were carried out by the Japanese First Army, but without success. They tried to mop up Communist forces in the mountainous districts to the west of Beijing along the borders of Shanxi and Hebei provinces in the final quarter of 1940. But, as an official Japanese account put it, 'the clever tactics employed by the Communists in taking cover prevented the area from obtaining its objective ...'.

No sooner did the Japanese acquire new ground in these mopping-up operations than they had to establish peace and order there, knowing that the territory was already too large for the available garrisons. This made it easy for both Guomindang and Communist forces to infiltrate and disturb Japan's possession.

But the Japanese took comfort from the fact that China's rival Red and anti-Communist forces could not reconcile their ideological differences and expended a great deal of energy – more and more as the war went on – trying to widen their respective spheres of influence, especially in Shandong, Jiangxi and Anhui, to gain advantage for the civil war to come.

The Communists publicized their Hundred Regiments offensive at the time as a great victory, claiming that it took the Japanese six months to restore their north China rail communications. They also claimed, less believably, 20,000 Japanese dead. But the Japanese too learned lessons from this famous engagement, and the Chinese Communists were never again able to launch an offensive of this magnitude against the Japanese.

The Chinese gains were short term, and within half a year the Japanese were back again with their forts rebuilt even more strongly. For this brief advantage the Red Army sacrificed too many men and too much ammunition, as they themselves later admitted. One of the Japanese staff officers in this sector described the Hundred Regiments campaign as the Chinese Communists' biggest blunder, and twenty years later the Chinese Communist Party wrote it down to megalomania on the part of General Peng Dehuai.

It is possible that the other Chinese Communist leaders went along with Peng at the time, in spite of their military reservations, for political reasons. They may have wished to turn Chinese opinion against any *rapprochement* between the National Chinese government in which they were participating, on the one hand, and the rival 'puppet' Japanese-sponsored regime of Wang Jingwei on the other. The Hundred Regiments offensive at least made a mockery of Guomindang propaganda about the Communists not fighting the Japanese – even if they were increasingly active against the Guomindang as well.

10

No End in Sight

The tension in the Chinese ranks, between the rival followers of Jiang Jieshi and Mao Zedong, exploded in the first week of 1941 into massive violence of the kind that could only help Japan. At issue was the role and territorial integrity of the so-called New Fourth Army.

The unfortunate Communist force was the heir to that phase of China's civil war in 1933–4 which had seen five successive campaigns by Jiang Jieshi's government to encircle and exterminate the Communists in Jiangxi in central China.

The main body of the Red forces with Mao had escaped on the Long March and gone northwards to Shaanxi, but a remnant was left behind which was now uneasily corralled with Guomindang forces into China's central defence system. Control over it was a heated point of dissension between the Communists and Guomindang.

By the end of 1940 the New Fourth Army was occupying a considerable area of Jiangsu and Anhui and boasted 35,000 men under arms. Chen Yi, later to succeed Zhou Enlai as Mao's Foreign Minister, was one of the divisional commanders who, following Mao's instructions, played the deadly game of combining baiting the Japanese with harassing the Guomindang.

A visitor to this army found its dedication commendable. In the kit bag of one of the soldiers, set out for morning inspection, was:

One short piece of candle, half a tube of toothpaste, an old toothbrush, a scrap of soap carefully wrapped in a rag, one letter from his family written by a letter-writer, a seal, three pencils, thirteen books and pamphlets, six lecture note books and copies of the army newspaper (with passages marked). Of books he had *Protracted Warfare* and the *New Stage in the War*, both by Mao Zedong ... and texts on strategy and tactics, military science, elements of social science and natural science. Of army pamphlets he had *Political Work in the Puppet Armies*, *Work Among the Enemy*, *Japanese Primer*, *Army Rules*, *Army Song Book*, *How to Write for the Wall Newspapers* and *Wartime Child Education*.

Not all the members of the army were peasants like this one. The director of the Anhui Student Army HQ was a West Point graduate and boasted that he had once given a banquet for a European crown prince consisting of 700 courses and lasting more than ten hours.

A crisis developed at the end of 1940 when the central government ordered this ambivalent New Fourth Army to evacuate the lower Yangzi valley and move into the region north of the Yellow River where there was flooding. This would have meant negotiating several Guomindang-controlled river crossings on the way. On top of that, the Communists' request for winter uniforms, funds and ammunition for the journey was summarily rejected.

Gradually some detachments from the New Fourth Army obeyed the Generalissimo's orders and started to cross the Yangzi northwards. But blows were exchanged between the remaining units and their Guomindang neighbours.

On 5 January full-scale fighting broke out between the New Fourth Army and the Guomindang's Fortieth Division, both sides blaming the other for the outburst. In the next few days the central forces tried to disband this Communist army, and on 17 January the National Military Council in Chongqing de-activated it and arrested its commander, General Ye Ting, for court martial. But the main body of the New Fourth Army remained in Jiangsu and Anhui until the end of the war.

Relations between the two parties supposedly in alliance against Japan now worsened to a point where no further military collaboration was possible, fatally weakening the Chinese war effort.

Later in January 1941 a battle began in southern Henan, where the Japanese tried to make Wuhan safer from threatening Chinese forces. Three Japanese divisions broke through the first Chinese line of defence north of Changtaiguan on 25 January, and five days later they reached Wuyang. Another Japanese force broke through the Chinese line at Minggang along the railway on the following day and advanced northwards against positions at Zhumadian.

Meanwhile the main Japanese force advanced to Suiping and crossed the Ru River, where it was blocked by strong Chinese troops. But the Japanese captured Wucheng and the Chinese had to retreat on 2 February.

The Japanese now crossed the Hong River to assault Xiangcheng. Another Japanese force attacking along the Sha River was, however, forced to retreat. At the beginning of February the Japanese forces involved in this whole operation united to attack Fangcheng, where they suffered heavy losses. Some of the Japanese retreated south to Tanghe, while others occupied Nanyang but then had to retreat to the railway again. By 10 February the Chinese had reoccupied all points north of Xinyang, along the railway and on both sides of it.

A month later a severe battle broke out in northern Jiangxi, near Nanchang, when the Japanese tried to capture Shanggao. The Japanese sent 50,000 men out in three columns from Anyi and from the banks of the Gan River opposite Nanchang on 15 March. Four days afterwards the Chinese counter-attacked with eight divisions, and in the course of a three-day battle the Japanese retired.

Meanwhile the Japanese left wing had advanced along the Jin River but was caught, along with other Japanese units, in a Chinese encirclement. By 28 March the Japanese were in full retreat. The Chinese claimed that they inflicted 15,000 casualties on the Japanese during the battle of Shanggao.

The desolate mountains of Zhongtiao just north of the Yellow River at the southern tip of Shanxi province provided the locale for the next major battle, which raged throughout May 1941.

In these virtually uninhabited mountains, from 1000 to 2500

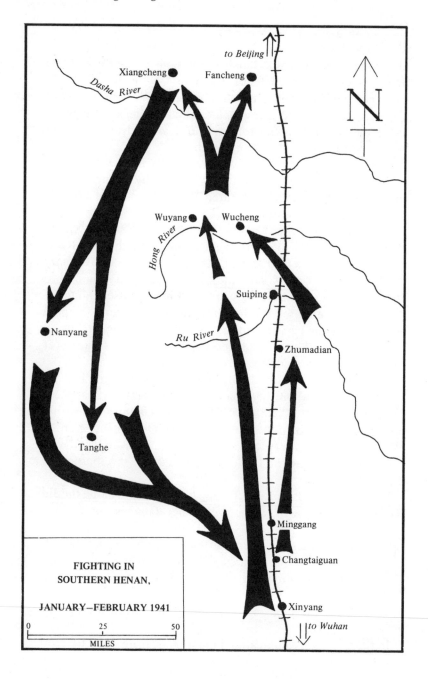

**FIGHTING IN
SOUTHERN HENAN,**

JANUARY–FEBRUARY 1941

0   25   50

MILES

metres high and with very few roads, an important group of Chinese forces had established a stronghold from which the Japanese sought to dislodge them. Six divisions and several additional brigades were massed for the siege of this mountain range, said to be the fourteenth attempt by Japan to clear the area of Chinese troops. The 100,000 Japanese began to advance from four points of the compass – from Maojindu on the Yellow River, from Jiyuan across the Henan border, and from Jiangxian and Qinshui to the north – on 7 May.

Supported by bombers, the columns from the north drove right across the mountains and over the other side to the Yellow River to capture Jiuyuanqu on 8 May. This, the most important crossing of the Yellow River in this sector, was captured in a creditable twenty-two hours.

The Chinese forces were thus split in half, and the Japanese tried to encircle each half. A western correspondent with the Japanese army commented that the Japanese force was now vulnerably hedged in on two sides. The Japanese military spokesman agreed, but laughed it off, saying that the Chinese would never close in. He was right.

Nevertheless the Japanese could not force the Chinese defences, and the bulk of the Chinese began to slip out of the net, moving northwestwards to the Jiwang mountains on the other side of the railway. The battle was thus indecisive.

The Japanese were outnumbered by three to one, and so their strategy had to be precise. It was 'to envelop the enemy forces completely, by blocking their routes of retreat with advance forces, and by taking advantage of the already existing positions on the front, the natural obstacles of the Yellow River and breakthrough actions from both flanks'.

By the Japanese own criteria the battle of southern Shanxi was a failure, and it petered out on 27 May.

Elsewhere in Shanxi the new Japanese commander, General Okamura Neiji, described by the Chinese Communists as 'one of the three ablest generals in the Japanese army, a devil whose bloody hands have murdered countless Korean and Manchurian people', took over in the middle of 1941 and further toughened the tactics against guerrillas. He dug even more

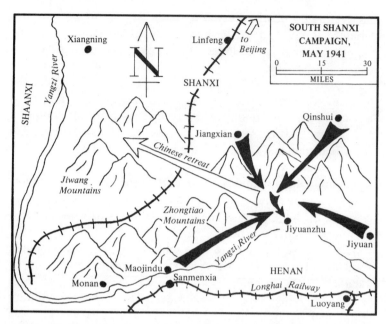

SOUTH SHANXI
CAMPAIGN,
MAY 1941

0   15   30

MILES

moats, built even more walls, and launched successive attacks
on the Communist guerrillas in the north. It was he who invented
the 'three-all' policy, dealing with Chinese villages by 'killing
all, burning all and looting all'. His chief of staff boasted that
there were more than 7000 miles of blockading moats (six times
as long as the Great Wall, or one-quarter of the circumference
of the earth) and nearly 10,000 fortresses in northern China.

Meanwhile the fifth major air operation of the Japanese,
known as Operation 102, saw a resumption of heavy bombing
of Chongqing and its surrounding region from Anyi on the
Yellow River, and from Wuhan and Jingmen on the River
Yangzi. This began early in August 1941, but was interrupted a
month later when the Japanese had to face about in order to
deal with the Americans.

In the early autumn of 1941 the Japanese high command
decided on another offensive, in spite of numerous adverse
circumstances. The new favourable factor was Hitler's invasion
of Russia in June, which fully tied Stalin's hands and allowed
Japan a golden opportunity to strike in China without having to

look over her back at Russia. Unfortunately it came too late. The Japanese were now tired, with their best strength bogged down in the China theatre and growing more and more short of oil and other strategic material.

Diplomatic events favoured China. The British had reopened the Burma Road in the autumn of 1940 so that supplies could be resumed for the Chinese army, and in the spring of 1941 Britain and the USA gave substantial economic assistance to the Chinese government. In July Japan occupied the southern part of Vietnam, as a result of which the Anglo-Americans froze Japanese assets.

In August the Japanese made an appraisal that the Russian–German war would be a long one, and so they planned to extend their own control southwards in east Asia. The showpiece of the new campaign would be the capture, at the second attempt, of the Hunanese provincial capital city of Changsha.

It was the re-emergence of the Chinese Ninth War Zone forces which finally led the Japanese into their adventure. These Chinese armies had not been used in battle for two years, but had now restored their strength so that they boasted thirty divisions of well-trained and well-equipped men drawn up along the Guangzhou–Wuhan railway with strong defences between the Xinqiang and Liuyang Rivers as well as along the Dongting Lake.

Among other activities, they were destroying the roads, leaving only the ridges between the rice fields as means of transportation, and the topography of this region prevented the Japanese from building motorable roads capable of standing up during the rainy season.

The Japanese Eleventh Army which had been in occupation of Wuhan since the end of 1938 proposed a second campaign against the Changsha area with the general aim of destroying Chinese strength, reducing the Chinese will to continue fighting and bringing the Ninth War Zone down to size.

The Eleventh Army Commander was General Anami Korechika, later to become the last of the unfortunate generals to enter, in 1945, the government as Minister for War. He ordered the new offensive to begin on 18 September.

During the night of 17–18 September the Japanese crossed the Xinqiang River at four points. The Chinese main strength went to the flank and trailed the advancing Japanese as they swept south. On the second day the Japanese reached the Miluo River which they crossed at numerous points, and once they were over on the south bank they tried to encircle the Chinese field forces with flanking movements. But the Chinese withdrew to the Laodao and Liuyang River regions closely followed by the Japanese, who then, on 26 September, made further flanking movements to encircle the city of Changsha itself. Paratroops were dropped from the air for the first time in this war.

The glory of the capture of Changsha fell to the plain-clothes Hayabuchi detachment of only a few hundred picked men. They gained access to the city by the north gate, having crossed the Liuyang River using local material. Once inside the city, however, the Hayabuchi detachment was annihilated, as were small squads of Japanese troops who forced their way into the northeastern part of Changsha on the following day.

Meanwhile four Japanese engineering regiments struggled desperately to lay down roads, achieving sixty miles of them in ten days. But the continuous rain just before the battle on the left bank of the Shui River made the repaired roads impassable for most of the time, and the Japanese heavy artillery and tanks could not take part in the battle.

When Jiang Jieshi realized that the Japanese were putting in forty-six infantry battalions with more than 300 pieces of artillery in reserve, he ordered a diversionary strike north of the Yangzi to take advantage of the reduced strength of the Japanese garrisons there. General Chen Cheng, the 'Crown Prince', was told to recapture Yichang within three days regardless of cost. By 6 October three Chinese divisions had indeed penetrated the east side of Yichang, but the Japanese brought up two extra divisions to protect their position there.

On the afternoon of 30 September the Japanese began to retreat from Changsha, suffering heavy casualties on their way to the Xinqiang River. A week later the Chinese pushed right to the gates of Yueyang, bringing the Japanese back to where they had started, and claiming 41,000 killed and wounded Japanese. The other main area of Japanese offensive in the autumn of 1941 was at Zhengzhou, the junction of the Beijing–Wuhan and Longhai railways in Henan province. For three years Zhengzhou had eluded the Japanese. At one point Generalissimo Jiang ordered a Chinese division to stand in the city and fight to the last man, while two other divisions withdrew about fifty miles to the rear.

The Japanese attacked the single division which stood in their path and cut it down, but then advanced no farther. Jiang explained to an American adviser that this was a matter of psychology. The Japanese had been so impressed by the determination of the one division they had wiped out, that they refrained from advancing on the other two. The Generalissimo reckoned to have stopped the Japanese advance at a cost of only one-third of his overall force.

But a final Japanese strike at Zhengzhou in October succeeded in capturing this obstinate city. Japan was thus brought within a dangerously short space of Xi'an, the crucial staging post through which Russian supplies came to help the Chinese armies. But the Japanese soon cut their losses and evacuated this city, returning to their original base across the Yellow River.

The campaigns of 1941 did not, therefore, substantially advance Japan's strategic position in the country she found so easy to invade but impossible to conquer. A Japanese army spokesman told an American correspondent, 'We see no end in sight. However, we Japanese intend to finish the job we began if we have to stay in China forever.' The American noted that this was a Columbia graduate speaking.

And then, on 7 December 1941, Japan switched the war about by bombing Pearl Harbor. From now on the war in China would be fought under the shadow of a more important and more fiercely contested war ranging right across the western Pacific and down to Malaya, the Dutch East Indies, New Guinea, the Philippines and the Pacific islands.

11

Allies at Last

The adventurists in the Japanese high command had taken a disastrous gamble. With the Russians reeling from Hitler's invasion, Asia was left entirely free from any European intervention. The war party in Tokyo argued that the Germans would now tie Stalin down, just as the Japanese themselves had, so they thought, destroyed China's capacity for an international military role.

Japan suddenly had the free hand in Asia for which she had yearned so long. Why not keep up the momentum and widen the war to enforce the exclusion from Asia of the only other world power which had thwarted Japan's political ambitions during the two decades since Versailles – the United States?

The army had already in October 1941 dropped Prince Konoye. He had collaborated with the militarists well enough, but was not himself a warrior and had an irritating propensity to urge compromise and political solutions just when the Japanese generals believed they were in sight of military victory.

Konoye was replaced as Premier by General Tojo Hideki, a member of the Japanese command in Manchuria and a former War Minister, with Togo Shigenori as his Foreign Minister. This was now a government openly and unambiguously out for a total military victory against China and other enemies.

The effect on China of the bombing of Pearl Harbor by Japanese planes on 7 December was to fill the leadership with new enthusiasm. Within hours Generalissimo Jiang Jieshi ordered all his armies systematically to attack and tie down Japanese forces on a rotation basis, to prevent them being used in other theatres.

In the Guangzhou area Chinese troops were sent to back up the British defence of Hong Kong, first victim of the post-Pearl Harbor offensive. Several Chinese units were moved from Guangxi and Sichuan in readiness to take part in the defence of Burma, now under Japanese attack, and others were brought down from Hunan to Guangdong and Guangxi as reinforcements.

At eight o'clock in the morning of 8 December 1941, while Japanese bombs were raining on Pearl Harbor on the other side of the International Date Line,* a dozen Japanese bombers with fighter escort bombed the Kai Tak airfield in Hong Kong, putting out of operation all the five RAF planes there as well as eight civilian aircraft. The Japanese pilots had been worried because their aircraft were out of date, but this pre-emptive attack was highly satisfactory. Their bombing was accurate and skilful.

At the same time three Japanese regiments crossed the Shenzhen River on temporary bridges into Hong Kong's New Territories. The British colonial government had only six battalions available to meet them – one of the Royal Scots Guards, a Middlesex battalion, a Rajput and a Punjabi battalion and two Canadian units. Against this motley and mostly ill-trained force the Japanese fielded only three regiments.

A 1932 Olympic Games' swimming medallist, Reizo Koike, swam out into Hong Kong harbour with other expert swimmers, keeping their guns and ammunition dry. The fired their rifles at the British mines from the water, and thus allowed the Japanese transports to sail into Hong Kong safely.

Within five days the British forces had to withdraw from the Kowloon mainland to Hong Kong Island itself. General Sakai then demanded the surrender of the island, otherwise, 'repressing my tears', as he put it, he would be obliged to attack it.

The British were depressed by the loss of their battleships *Prince of Wales* and *Repulse*, but news came from Guangzhou that 60,000 Chinese troops were on the march to relieve Hong

*Because of the International Date Line in the Pacific, 7 December in Hawaii was 8 December in Hong Kong.

Kong and the governor stood firm. On 18 December the Japanese launched their attack on Hong Kong Island itself but it took them a long week to crack its defences. By Christmas Day the British were holding out only in the centre of Victoria and at Stanley on the other side of the island. The British governor ordered his men to surrender, walking to Queen's Pier to receive General Sakai and become his prisoner. The British estimated their own casualties at 2113 dead or missing, the Japanese at 3000 dead.

There were several cases of cruelty by Japanese soldiers. The nurses and staff of the St Albert's Convent Hospital were tied up and about to be machine-gunned when the Japanese discovered that one of their own officers was being treated for wounds there and being well looked after, whereupon the staff were released. At another emergency hospital at Stanley more than fifty wounded Britons and Canadians were bayoneted in their beds on Christmas morning.

But the British survivors of the capture of Hong Kong were reluctant to condemn the Japanese afterwards, and regarded most of the bad incidents as the result of breakdowns in unit discipline. The worst fate was that of some local Chinese civilians who, in the words of the British historian of this episode, 'were used for bayonet or shooting practice, or for jujitsu practice, being thrown heavily a number of times, and bayoneted when unable to move'.

The other side of this coin was the way in which Japanese soldiers were impressed by the courage of their enemies and treated those who they felt had made a good fight with respect, even with deference. The capture of the British colony was nevertheless a tragedy of massive proportions, in line with those of earlier cities similarly dislocated. From Hong Kong about a million Chinese, many of them people who had escaped to Hong Kong from the Japanese in the first instance, were put to flight – by air and by sea, but mostly inland – under appallingly distressing conditions.

An American observer noted, in connection with the frequency of rapes after the capture of Hong Kong, that it was Chinese women rather than British who were thus attacked.

'Either the men were being held in,' she added, ' – the Japs certainly did have in mind the idea of showing those snooty British that they could be gentlemen too – or they just preferred Chinese women to British. . . .'

The same writer noted how Japanese soldiers urinated everywhere in the houses they occupied, especially on the floor, and she regarded this as an intended insult. She cited the experience of a British woman friend in whose living room Japanese troops had made a ring of her best linen doilies, carefully shat on each one and then showed her the results. Her friend was puzzled, but the writer read some symbolism into it.

Japan also occupied the International Concessions in Shanghai and other Chinese Treaty Ports which until then had been controlled by various western powers. Among other things the extraordinary success of the Chinese intelligence agent in Shanghai called He Yizhi came to an abrupt end.

He was a northerner who had graduated in political science from the highest Japanese academy the Imperial University in Tokyo. Because of his fluent Japanese and high academic qualifications, the Japanese army sent him as an interpreter to south China, where he became friendly with such military leaders as Doihara, Itagaki and Colonel Wachi Takaji.

When General Li Zongren met this Chinese interpreter and reproached him for serving his country's enemy, the young man burst into tears, and offered to serve, without any remuneration, as an intelligence agent for Li within the Japanese command.

Wachi was one of those Japanese officers who felt strongly that his country should be attacking Russia rather than China. The aggression against China, in the view of these officers, was a great mistake on Japan's part, since China would be a valuable ally against the Soviet Union.

One of the Chinese officers whom Wachi befriended was General Li, who had equally independent political opinions, and gradually Wachi began to pass on Japanese military secrets to the Chinese intelligence, notably to He Yizhi.

He constructed a secret radio transmitter in the home of a Japanese friend in the French Concession of Shanghai, and in the early months of the war the speed and accuracy of his reports on Japanese strategy were unparalleled. He gave the Chinese high command advance information on the Japanese deployment in many battles, from Xuzhou to Wuhan.

When General Wachi was transferred for his unorthodox opinions, he introduced He to another colleague, and so the intelligence reports continued until 1941, when the Japanese occupied the International Settlement in Shanghai and forced He to flee the city, suspected of espionage.

One of the consequences of Pearl Harbor was that China could formally declare war on Japan on 9 December 1941. She was no longer fighting the invader single-handedly, but became one of many allies on many continents dedicated to defeating Japan in war. A few days later Jiang Jieshi presided over a conference of Chinese, British and American military representatives about the conduct of future military operations.

'China and Britain', he told the British delegate, 'neither must fail. If China should fail, Britain's India will be endangered.' Earlier lapses by the British in withholding American Lend-Lease aid in Rangoon were now officially forgiven.

At the end of the year President Roosevelt cabled to Jiang Jieshi proposing, with the previous support of the other western Allies, to set up a China theatre of which the Generalissimo himself would be the supreme commander. China joined twenty-five other Allies in Washington in a joint declaration promising that there would be no separate peace with Japan.

Jiang had to find a chief of staff for the Allied Forces headquarters in the China theatre which was now under his command, and which included parts of Thailand and Vietnam. He cabled Roosevelt on 2 January 1942 asking him to recommend a trusted general to serve in this position. The Americans nominated Joseph W. Stilwell – 'Vinegar Joe' – a West Point graduate, born in the same year as Mao Zedong.

Stilwell had served in China for several years, as a language officer, with the American Fifteenth Infantry Regiment in Tianjin, and as US military attaché. He had supervised the building of the modern highway from Taiyuan in Shanxi province to the Yellow River, which ironically was used seventeen years later by the Japanese as their way of triumph into China.

He had also been an eyewitness of the 1911 revolution, and knew and spoke Chinese, although one of his Chinese critics complained that he 'lacked real knowledge of Chinese culture, politics, the aspirations of the Chinese and the ability to evaluate these'.

It was conceded that Stilwell had a rough temper, was rude to his superiors and had only reached the rank of divisional commander. He was said on the other hand to be skilful in troop training and courageous on the battlefield, and he was a very close friend of General George C. Marshall, Roosevelt's chief of staff. He arrived in China to take up a role which proved extremely controversial, not least because the Americans insisted that he should act not only as the Allied chief of staff but also as the US army representative and the supervisor of US Lend-Lease material for China.

It was a symptom of Stilwell's ineptness that for the first fifteen months in China he never used his title as chief of staff of the Allied forces, which was so important to the Chinese. When Jiang finally asked him outright about this Stilwell replied: 'I am your chief of staff and under your direct command.' But his heart was not in serving a commander he could not admire.

Jiang soon discovered that Stilwell had very little practical war experience or knowledge of basic military principles. He nevertheless made the best of his American recruit and appointed him commander-in-chief of the Chinese Expeditionary Forces in Burma, where the Chinese had to co-operate with British and American forces in a fully international campaign.

A few days after Pearl Harbor the Chinese, at the request of their new allies, had organized an expeditionary force for Burma which crossed the frontier to take over the defence of the border areas with northern Thailand and Vietnam. The British were particularly insistent in their call for more Chinese reinforcements to help bolster their weak position in Burma.

General Iida, commander of the Japanese Fifteenth Army,

was now concentrating more than 100,000 men on the Thai border to invade Burma and cut off China's supply road from India. In February 1942 Japanese troops landed in Rangoon from the sea, creating a critical condition for the Allied defence.

The Generalissimo paid a visit to India, meeting both Nehru and Gandhi. The latter lectured the Chinese leader in Calcutta on 18 February on the merits of opposing Japan by non-violence. Jiang took little notice of this, but another of the Mahatma's remarks was well remembered afterwards. 'The West,' he told Jiang, 'will never voluntarily treat us orientals as equals. Why, they do not even admit your country to their Combined Chiefs-of-Staff conferences.' Jiang for his part continued to berate the British for withholding self-rule from India.

Some of the Chinese forces in Burma were cast in an antique mould. Once in the Burmese theatre a particularly old-fashioned minor Chinese general played a macabre game with some of his soldiers. Coming across them in his sedan chair as they were resting a few days before battle, he smilingly asked whether they were prepared to die for China. Those who were ready stepped forward, and the general nodded approvingly. He was about to climb back into his sedan chair when another idea occurred to him. He turned back, fixed the men with his eye and said: 'As a test of your loyalty to your general, I have one more question to ask. Who will sacrifice his life for me?'

At first nobody moved, but eventually, after a good five minutes, some of them stepped tentatively forward, as if in a daze.

To the five who stepped forward from the front rank the general asked again: 'You are prepared to die for me?'

The soldiers did not answer, but they threw up their heads in a way which meant, 'Yes.' Then, walking slowly down the line and pausing before each man, the general shot the five who were ready to die for him, one by one. Afterwards he barked: 'Dismiss.'

He returned to his sedan chair, turned back and smiled broadly at the soldiers – upon which they set upon him and trampled him to death.

The Chinese Expeditionary Force in Burma consisted of

three armies, the Fifth (under General Du Yuming), Sixth and Sixty-Sixth. Their senior Chinese commander was General Luo Chuoying, but Stilwell was put in overall command of them in orders signed by the Generalissimo on 11 March. Chiang explained to the American that the Fifth and Sixth Armies were among China's best, and that the Chinese expedition to Burma must at all costs be successful.

The ambiguity of Stilwell's role was illuminated by General Du when he explained to the British Governor-General of Burma that Stilwell 'only thinks that he is commanding. If fact he is doing no such thing. . . . We Chinese think that the only way to keep the Americans in the war is to give them a few commands on paper. They will not do much harm as long as we do the work.'

The Chinese were given positions to the east of the Rangoon–Mandalay railway, extending 450 miles to the Thai frontier. When the Japanese attacked Pegu, the Chinese forces moved down from the border into central Burma, but by then the situation on the Irrawaddy front had already become critical. The Chinese began digging themselves in around Toungoo in muddy fields during the second week of March, and engaged with a Japanese motorized division supported by other regiments, but it had to withdraw under intensive shelling and relay bombing.

Stilwell noted of the Chinese tank battalion: 'They are green men in the military sense, and many of them have come from China's paddy fields to drive a motor-driven vehicle for the first time in their lives. . . .' He went on to praise its performance in the Hukawng valley later.

Stilwell had already got into a fierce argument with the Generalissimo about strategy. The American wanted the Fifth Army to remain where it was at Toungoo, whereas the Generalissimo gave orders for some of its units to go to the defence of Mandalay. It then became apparent that the British might not be able to hold Prome and that Toungoo's security could thus be threatened.

The Japanese indeed took Toungoo on 26 March, forcing the Chinese to retreat northwards. The British commander, Field

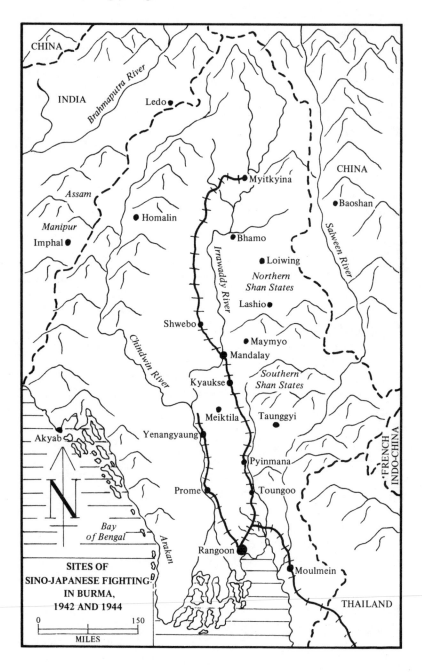

CHINA

INDIA

Brahmaputra River

Ledo

Assam

Homalin

Manipur

Imphal

Myitkyina

CHINA

Baoshan

Bhamo

Loiwing

Irrawaddy River

Northern
Shan States

Salween River

Lashio

Shwebo

Maymyo

Mandalay

Chindwin River

Kyaukse

Southern
Shan States

Meiktila

Taunggyi

Akyab

Yenangyaung

Pyinmana

FRENCH INDO-CHINA

Prome

Toungoo

Bay
of Bengal

Arakan

Rangoon

Moulmein

**SITES OF
SINO-JAPANESE FIGHTING
IN BURMA,
1942 AND 1944**

THAILAND

0   150

MILES

Marshal Alexander, taxed General Du about the Chinese field guns, which had been observed the day before the battle, carefully dug in, well sighted and expertly camouflaged. Du explained that the guns had been withdrawn to safety.

'Then you mean that they will take no part in the battle?'

'Exactly.'

'Then what use are they?'

'The Fifth Army,' the Chinese general explained to his British colleague, 'is our best army because it is the only one which has any field guns, and I cannot afford to risk those guns. If I lose them the Fifth Army will no longer be our best.'

Stilwell came under criticism later from the Chinese for having ordered the Fifth Army into combat in these circumstances, after Jiang Jieshi had warned him not to underrate Japanese strength and not to advance at will. The Generalissimo bombarded Stilwell and the other commanders with detailed orders as to where they should march and what they should do, making Vinegar Joe's position impossible.

On 1 April Stilwell flew back to Chongqing and complained to Jiang that the Chinese forces had lost three opportunities to counter-attack because the Twenty-Second Division had disobeyed his orders and General Du Yuming had not carried out his instruction faithfully. Stilwell threatened to resign.

In this early test of wills, the Generalissimo prevaricated. He obliged Stilwell by court-martialling the divisional commander and sending an envoy to investigate the other complaints. He reaffirmed Stilwell's authority and clarified General Luo Chuoying's role as the Chinese commander of the expeditionary forces. The idea was that General Luo would take orders from Stilwell, while all the other Chinese commanders would take orders from Luo.

Feeling vindicated, Stilwell returned to Burma to lead the Chinese Expeditionary Force in a critical battle against the Japanese in central Burma, this time in an endeavour to save the encircled British troops at the Yenangyaung oilfields. The Japanese Thirty-Third Division had broken through the British positions at Prome and pressed the British back to Yenangyaung, which the Japanese captured on 16 April, surrounding two British brigades and a tank battalion. Stilwell rushed the one and only Chinese armoured division from Lashio to the rescue.

After a desperate forty-eight-hour fight on 17–18 April this force under General Sun Liren routed the Japanese Thirty-Third Division and recaptured Yenangyaung, killing more than 1000 Japanese and rescuing more than 7000 British and Indian soldiers, not to mention 500 prisoners, American missionaries and reporters, besides recovering many tanks and horses. 'A new record was established,' a Chinese military historian commented proudly, 'in the revolutionary history of the Chinese armed forces in which Chinese forces achieved distinction abroad.'

But the sudden dash of this armoured division from its original station left the right wing of the main Chinese forces unprotected. The Japanese were quick to exploit the weakness and the whole Chinese defence line began to crack. The general commanding the 200th Division died of wounds during this retreat.

At the same time, the Japanese pressed heavily on the left wing to attack the Chinese in the northern Shan states of Burma, entering Taunggyi on 20 April. The Chinese drove this column back, but the Japanese effectively cut off the Chinese lines of communication in their rear by seizing Lashio, forcing the Chinese under heavy shelling and bombing to evacuate the town on the 29th.

Stilwell, complete with his First World War hat and government-issue khaki which he wore, out of inverse snobbery, without any insignia or decorations, conferred with Alexander and Generals Luo and Du at Kyaukse at the end of April. The two Chinese generals, Stilwell confided to his diary, looked 'plump and unhappy', and 'uncertain and sulky', and no wonder. There was nothing they could do to stem the retreat.

Early in May the main Japanese force drove northwards up the Irrawaddy to capture Myitkyina. Two other Chinese divisions defended the eastern bank of the Nu River, and ultimately there was a stalemate between the Chinese and Japanese troops at this point.

One Japanese column advanced along the Burma Road and crossed the Salween River into Yunnan province on 3 May. It was eliminated by Chinese defenders, but another reinforced Japanese column took Tengchong in west Yunnan on 11 May.

In Burma itself the Japanese systematically occupied all the strategic cities, to control the whole country by June. Part of the Chinese Expeditionary Force crossed the high mountains into India for reorganization and training, while the main force retreated into western Yunnan.

Before Myitkyina fell, Jiang had cabled to Stilwell and Luo to move their main forces to Myitkyina and Hpimaw. General Du could have assembled three divisions by this strategy and something might have been retrieved from the situation. But Stilwell and Luo continued instead to move about inconclusively between Mandalay and Shwebo, ignoring Jiang's command, until all routes of retreat were blocked and the Myitkyina railway was no longer available.

Tens of thousands of Chinese troops were thus bogged down in northern Burma and several thousands of them died from hunger and cold. Stilwell's Chinese army was broken into two and suffered a significant defeat while its route of retreat was obstructed.

Realizing that Lashio had been lost, the position at Wanding had become critical and even Bhamo was in danger, Stilwell had decided in late April to evacuate to Imphal in India. On the afternoon of 5 May he parted company with General Luo at Banmauk, Stilwell leading his forces westward on foot, and Luo remaining to take care of the wounded and the laggards.

One of the American transport planes flying the Hump – the airlift route from India – had been ordered urgently to fly to Shwebo to evacuate General Stilwell and his staff. When it arrived he said stiffly: 'The air force didn't bring me in here and it doesn't have to fly me out either . . . I'll walk!'

And he did. His staff officers went on the plane which had come for them, but Stilwell doggedly walked out on his own two feet depriving the whole theatre of its commander for three weeks, since nobody knew exactly where he was. He emerged in India twenty-one days later emaciated, sick from dysentery and malaria and down to eighty pounds. 'He was a brave man, all right,' one of the Americans with him commented, 'but he was fighting the wrong war.'

Stilwell had that rare quality of being able to command men under fire and make them want to follow him. He was an outstanding battlefield commander, but he could not do justice to the responsibility of a theatre command. Not for nothing did he become known as the 'best damned four-star battalion commander in the army'.

General Du Yuming knew that an evacuation to India would make Jiang angry, and he therefore considered throwing his Fifth Army into a life-or-death struggle with the Japanese at Bhamo and Myitkyina. If it succeeded, well and good, and if not, then the Chinese could still return to China via Tengchong. But when General Luo learned of the Japanese capture of Bhamo, leaving the Chinese forces entirely at a disadvantage, he instructed General Du to withdraw the Fifth Army to Homalin according to the original plan.

With superior equipment, a superior air force and unified strategy, the Japanese with ten infantry divisions and two armoured battalions were thus able to defeat the combined forces of China, Britain, India and Burma and cut off the international communications line of China in one brilliant campaign. They lost 1200 men dead and over 3000 wounded, while the Chinese losses alone exceeded 10,000.

During this difficult campaign the Chinese forces won a number of individual victories over an enemy superior in numbers, notably in Toungoo, Yedashe and Yenangyaung. But the overall result was a failure, mainly because the various Allied troops had no unified command, and lacked adequate air cover, intelligence or reconnaissance. As a Chinese general commented: 'The Allied powers have no concrete agreement or operational preparation. After the fall of Rangoon, the main British force was moved west of the railroad and the Chinese troops undertook to engage the enemy east of the railroad. . . . The Chinese forces could not be massed in time and their strength therefore was not fully utilized. As a result, the Chinese fought passively from the beginning to the end.'

Stilwell's dramatic rush to rescue the trapped British was heartily disapproved by the Generalissimo, to whom it appeared that the Chinese counter-offensive had been sacrificed merely to save a few hundred British soldiers. As General Chennault, who knew Jiang well, explained afterwards: 'To a man with the Generalissimo's experience and temperament, Stilwell's pulling the props from under the Chinese offensive seemed the sheerest sentimentality and incredible military callowness. From that day forward the Generalissimo had little respect for Stilwell's ability as a field commander and his faith in Stilwell's integrity began to crumble....'

More importantly, the loss of the two key Chinese armies in this first Burma campaign represented a grave setback in the war in China itself. Partly trained and equipped by Germany, they were among the best which the Chinese government had at its disposal.

Until they were lost in Burma, these two armies had served Generalissimo Jiang Jieshi as roving trouble-shooters, able to plug critical breaches in China's defences as they occurred before the onslaught of Japanese offensives. Their loss in Burma deprived China of more than one-third of her strategic reserve.

It was in this campaign that Vinegar Joe Stilwell established his reputation for going incommunicado. Throughout the campaign the only message he ever sent to the Generalissimo in Chongqing was right at the end, during his flight to India, on 6 May.

'With a party of about 100,' it read laconically, 'we are travelling on foot towards Homalin.... From there we shall proceed to Imphal. There is no need to worry, we are armed and have food. The Chinese troops have pretty well disintegrated and control has passed to small units. It is useless to try to exercise command over them....'

Jiang noted bitterly in his private file on Stilwell: 'Does not know discipline.'

Stilwell's own comment on his first Burma campaign was: 'We got a hell of a beating. We got run out of Burma and it is humiliating. We ought to find out why it happened, go back and retake it.' Nothing could be done during the monsoon rains which flooded Burma from May to October, but Stilwell was set on returning there.

He worked out detailed plans for opening up a new road through northern Burma to break the Japanese blockade of China, and to build up three Chinese divisions to cross the high mountains of Ledo in India where they were training, into northern Burma at the beginning of the dry season. This could be dovetailed with a British invasion of southern and central Burma, and also an attack by Chinese forces from Yunnan towards Myitkyina.

But each of these three forces in Stilwell's grand strategy would need a year in which to reorganize and prepare, and so October 1943 was Stilwell's target date for launching the recapture of Burma.

12

The Flying Tigers

Another outstanding foreign character in the Chinese cast now came forward. In 1937 Captain Claire L. Chennault, an able but non-conformist Texan in the US air force, had been retired for deafness, which was taken as disqualifying him from flying. Madame Jiang Jieshi had just been appointed China's National Secretary for Aviation, and she invited Chennault to China to help her. He arrived too late to rescue the American flying school in China: it was the Italian academy at Luoyang run by officers of Mussolini which had just been given the major role in China's air effort, along with the Nanchang Fiat fighter assembly plant. Chennault nevertheless came to act as air chief-of-staff to the Generalissimo, and chief trainer of the Chinese air force. The pilots he was given to coach were sadly incompetent, however, and many of the new planes which China had acquired from abroad were smashed up during training.

The American therefore pressed his own country to help the Chinese air force, and finally succeeded in 1941 in acquiring a hundred US-financed P-40s which had been rejected by the British as obsolete. He then caught the ear of one of President Roosevelt's advisers and won approval for the famous American Volunteer Group, or Flying Tigers – a Foreign Legion of the sky. The first hundred volunteers assembled secretly in San Francisco, set sail on a Dutch ship, switching to a Norwegian boat to disembark in Rangoon and thence to China in September 1941.

Chennault trained his men methodically to hunt the Japanese enemy. 'The Japanese,' he told them, 'are superbly trained pilots. They are mechanical, yes, when compared to Americans with their individuality. But mechanical flying can be effective and dangerous to you when it is combined with expert air discipline, as you'll discover in the Japanese. It can only be beaten by your own initiative backed with superior judgement.

'The Japanese can stick together longer in their formations than any of you have ever thought possible. You will have to break them up. Then, and only then, will you be able to make them fight according to your own desires. Then and only then can you win. Once you are able to do that breaking up you will have him in trouble. He lacks the ability to improvise readily, but just the same never underestimate him....'

One night in the autumn of 1942 Radio Tokyo declared that Chennault's 200 fighters would be destroyed. It was the biggest compliment the American could have wished for, because his strength at that time was only twenty-nine aircraft. The digits of their numbers had been reversed, the colours of the propeller spinners changed so often that even the pilots themselves did not know how many actual fighters there were.

The new American Volunteer Group divided into three squadrons, two initially based at Kunming and the third in Toungoo in Burma. The Flying Tigers had frequent engagements with the Japanese over Burma in the spring of 1942, with very few losses. During the year 1942 they sank about 50,000 tons of Japanese shipping and provided effective air cover for the Chinese infantry in the battles of Changsha, Zhejiang and Jiangxi. Chennault himself was credited with some of the 'hits' in spite of his alleged bad ear.

In October Chennault went further, asking Roosevelt to supply a 'very small American air force – 105 fighter aircraft of modern design, thirty medium bombers and in the last phase, some months from now, twelve heavy bombers....' If such a force could be supplied, Chennault pledged the downfall of Japan. Roosevelt liked the idea, but Marshall and Stilwell opposed it and in the end there was a compromise arrangement for only a gradual increase in Chennault's complement.

The airlift over the Hump from India, so vital to China's war supplies, was also performed by American pilots in Douglas and

Curtiss Commando transports.

In China itself the first battle following Pearl Harbor was being fought around Changsha, the capital of Hunan province, which the Japanese were trying for the third time to capture. On this occasion they had the additional objective of preventing Jiang from reinforcing the Hong Kong and Burmese theatres.

At the end of December 1941 three Japanese divisions were massed at Yueyang to advance southwards towards the Hunanese capital, in the belief that many of its defenders of October had been sent south. This force of about 70,000 men crossed the first Chinese line of defence, the Xinqiang River, on Christmas Eve and the Miluo River on 27–28 December. Between the Miluo and Changsha the Chinese had set traps, and the Japanese columns had to make detours.

On 31 December the first Japanese forces arrived at the outskirts of the city, which by then had been almost completely evacuated. But they made little headway, and began to be surrounded by Chinese reinforcements as well as being shelled by Chinese heavy guns, much to the Japanese surprise. The Japanese attack collapsed on 4 January, and not even the injection of another brigade from Yueyang could save the day. In the course of retreating across the Liuyang River the Japanese suffered heavy casualties and the whole operation was a dismal failure.

Jiang immediately declared it one of the decisive battles of the war: an entire Japanese army had been cut to pieces and 57,000 Japanese had died or been wounded. Foreign correspondents were rushed to the scene to see Japanese bodies stripped of their clothes on the frozen battlefield, and evidence that the Japanese army had penetrated into the outskirts of Changsha – even, in small numbers, into the heart of the city. *The Times* correspondent reconstructed the battle. 'The young Chinese soldiers in blue, the Japanese in brown, with steel helmets, which few of the Chinese possessed. The Japanese wore leather sandals, the Chinese wore sandals of bark or rice-straw. The Japanese were far from their homes, the Chinese were fighting outside of the walls of their homes.'

The Japanese were young, which another correspondent

found extraordinary. 'The older and more experienced must have been sent down to fight against Malaya and the Philippines. They were superbly confident that they could capture Changsha without trained men. Yet the Chinese were even younger.'

When they came to the dead Japanese and Chinese lying by the roadside 'in small companionable groups, like lovers', the foreign pressmen found that most of the Japanese corpses were naked, stripped of their clothes by Chinese soldiers who knew the coldness of the long winter nights around Changsha.

One Chinese soldier, 'who cannot have been more than 12 years old', led Robert Payne, the British journalist, to the body of a Japanese officer whose fingers had been broken and whose teeth were clenched tightly over five bullets.

'He fought to the end,' the young Chinese said. 'Look at the bullets in his teeth. We had to cut off his fingers to get at his revolver, so tightly did he hold it.'

The newsmen concluded that only a relatively small column of Japanese had blundered into a trap, leaving perhaps 6000 or 7000 dead in what looked more like a series of hard-fought skirmishes – hardly a full-scale battle.

But the Gimo insisted to the end that the battle of Changsha was a turning point. The Chinese, he wrote in his autobiography, had 'dealt a crushing defeat to the Japanese at the battle of Changsha', a blow so fatal to Japan that it was now 'impossible for her to recover her strength in China'. Personally Jiang needed to exaggerate the Chinese success to strengthen his own hand with his new western allies.

Another important consequence of the internationalization of the war was the bombing of targets in Japan by American aircraft using Chinese airfields. During the early part of 1942 the Chinese strengthened their own air force in south China and extended the runways or built new ones at several places. The Japanese frequently damaged these airfields, but the Chinese were always able to rebuild them.

On 18 April American bombers under General James Doolittle, launched from aircraft carriers at sea, began to bomb Tokyo and other Japanese cities, landing afterwards at Chinese airfields in Zhejiang or Jiangxi. Imperial GHQ in Tokyo immediately ordered the Japanese air force to destroy these bases, using their newly acquired Hayabusa Type 1 fighters, and sent more than 100,000 soldiers to capture cities in Zhejiang which had helped the American pilots and crews of planes which had crashed.

The Americans did not give China enough notice of the Doolittle raids for adequate defences of the relevant airfields to be prepared. Chiang asked for a postponement or else for a change in the airfields to be used, but the aircraft carriers had already sailed and the orders could not be changed.

As a result the whole of Zhejiang province was shaken and General Marshall had to send apologies to Jiang Jieshi. A senior American officer observed of the retaliatory Japanese campaign in Zhejiang: 'A quarter-million Chinese soldiers and civilians were killed in the three-month campaign. The Chinese paid a terrible price for the Doolittle raid, but they never complained.'

At the end of May other Japanese troops moved from Nanchang in Jiangxi province to meet the Japanese units from Zhejiang in the first week of July, thus gaining a control of the Zhejiang–Jiangxi railway which was to prove only temporary. For a brief moment the Japanese could dream of commanding a Tokyo–Singapore railway using the Shanghai–Hangzhou, Zhejiang–Jiangxi, Hunan–Guangxi, Vietnam and Thailand railways.

But early in August the Chinese counter-attacked, quickly recovering several cities and airfields. Such towns as Lishui and Wenzhou changed hands several times during this campaign. The Chinese recaptured Quxian on 28 August. Apart from retaining the vital air bases which enabled the Americans to bomb Japan, the Chinese during this campaign also frustrated the grandiose plan for a continuous railway to Singapore.

The principal priority of the Japanese command in China was still to crush the Chinese government and army by invading its last fortress, Sichuan province. In the spring of 1942 the Japanese generals in China suggested that sixteen divisions be brought into south-central China from Japan itself, Manchuria and the South Seas to reinforce the Japanese Expeditionary Force and allow it to attack Sichuan, using ten divisions of its main strength from southern Shanxi and another six at Yichang in the spring of 1943.

But the events of the months that followed made it less and less likely that this final coup could be brought off. In the summer of 1942 the Japanese were defeated in the Pacific at Midway and the Americans landed at Guadalcanal. In September preparations for the Sichuan campaign were postponed, and after it became clear in November from the total defeat on Guadalcanal that Japan's freedom of manoeuvre in switching forces around was greatly reduced, the plan was completely scrapped.

Meanwhile Vinegar Joe Stilwell was still brooding over his setback in Burma. He had a spirited post-mortem with the Generalissimo on 4 June, at which he blamed the reverses on the lack of air support and criticized the commanders of the Fifty-Fifth and Ninety-Sixth Divisions as well as the Fifth Army's quarter-master general – though he did single out the Thirty-Seventh and 200th divisional commanders for praise.

Jiang Jieshi dismissed and court-martialled two of the three offending commanders, but refused to transfer General Du Yuming, the Fifth Army commander. Stilwell now concentrated on the programme for training Chinese troops in India, together with the reorganization of the Chinese forces along the lines of 'weeding out the weak and retaining the strong, quality before quantity, appointment of the capable and delegation of authority and responsibility to the trustworthy' – points which the German military advisers had been vainly pressing ten years earlier.

For his part Jiang tried to educate Stilwell into a wider view of his responsibilities. On 24 June he told the American: 'The Burma operations were under way when you arrived in China. You hurried to Burma to take command and assumed only a small part of the responsibility for Chinese military affairs. As my chief-of-staff you should prepare an overall plan for all military operations and not concentrate your mind on a single locality. Air power and the tonnage of air transport between

India and China are crucial in maintaining the status quo of the China theatre. I hope you will dedicate yourself to these matters.'

Yet only two days later a batch of American Flying Fortresses originally assigned to the China theatre was transferred instead to support the British in Egypt, without prior consultation with the Chinese. The Generalissimo stormed at Stilwell, who sent an agitated cable to Roosevelt: 'Jiang feels that Allies do not regard China as part of Allied war effort. China has done her best for five years. Questions whether Allies are doing their best for China.... Do the Allies want the China theatre maintained?'

After this Jiang and Stilwell hardly spoke to each other. The Generalissimo complained to an envoy of Roosevelt: 'To me he behaves as if he were my boss....'

Stilwell busied himself with plans for a counter-attack in Burma, in which he had now acquired a strong personal interest as well as a need to regain lost prestige. Zhou Enlai, the Communist representative in Chongqing, offered to lead Red Army troops in a campaign to retake Burma, adding significantly that, '*I* would obey General Stilwell's orders!' The British, of course, preferred to wait to take Burma themselves rather than let it be liberated by troops of an independent Asian country; Stilwell did not fully comprehend the subtleties of Anglo-Chinese differences over Burma.

Fighting flared across north China during 1942. General Ye Jianying of the Communist armies reported that the Eighteenth Group Army fought six major offensives in the first half of 1942. In one of these the Japanese General Sakamoto was killed, and in another the deputy chief of staff of the Eighteenth Group Army also died. Very large casualties were suffered on both sides in these 'mopping-up' campaigns.

General Zhu De, the Communist commander-in-chief, claimed on 7 July that the two Chinese Communist armies had during 1941–2 engaged more than twenty-four Japanese divisions, or 44 per cent of the total Japanese troops in China.

Meanwhile throughout Japanese-occupied China guerrilla resistance continued. More often than not the Chinese partisans owed their successes to their wits rather than their equipment or numbers. The night attack on Xiangyangdian in September 1942 by the Seventh Independent Regiment of the 358th Brigade was a case in point.

This was a citadel of a town, only a few miles upriver from the Shanxi province capital of Taiyuan. It was protected on all sides by strong Japanese fortifications, so that in the event of a crisis reinforcements could reach it in less than half an hour. So confident were the Japanese that the Eighth Route Army would never dare to attack it that they left a few dozen Chinese 'puppet' soldiers in charge.

Xu Wenli, a political instructor, discussed with his colleagues how they could take Xiangyangdian. Lieutenant Wu Shihzheng, who had killed fifty-eight Japanese without even being wounded himself, proposed a way of disarming the puppet garrison without a single shot being fired.

'We had captured,' Xu recalled, 'regulation Japanese tunics, overcoats, leather boots, sabres, binoculars, pistols and many uniforms of both Japanese and puppet soldiers. I was disguised as a Japanese captain, Wu as a lieutenant and the rest of the squad looked like either Japanese or puppet soldiers.'

They set out at dusk and reached the town gate at midnight. They formed a human ladder to climb the wall, and the resourceful Lieutenant Wu went first. 'Being small and agile, he stepped on the "human ladder" quickly. The men below supported his feet with the butts of their rifles and gave him an upward push, on the force of which he jumped on to the top of the wall. From there he hauled the other men up, one by one, with the aid of a rope. Since we were all disguised as either Japanese or puppet soldiers, I asked everyone to tie a strip of white cloth around his leg, so that he would be able to distinguish our own men from the enemy in case of a skirmish.'

Once inside, they went to the house of a local supporter. He took them to search out the sentry who could open the gate to allow a speedy getaway if necessary.

They did not get far before hearing the click of a rifle bolt.

'Who goes there?' a fierce voice pierced the stillness of the night. Perched on top of a house just in front of them was a sentry box, and a puppet soldier was levelling his rifle at them.

'Sentry! Quick, come down!' called Wu, mimicking the peculiar broken Chinese which was usually spoken by the Japanese.

The puppet soldier saw two Japanese and a local inhabitant, and he hastily climbed down from the roof of the house. Without waiting for him to come close, Wu stepped up and boxed his ears.

'*Bakayaro!* [fool] Too bad!' exclaimed Wu, and grabbed his rifle.

The local resident who had come with them was quick-witted. He promptly said to the soldier, 'His Honour wants you to open the town gate.'

'Yes! Yes!' the puppet soldier replied, and immediately pulled out of his pocket the key for the big padlock on the town gate. Wu snatched the key from his hand and, ordering him to walk in front, went with him to open the gate.

'Back at the alley,' one of the partisans recollected, 'we rejoined our men and ordered the puppet soldier to bring us to the place where the other puppet soldiers were. On arriving at the house where the other puppet soldiers were lodged, the fellow yelled, "Open the door, the Japanese have come!"

'Thinking that he had announced us improperly, Wu acted as though he were very angry and kicked him.

'"*Baka!* You say, 'Your Honour!'" Wu shouted. Had the man been clever, it would not have been difficult for him to have detected some slip in Wu's Japanese-Chinese gibberish, but he was scared out of his wits by Wu's behaviour from the moment he met them, and bowed and scraped, saying repeatedly, "Yes, yes, Your Honour!"

'The row that we made outside woke up the puppet soldiers in the house, and we clearly heard the click of rifles. I was worried that if those fellows inside should start to fire all would be spoiled. There must be no delay!

'"Whoever delivers the first blow will be the winner," the old saying goes, so I instantly kicked the door with my heavy Japanese boots. The door yielded with a bang and fell in with a crash. One puppet soldier behind the door, seeing us strut around in a blazing rage, was scared stiff and stood to one side speechless. But we were afraid of talking too much ourselves, lest we give away the show. Wu saw a leather belt hanging on the wall. He took it down and started to whip the puppet soldier with it. The fellow was bewildered. Protecting his head with both arms, he asked in a trembling voice, "Is it that we are all to assemble, Your Honour?"

'He blew a whistle and all the puppet soldiers in the house came out holding rifles and fell in a straight line. I saw that they all had rifles in their hands and wondered how we could disarm them.

'Wu gave the visor of his military cap a downward pull, walked up to the puppet soldier who had blown the whistle and gave him a resounding blow on the chest.

'"*Bakayaro!*" shouted Wu, staring round round-eyed. "Too bad! When assembled, why hold rifles?"

'The puppet soldiers hastily put their rifles against the wall. Our men came up quickly and collected all the rifles and unloaded them. Now we became even bolder.

'The sound of a telephone ringing interrupted us. A puppet soldier was trying to get through to Lancun to find out what had happened there. I ordered one of the men to pull the receiver out of his hand and cut the wires. One of the puppet soldiers, seeing that we were to destroy the telephone, said with a tremble in his voice:

'"Beg to report, Your Honour! Without the telephone we won't be able to communicate with Lancun and Taiyong in case of an emergency."

'I acted as if I had not heard and told them all, "You! Too bad, too bad! The Imperial Army will bring you, all of you, back to Lancun!"

'The puppet soldiers were bewildered, yet, not daring to utter a words of protest, they left immediately, obediently, one by one, under the custody of our men. Sadly they said goodbye to Xiangyangdian.

'After we had gone a mile or so out of the town the road took a turn and we soon found ourselves walking along a narrow path beside the fields.

'Now one of the puppet soldiers became impatient and he blurted out, "We have taken the wrong way, Your Honour. This is not the right way to Lancun."

'Since the danger was not so great now, I wanted Wu to let them rest awhile and then tell them the truth.

'Wu resumed his normal easy manner, and said to them with a grin, "Now I'll tell you the truth! We are not 'Your Honour' or Japanese soldiers. We are none other than the Eighth Route Army men!" His voice grew serious, as he continued, "You thought that you could take liberties with the peasants and do all sorts of evil things under the wing of the Japanese invaders because you were stationed at Xiangyangdian, surrounded by big Japanese forts. You thought that the Eighth Route Army could not come. But you were wrong! The Eighth Route Army could come at any time it was ready to punish you! Now come along with us and be obedient. You will still have an opportunity to redeem yourselves if you are willing to make a fresh start and atone for your crimes."

'At this disclosure the puppet soldiers were startled and dumbfounded. Ever since this incident the story of a mysterious engagement in which not a single shot was fired took wing and was related in all the enemy bases in the Shanxi plain. The countryfolk said that it was the "heavenly troops descending from the sky". It put the enemy soldiers in all the enemy bases on guard and they were uneasy for a long time....'

On another occasion six Chinese partisans dressed as Japanese gendarmes, with their hair cut in the Japanese style, wearing spectacles and leading a dog on a leash, approached a village run by puppet Chinese soldiers. They went to the office of the village head, who was a collaborator, and said to him sternly: 'The Eighth Route Army has come, but you have never supplied any information on their movements. How is your intelligence service organized? Can you capture the leading Communist in the district?'

The village head was delighted at the opportunity to ingratiate himself with the Japanese. He made a detailed report on his intelligence network and, at the request of his visitors, assembled all his intelligence agents in the surrounding area. The gendarmes thereupon said that they would take them to see their commander.

The village head and his intelligence agents were thrilled. They tidied their clothes in expectation and followed the gendarmes towards the railway station. But when they reached a hilltop the gendarmes abruptly pointed their pistols at the breasts of the intelligence agents, who were thus taken by the Chinese Communists without a single shot being fired.

13

Defence of Changde

In the spring of 1943 the Japanese North China Army launched a powerful campaign against the Chinese Eighteenth and Twenty-Fourth Group Armies – the former Communist, the latter Guomindang – in the Taihang mountains on the northern Shanxi–Hebei border. The Nationalist forces were defeated at the battle of Zhongyang in Shanxi in circumstances where each of the rival Chinese factions accused the other of sabotage. The Nationalist troops had to retreat south of the Yellow River, and their morale was reported by the Japanese to have been seriously undermined.

In the summer the Japanese carried the campaign to the southern Taihang region to fight the remnants of the Chinese Twenty-Seventh Army there. According to General Jiang Dingwen, this Nationalist Army was surrounded and outnumbered by the Japanese on three sides with the Communists on the fourth. General Jiang alleged that the Chinese Communists then acquiesced in the Japanese destruction of the Twenty-Seventh Army by allowing them to ambush it on 8 July.

The Japanese reports made it clear that it was now the Communists who were offering the heavier resistance. Three-quarters of the engagements in north China were against Communist troops. 'Half the corpses collected', an *Asahi Shimbun* report declared, 'were Communist, while among the 74,000 prisoners captured only 35 per cent were Communist.' The Nationalist troops were weakening, while the morale and fighting spirit of the Red Army seemed to grow, the report went on. Except for one group under General Yu Xuezhong, the Nationalist troops were dispirited, while the operations against the Communists had now become the main mission of Japan's North China Army.

General Ye Jianying of the Eighteenth Group Army claimed that the Communist forces in north China were keeping more than fourteen divisions of Japanese troops constantly in action, meaning almost a half of all the Japanese forces in China were bogged down there, 'unable to set themselves free either to operate on other fronts in China or in the Pacific'.

The loss of morale among the Nationalist armies could not be disguised in Chongqing, where General Stilwell fumed about the situation. Called to Washington in May to a military-style conference convened by Roosevelt and Churchill, Stilwell publicly slandered the ability of the Chinese army, questioned its readiness to fight and denounced Jiang Jieshi's arbitrary decisions and frequent changes of mind.

In his diary Stilwell confided: 'No matter what Peanut agrees to, if something is not done about the Chinese High Command the effort is wasted.'

While Stilwell was denouncing the Chinese behind their backs, Chinese forces scored a major victory in western Hubei. In another attempt to take control of Sichuan, a large Japanese force totalling 90,000 men in south-central Hubei near the Hunan border launched on 5 May an attack on the Chinese river defences along the upper Yangzi. The main Japanese force straddling the Hubei–Hunan border moved south to capture Nanxian and Anxiang on 8 May, but was then stopped by strong resistance.

Another force of Japanese crossed to the south bank of the Yangzi from Majiadian on 13 May, in parallel with another unit which drove south from Mituosi to capture Doushi. All these Japanese columns now planned to break through the prepared Chinese positions along the road going south towards Hunan from Yidu on the Yangzi. Meanwhile the Japanese forces at Yichang also crossed the Yangzi and drove southwards to take Changyang before converging on the Shipai forts on the Yangzi River's south bank on 28 May.

On the following day, however, the Chinese were able to recapture Yuyangguan, the westernmost town to fall into

Japanese hands, after forty-eight hours of intense fighting. This was the signal for a general Chinese counter-attack. By now the Flying Tigers under General Chennault were giving support by bombing and strafing the retreating Japanese and attacking their bases and supply lines. By 14 June the Chinese had recaptured all the positions which they had held at the outset of the Japanese offensive.

The Japanese had to retreat with heavy casualties, and they lay low for the next five months. At about this time Colonel Miyazaki Shunichi of the China Expeditionary Forces HQ estimated that whereas the Chinese were now fielding 1.9 million men, the Japanese soldiers in China totalled only 620,000, with 130,000 horses and 18,000 vehicles.

It was also at this time that the Japanese China Expeditionary Forces sent a staff officer to Tokyo to argue the case again for the destruction of the Chongqing regime by an invasion of Sichuan. But Imperial GHQ in Tokyo rejected the plan because of the urgent needs of the Japanese in Southeast Asia.

The partisans continued meanwhile to tease the Japanese and hold them down, but not always without losses on the Chinese side. In the summer of 1943 in central Hebei a Chinese partisan was caught offguard by the Japanese arriving in the main street of the village where he was hiding with a Chinese general, his wife and their six-month-old baby. Their presence had been given away by spies. The Chinese resistance group tried to escape through a tunnel leading out of the house, but there was no time to cover up the entrance after them.

When the Japanese came to the house and saw the entrance to the tunnel they asked the householder, an old woman, who her visitors had been, but she would reply only that there were no soldiers there. The Japanese took up a meat axe and cut off one of her fingers from her left hand and asked her again. She gave them the same reply five times, and they cut off all five fingers.

Meanwhile the resistance group struggled through the tunnels under the village. The Japanese dug trenches to try to intercept them and poured in poison gas, making the baby cry. The partisans stayed in the tunnels for thirteen hours with wet cloths over their mouths, constantly moving about seven feet below the surface, until they finally heard the Japanese leave, whereupon they emerged from their hiding place.

'We discovered then,' the guerrilla afterwards recalled, 'not before, that the general's wife had smothered the baby to death for fear that the Japanese would hear her cry.'

The success of the Flying Tigers sparked off an acrid argument between the Japanese infantry and air force in central China. Both agreed that there should be heavy bombing of the interior, especially Guilin, Kunming and Hengyang. But the Japanese Third Air Division insisted on a stronger fighter escort than the troops on the ground felt was justified, and the army supporters criticized the pilots for wasting resources on raids where Chinese aircraft were not destroyed.

Another issue was how Japanese air units should transfer from Wuhan to Guangzhou to assist in operations in Guangdong and Vietnam. The air force officers ordered their planes to go the long way round via Shanghai and Taiwan, to remain safe from Chinese attack. But the soldiers wanted to fly direct to save time. On 9 September General Nakasono died in an air engagement while flying directly from Guangzhou to Wuhan, illustrating the dangers of this route.

The Japanese estimated that the Americans and Chinese between them had more than 250 fighters and bombers in Yunnan and Sichuan at the beginning of 1943. By the end of the year they put the figure at 400.

In October 1943 the rains stopped in Burma, and the limelight fell once again on China's southernmost front. The Chinese forces in India, fresh from their training and supported by Allied engineers and fighter aircraft, began to cross the high mountains from Ledo to resume operations in northern Burma.

This was part of what Stilwell had hoped would be a tripartite attack in collaboration with a British advance into southern and central China and a Chinese attack from Yunnan towards Myitkyina. It was eighteen months since Stilwell and the Chinese had been run out of Burma, and that ought to have given enough time for all the parties concerned to get ready.

But Wavell, commanding the British forces, let Stilwell down.

The results of the Chindit operations under Wingate in the preceding winter had been disappointing, and the plan to advance to Arakan had failed. In China the Generalissimo also postponed his part of the offensive because of inadequate supplies coming in over the Hump for the Chinese forces. Stilwell characteristically decided to carry on alone with his Chinese troops from India.

Early in November the Chinese Thirty-Eighth Division reached Shinbwiyang in the Hukawng valley in northwestern Burma, while American engineers behind it pushed the road from Ledo towards Myitkyina. The Twenty-Second Division completed its training and was about to march in the Thirty-Eighth's footsteps. But at this point Japanese forces surrounded three battalions of the leading Chinese regiment, together with their American advisers.

Again characteristically, Stilwell rushed to the front and organized a rescue of his vanguard, ignoring the snipers in the surrounding jungle and calmly exposing himself to enemy fire in the front line, contrary to normal practice. He saved his men, but the advance was still maddeningly slow.

Jiang Jieshi was under pressure from a Japanese offensive in Hunan province designed to prevent the movement of Chinese forces from central China to the southern fronts in Yunnan, India and Burma. The Japanese also hoped to disrupt Chinese communications between their headquarters in Sichuan and the two neighbouring provinces of Hubei and Hunan, as well as destroy the preparations which the Japanese knew the Chinese high command was making for a counter-offensive.

This pre-emptive Japanese attack, which became known as the battle of Changde (the city in the central part of northern Hunan), began on 2 November when 100,000 Japanese troops massed along the south bank of the Yangzi River between Shashi on the Hubei side and Huarong in Hunan. Following the pattern of the earlier fighting in May and June, the Japanese sent columns southwards towards Doushi and Nanxian.

After ten days of bitter fighting in the mountains of north-western Hunan, the Japanese found it impossible to make any headway around Yichang and therefore turned southward to occupy Shimen and Lixian in northern Hunan in mid November.

Under artillery and air cover the Japanese crossed the Li River and converged with the other forces which had been marching southwest from Nanxian and Anxiang. The plan was for them to unite at Changde, the strategic city commanding northern Hunan on the Yuan River. The Japanese first captured a number of surrounding towns. including Taoyuan and Hanshou, and then the battle for Changde itself opened on 26 November.

Using gas, the Japanese broke into the city on 3 December and practically wiped out the Chinese Fifty-Seventh Division which was defending it. Street fighting continued although the Japanese set fire to the city, and a small group of defenders remained to fight the invaders. The Fifty-Seventh Division had been ordered by Jiang Jieshi to hold Changde to the last man, and its defence of Changde has been described as 'one of the most gallant and hopeless actions of this or any other war'.

Two American radio operators took up a position in the basement of a bank to send messages to the fourteen air force planes which were supporting the Chinese defence. Only when there were fewer than twenty Chinese defenders left in Changde did these two Americans agree to evacuate – whereupon the Chinese commander did too, and was later threatened with execution for literally disobeying Jiang's orders.

In fact reinforcements arrived at the moment the last defenders decided to leave. Four army corps from Jianxi and the south Yangzi area recaptured the city on 9 December. As the Chinese reinforcements from west, south and north streamed towards Changde, the Japanese beat a hasty retreat from this potential trap, heading northeast towards the point from which they had started. Even there they were intercepted and attacked by Chinese forces along the road and did not escape unharmed.

By Christmas Day the Chinese had recaptured all the places lost during this campaign, restoring the position as it had been before 2 November, but only at the cost of heavy casualties, including three divisional commanders killed.

This was a battle in which Chinese and American aircraft played a vital role, dropping supplies to the Chinese defenders during the siege of Changde, as well as bombing and strafing enemy vehicles, supplies and troop concentrations. To some extent these planes played the role of a mobile flying artillery, making up for the Chinese lack of heavy armament in the battle.

It was also during the battle of Changde, on the other hand, that the Japanese air force first succeeded in inflicting severe damage on the American and Chinese planes. On the two days of 10 and 11 December it destroyed more than forty American and Chinese aircraft in night-time raids on Hengyang and Lingling airfields.

In the middle of the battle of Changde, the Generalissimo, with his leading generals, including Stilwell, attended the Cairo Conference on 23–26 November to co-ordinate strategy with his allies. They delighted him by agreeing to restore 'all the Chinese territories that Japan has taken from China', specifying Manchuria, Taiwan and the Pescadores. Roosevelt supported Jiang as always, but Churchill resented the American President's 'exaggerated view of the Indian–Chinese sphere' and his absorption in the Chinese story, 'which was lengthy, complicated and minor'. At the same time Churchill admired the 'calm, reserved and efficient personality' of Jiang Jieshi.

Roosevelt himself, however, had private doubts. On 6 December he received Vinegar Joe Stilwell in Cairo to hear his news. Changde was about to fall to the Japanese, and Roosevelt wanted to know what the situation really was in China. Stilwell warned that Jiang's regime might not last.

'If Jiang Jieshi flops,' Roosevelt responded, 'back somebody else.'

When Stilwell returned to China from the Cairo Conference, greatly agitated, he revealed to his deputy, a fellow-American in Kunming, that this cavalier attitude to the Chinese President had gone even further.

'I have been directed,' Stilwell confided, 'to prepare a plan for the assassination of Jiang Jieshi. ... The order did not say to kill him, it said to prepare a plan. ... The Big Boy is fed up with

Jiang and his tantrums and said so. In fact he told me in that Olympian manner of his: "If you can't get along with Jiang and can't replace him, get rid of him once and for all. You know what I mean. Put in someone you can manage.'"

In fact there was a Young Generals' plot while Jiang Jieshi was away in Cairo. Their plan was to remove such corrupt and inefficient leaders as He Yingqin, but they failed.

14

Second Try in Burma

In the winter of 1943–4 the Chinese troops in Burma once more took the centre stage, and the world watched their fortunes under the direction of Vinegar Joe Stilwell. At the end of 1943, anticipating the dry season, the Chinese moved into Burma their New Thirty-Eighth and New Thirty-Second Divisions under Generals Sun Liren and Liao Yaoxiang, respectively, together with one regiment of the Thirtieth Division and a tank group commanded by an American colonel.

These made up the new so-called Chinese-Army-in-India, and Jiang had given it top-grade commanders. General Sun was a graduate of the Virginia Military Institute and had studied at Purdue University, while General Liao was a graduate of St Cyr.

Not everyone in the Chinese command, however, welcomed this transfer of troops to Burma with the goal of taking Rangoon and thus facilitating a delivery of American supplies. General Li Zongren, for one, advocated opening up a sea-route for Allied supplies in southern China itself, in Guangxi.

'We should cut the snake at its middle,' he argued, 'not strike at its head or tail.' Li was also thinking ahead to the Japanese surrender: the half-million Chinese troops held up in the mountains of Burma and the Yunnan border would not be able to influence post-surrender politics in northern China, which would thus pass to the Communists.

The advance of the Chinese into Burma had been held up, however, when the vanguard of General Sun's Thirty-Eighth Division was cut off and besieged for nearly a month on the road to Yupbang. Stilwell had rushed reinforcements to the scene and taken personal command of the battle, but the campaign was still held up for nearly a month. In the closing days of December the Thirty-Eighth Division bypassed the Japanese and attacked them at the rear, recapturing Yupbang at the cost of more than 300 dead.

By January 1944 the Thirty-Eighth Division had arrived on the west bank of the River Hka, and the Twenty-Second Division had moved up to join the battle. Stilwell himself returned to the front in February with the famous American Long-Range Penetration Group, known as 'Merrill's Marauders', which he proposed to use as a stimulus to make the Chinese units march faster this time. They would lose face if the Americans went ahead of them.

On 5 March, the Chinese, in their first campaign ever fought jointly with the Americans, captured Maingkwan, which was defended by the Japanese Eighteenth Division under Lieutenant-General Tanaka Shinichi. The Chinese attacked frontally while Merrill's Marauders encircled the Japanese unit. Only a very rapid retreat and skilful delaying actions enabled General Tanaka to save his men – and then Stilwell trapped him again further down the line at Shaduzup.

These two battles at Yupbang and Maingkwan enhanced the Japanese respect for China's combat ability. The Chinese-Army-in-India had shown that with good equipment, adequate training, professional leadership and sufficient medicine and supplies, Chinese troops were well capable of defeating the feared Japanese.

General Tojo, the Japanese Premier, admitted in 1944 that 'the Chinese-Army-in-India ... is a highly trained crack army to which we should give our close attention ... '.

Stilwell now ordered a temporary halt in the Chinese advance. The Japanese were attacking the Indian frontier at Imphal. Lieutenant-General Kawabe Shozo, the new commander of the Japanese forces in Burma, ordered the 100,000 veterans of his Fifteenth Army to cross the Chindwin River into India. If the Japanese managed to capture Dirnapur on the Assam railway all the supplies being flown across the Hump to China and to Stilwell's men in Burma would come to an abrupt halt.

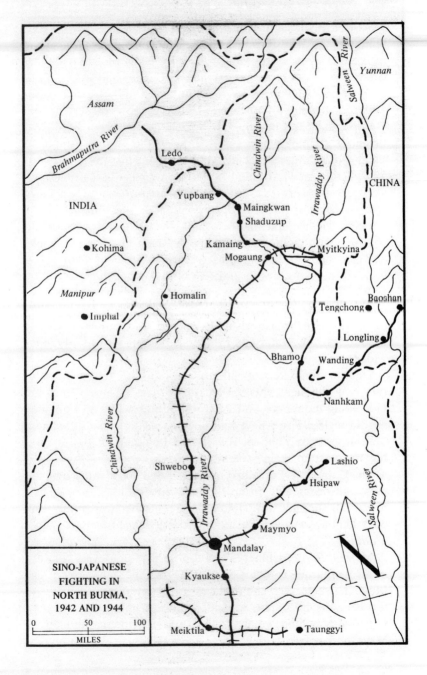

SINO-JAPANESE
FIGHTING IN
NORTH BURMA,
1942 AND 1944

0   50   100

MILES

Stilwell resumed his march in April, apparently confident that Slim, the British commander, could cope with the Japanese in Assam. Vinegar Joe sent his Chinese army on to Myitkyina, which was not only the town from which they had so ignominiously been expelled two years earlier but also the only hard-surfaced airfield in northern Burma capable of serving the Hump route into China.

Another Chinese force now entered the Burma campaign, the Y-Force under Marshal Wei Lihuang. This was an army of 72,000 men newly trained by the Americans in south China. The recruits were raw indeed. 'The majority of the men we receive,' one of the American commanders commented, 'are more fit for hospital than a training camp. Before we can do anything with them we have to fatten them up for a few weeks and give many of them medical treatment. Some of them walk a hundred miles to report, and God knows what they eat on the way.'

The Y-Force crossed the Salween River at night on 11 May on a broad front against a Japanese division which had only 15,000 men. It established bridgeheads along a front 100 miles wide.

Fighting in extremely difficult terrain and under constant rain, fog and sleet, the Y-Force drove the Japanese from the Gaoligong mountains and down the Shweli valley to Longling, an old walled city which had become an important Japanese base in western Yunnan. It captured Longling on 10 June but had to give it up again a week later.

The Chinese Y-Force had reached Tengchong by the time the monsoon rains fell from the heavens in late June. Their munitions supplies were held up and transportation of men and pack animals delayed, postponing the advance for more than a month.

Meanwhile the Chinese-Army-in-India was moving forward in two separate columns, one engaging the Japanese in the Mogaung sector and the other negotiating ravines and cliffs in the Kumang hills. This second column penetrated more than sixty miles behind Japanese lines near Myitkyina and on 17 May, after a twenty-day march over the Burmese mountains,

two Chinese regiments together with Merrill's Marauders astonished the Japanese by suddenly appearing at the Myitkyina
airfield. The Japanese had thought the mountains impassable.

The Chinese captured the airfield, upon which airborne
reinforcements arrived to lay siege to the town. Stilwell himself
landed at the Myitkyina airfield with part of the main forces of
China's Fifteenth and Fourteenth Divisions, but the Japanese
stubbornly held on to the town itself.

The battle of Myitkyina raged for several more weeks, but
meanwhile the capture of the airfield inspired two Chinese
divisions to storm Kamaing, which commands the Mogaung
valley, on 16 June after a seven-day siege.

The bayonet assault which clinched this success gave China
the first important Burmese city to be regained by the Allies in
this Second Burma Campaign. The Japanese Eighteenth Division under General Tanaka Shinichi, the brilliant commander
who had taken Singapore from the British in 1941, and whose
men were famed in the whole Japanese army for their courage
under fire, was forced to retreat, losing many prisoners and
guns.

This defeat was a great blow to Japanese morale. Mogaung
itself was the next town to fall, taken by the Chinese Thirty-
Eighth Division on 26 June in collaboration with the British
Chindits. But the siege of Myitkyina went on until 3 August,
when organized resistance at last collapsed. The Japanese dead
in the battle of Myitkyina were put at 3000, Allied casualties at
5000. Total Chinese casualties in the campaign were 2226
dead, and 6690 wounded.

The Chinese forces fought in northern Burma for seventeen
months, advancing more than 600 miles from their base in India
without sustaining a single defeat. 'Their tails are up,' Stilwell
exulted, 'and they tear into the Japs with full confidence that
they can beat the hell out of them. It is what you may call very
satisfying to say the least. Also, our score of dead Japs counted
is now over 20,000.' Colonel Rothwell H. Brown, who commanded the Chinese tank battalion, observed: 'The Chinese
are the bravest soldiers I have ever seen.' General Sun Liren
said that the victory in Burma was 'the happiest result of the

Chinese fighting spirit combined with American equipment and training ... '. It had been described by General George Marshall, after all, as 'the most difficult campaign of World War II'.

Meanwhile the Y-Force had taken over the old walled town of Tengchong at the beginning of August through a breach made by Chennault's Flying Tigers, but had then to relinquish it again. At the beginning of September the forward units of the Y-Force made contact with the Chinese-Army-in-India on the 2500-metre Gaoligong pass on the border between Yunnan and Burma, representing the first overland contact between China and the Southeast Asia theatre since the Japanese had first occupied Burma in 1942.

On the next day the Chinese troops in western Yunnan captured Songshan, the Gibraltar of the Burma Road, going on to recapture Tengchong a week later after a siege of two months. The Japanese garrison at Tengchong was killed to the last man.

At this point the Japanese Fifty-Sixth Division counter-attacked at Liuling, driving the Chinese in that area back towards the Salween River. But that was only a small setback in the overall Chinese advance. Chinese troops during November cleared the remaining strongpoints of the Japanese defence in western Yunnan, and in December the Chinese-Army-in-India recaptured Bhamo, going down to take Nanhkam on 15 January 1945.

But these famous victories in Burma had been won, at least in part, at the expense of the Sino-Japanese fighting in China itself. Once the Burma operations had begun, Stilwell diverted supplies being airlifted from India over the Hump to the Burmese theatre, depriving other Chinese forces and Chennault's Flying Tigers of their expected share. This enabled the Japanese to launch offensives in central China during 1944 and to have unexpected successes in them.

In April 1944, while Stilwell was vindicating his honour at Myitkyina, General Chennault wrote several times to his American colleague warning him about massive Japanese troop movements in preparation for a pincer attack in Henan and an offensive against Changsha. He warned that unless he could be assured of supplies of up to 10,000 tons a month, his aircraft could not repel a strong Japanese air offensive and still give adequate support to the Chinese armies.

But Stilwell simply did not believe Chennault's reports about the military dangers in eastern and central China, preferring the view that the Japanese were merely after food supplies. This was a major error of judgement.

While Stilwell was enjoying his successes in Burma, his status was being reconsidered by Generalissimo Jiang Jieshi. The Americans had become worried about the growing military polarization in the Chinese army between the Guomindang and Communist troops. General Marshall wanted Roosevelt to press Jiang Jieshi to put Stilwell in command of all Chinese forces in order to pull them together.

'The serious pass', he wrote, 'to which China has come is due in some measure to mismanagement and neglect of the army Until her every resource, including the divisions at present confronting the Communists, is devoted to the war against the Japanese, there is little hope that she continue to operate with any effectiveness until the end of the war. The time has come ... when all military power and resources remaining to China must be entrusted to one individual capable of directing that effort in a fruitful way against the Japanese. There is no one in the Chinese government or armed forces capable....'

In fact the Chinese situation was not quite as bad as Marshall painted it. General Fang Xianjue's troops had defended Hengyang for forty-seven days at this point, while General Xue Yue had made a good counter-attack at Changsha.

But Roosevelt was impressed by Marshall's thesis. On 7 July 1944 he promoted Vinegar Joe to be a full general, and he relayed to the Generalissimo the American advice to give Stilwell full charge of all Chinese forces – though the Gimo had told Vice-President Wallace only ten days earlier that he 'lacked confidence in General Stilwell's judgement'.

A week later Dr H. H. Gong, Jiang's brother-in-law and confidant, explained to Roosevelt at the White House why the American idea was a non-starter.

'I advanced the view,' he reported to Jiang afterwards, 'that the Chinese forces, because of the complexity of their background and history, geography and command relations, are usually governed by the friendship of individual persons in addition to laws and regulations. In selecting a commander for such forces it is important to take into consideration such factors as personal prestige, qualifications and personal relationships. A foreign general could not expect to exercise effective command simply by giving orders under the law. . . .'

Needless to say, Jiang ignored Roosevelt's advice, and the final confrontation between the two men loomed nearer. During September, in the course of their offensives within China itself, the Japanese poised seven divisions of their Eleventh Army for a thrust southward from Hengyang in Hunan, while another two divisions of the Twenty-Third Army were ready to push inland from northern Guangdong. These two prongs were aimed at Lingling, the gateway to Guangxi province where the Americans had their chief air bases, at Guilin and Liuzhou. Meanwhile the Japanese in northern Burma were also stepping up their attacks along the Salween River front.

Jiang Jieshi asked Stilwell on 15 September to expedite a planned diversionary attack on Bhamo by the Chinese troops at Myitkyina, in order to save Lingling. If this was not feasible, then the Y-Force ought to be moved back to guard Kunming, the capital of Yunnan, and thus avert a débâcle on the south China front.

But Vinegar Joe insisted that his Chinese at Myitkyina needed rest after their hard battle, and that, far from being withdrawn from the Burma campaign, the Y-Force should actually be reinforced. Why not release, he suggested, the troops under General Hu Zongnan, who were containing the Chinese Communists in north Shanxi, to come south to halt the Japanese advance?

Roosevelt made matters worse as far as Jiang Jieshi was concerned in a message of congratulation sent on 18 September about the contribution which the Y-Force had made to the north Burma campaign. Having sung the praises of the Y-Force, Roosevelt went on to tell the Generalissimo:

'But we feel that unless they are reinforced and supported with your every capacity you cannot expect to reap any fruits from their sacrifices, which will be valueless unless they go on to assist in opening the Burma Road. Furthermore, any pause in your attack across the Salween or suggestion of withdrawal, is exactly what the Jap has been striving to cause you to do by his operations in eastern China.

'He knows that if you continue to attack, co-operating with Mountbatten's coming offensive, the land line to China will be opened in early 1945 and the continued resistance of China and maintenance of your control will be assured....' Roosevelt repeated his demand for Stilwell's appointment.

Vinegar Joe came to the Gimo's residence in Chongqing at four o'clock in the afternoon to deliver this tactless message from Roosevelt, just as the Gimo was reluctantly ironing out the details of an announcement conceding the appointment of Stilwell. But the tone of the American President's message was so patronizing and insulting that Jiang took final offence. There was no more hope for Vinegar Joe. The Generalissimo asked the Americans instead to replace him.

Ironically, Jiang had been on the point of accepting the major American demands about the conduct of the war. 'It is obvious', Stilwell had written just before this incident, 'that CKS [Jiang Jieshi] is listening to our recommendations. He changed his plan at Guilin, he put Bai Chongxi back in. He executed the commander of the Ninety-Third Army and he is going to move six divisions down to the southeast. Apparently he is ready to pass command, and will use the Reds, if they acknowledge the authority of the central government....'

But the combination of Stilwell's insubordination and bad judgement in Burma, together with the intemperance of American pressure from Washington, provoked Jiang into reasserting his independence, and that meant the end of Stilwell's ambitions in China.

'The victory of the battle of Myitkyina', a Chinese historian concludes, 'made Stilwell a great hero in the eyes of the American people, but this reputation of heroism was built, not only on the tens of thousands of corpses of Chinese soldiers in

India, but also on the compilation of blood, sweat and lives of millions of Chinese people in Changsha, Hengyang, Guilin and Liuzhou.'

Jiang Jieshi himself told Roosevelt on 9 October that 'the Myitkyina victory could not compensate for the losses of the eastern battlefield.... We have taken Myitkyina but we have lost almost all of east China, and in this General Stilwell cannot be absolved of great responsibility. Even now he appears to be unaware of the implications of this fact and the grave damage to the prestige and morale of the Chinese army.'

In Burma in mid October Stilwell issued his last order, for his five Chinese divisions to launch their last offensive against the Japanese Thirty-Third Army. The Chinese Thirty-Eighth Division moved south along the east bank of the Irrawaddy River towards Bhamo, and the other four Chinese divisions crossed the Irrawaddy at Shwegu, to swing southeast through the jungle towards Lashio with the object of encircling the Japanese Thirty-Third Army.

But on 18 October, just as this final stage of the recapture of Burma was opening, Stilwell was recalled to Chongqing, to be informed by the US War Department of his recall from China. He was told to leave the Chinese capital, in total secrecy and without publicity, within forty-eight hours. General Dan Sultan took over as commander of the India–Burma theatre, while General Wedemeyer was appointed to replace Stilwell in Chongqing.

At least one Chinese commander had a good word for Stilwell. General Zeng Xigui told him when they parted: 'For at least three years you have made things possible out of impossibilities.'

In the middle of November two of the Chinese divisions in Burma were flown back over the Hump, at Wedemeyer's request, to join a Chinese counter-attack east of Guiyang. This was necessary to save the day in China itself, but it spoilt the final stage of Stilwell's planned offensive in Burma. In mid December 800 Japanese survivors left Bhamo just before dawn to fight their way out into the mountains rather than surrender to the Chinese.

The last town on the western Yunnan–Burma border to remain in Japanese hands, the walled town of Wanding, was recaptured by the Chinese on 20 January 1945. Soon afterwards the Chinese Thirty-Eighth Division met units of the Y-Force at Mongyu, the last Japanese pocket threatening the new road. The Ledo and Burma roads were now joined together, and on 4 February the first convoy from Ledo in India to Kunming in China arrived. It was soon bringing more than 50,000 tons of vital petrol a month into China.

Jiang Jicshi was not vindictive. He had a shrewd and realistic judgement of Stilwell's successes, as well as Stilwell's failures. It was at his suggestion that the new joint road was christened after its original architect: 'Let us name this road after General Joseph Stilwell in memory of his distinctive contribution. . . .'

15

The Ichi-go Offensive

'Imperial GHQ desires to destroy the main enemy air bases in southwest China.' Such was the order received from Tokyo on 25 January 1944 by General Matsui, the Chief of Staff in China, unleashing the final grand Japanese offensive of the war, code-named Ichi-go, or Operation Number One. Its overall goal was to capture the strategic areas still resisting Japanese control along the main north–south trunk railway from Beijing to Wuhan and Guangzhou, together with its feeder line from Hengyang in Hunan province to Guilin and Liuzhou in the southernmost province of Guangxi, where the Americans were using Chinese airfields to such devastating effect on Japanese targets.

By early 1944 the Americans had 340 military aircraft in China. The Japanese airforce in China was getting fifty new planes a month from Japan but had to send its own crews to fly them back to China, which hindered their training programme. Ominously, the Japanese aeroplanes had only six months' supply of fuel. They were also short of machine-guns and automatic cannon ammunition.

The war had now turned against Japan. Across the Pacific, her western enemy, the USA, so rashly provoked at Pearl Harbor, was now advancing implacably towards her. The purpose of Ichi-go was limited to consolidating the Japanese position in China by creating a dependable line of communications from north to south and taking out the American air bases. If there were a surrender of the Chinese government into the bargain, so much the better.

Operation Ichi-go was divided into two parts, Operation

Ko-go in the Beijing–Wuhan railway sector in the north, chiefly in Henan province, and Operation To-go in the southern sector centered on Hunan. It was the northern campaign which opened first. In mid April the Japanese took the offensive in Henan with a view to gaining control of the railway and destroying the Chinese field forces in the vicinity. Mustering more than 100,000 men supported by numerous planes and special arms, the Japanese took advantage of the flat Henan plain to deploy their tanks on a big scale.

The offensive began at Zhongmou on the south bank of the Yellow River where the famous breach of the dykes had occurred in 1938. The Japanese struck westwards against Zhengzhou, although they were disconcerted by American bombing.

Other Japanese forces at Xinyang in south Henan moved northwards along the railway to join the fight. The Japanese maintained between 400 and 500 tanks and armoured cars and between 2000 and 3000 trucks in this campaign. They captured Zhengzhou on 22 April and then kept up their westward offensive along the spur railway line to Mixian and beyond it to the strategic mountain city of Dengfeng.

This brought them to the ancient city of Luoyang on the east–west railway in the first week of May. Simultaneously Japanese forces in southern Shanxi province on the other side of the Yellow River crossed at Jiuyuanqu, and then divided into two columns, one taking Mianchi on the railway on 12 May and the other marching east to converge with the main Japanese forces on Luoyang on 10 May. The men of the Japanese First Army and Twelfth Army thus united, linking the Japanese forces in central and northern China to fight a notably fierce battle for Luoyang, which was defended against heavy odds by the Chinese for more than two weeks. They surrendered on 25 May.

The Japanese continued to press to the west, hoping to cover the right flank of their main operation which was to control the railway from Zhengzhou south to Wuhan. They captured Lingbao at the westernmost tip of Henan province on 11 June. But now the Japanese lines were stretched and the mountains

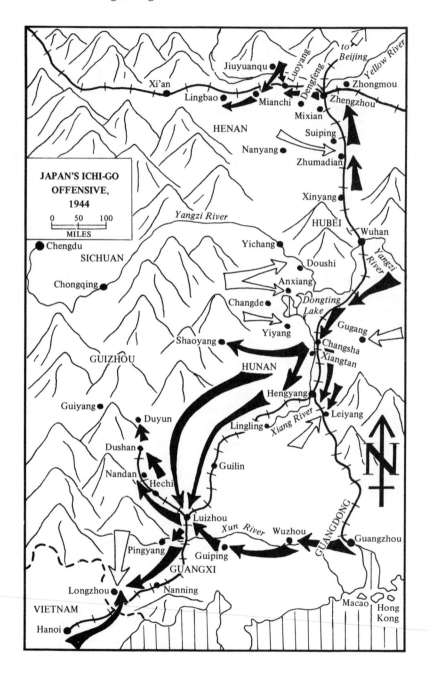

were making it difficult for their tanks. By the middle of June the Chinese recaptured Lingbao and other towns. According to the Guomindang accounts, a Chinese plan to recapture Luoyang was sabotaged by Communist forces taking advantage of the Chinese weakness in the rear areas to expand their own influence, looting and attacking local militia. But the Guomindang also admitted that its own government of famine-ridden Henan province was so inept and unpopular that the people were in some cases helping the Japanese.

The thirty-four Chinese divisions in Henan showed little interest now in resisting the Japanese. They melted away before the invaders, leaving anarchy and sometimes the Red Army in control behind them.

In addition to their main westward attack from Zhengzhou, the Japanese also attacked southwards along the Beijing–Wuhan railway from the end of April, co-ordinating with the units advancing northwards from Xinyang. By 9 May the entire length of this strategic railway was in Japanese hands, but it was cut again by the Chinese only four days later when Suiping and Zhumadian were also recaptured. The Japanese then, however, repossessed the entire railway a month later. It gave them great satisfaction when the first Japanese-run Beijing–Wuhan train eventually arrived at its destination on 10 October.

The air forces on both sides played an important part in this battle of central Henan, but there were heavy casualties. The general commanding the Chinese Thirty-Sixth Group Army was one of those killed in action.

But the emphasis now shifted to the sector south of the Yangzi, where the decommissioning of Chinese airfields was of such great importance. On the day the battle of central Henan ended, with the Chinese recapture of Luoyang on 15 June, American B-29 planes made their first raid on Japanese cities from Chengdu in Sichuan province. By the middle of August there were 150 B-29s in China, and by October there were 200, so this made action against Chinese airfields all the more urgent.

The Japanese fighters' interception of the B-29s was weak.

Japanese radar had teething troubles and not every fighter had it installed. Not until 8 September did the Japanese air force raise a bombing party against Chengdu airfield. Eighteen Japanese bombers then took out eighteen B-29s at a loss of two of their own planes.

At the end of May, with fighting still going on in Henan, the Japanese opened the second part of their Ichi-go offensive in Hunan province, south of the Yangzi River. In this, the fourth successive Japanese offensive in Hunan, the goal was to clear the railway along the entire length of the Wuhan–Guangzhou sector and establish an uninterrupted land route of communication from north to south.

A subsidiary objective was to divide the Chinese into two separate and isolated forces, one based at Chongqing and the other between Hunan and the coast. The Japanese also intended to destroy various Chinese supply points and air bases, not only in Hunan itself but in Zhejiang, Fujian and Jiangxi as well.

For this offensive more than 200,000 Japanese were massed in the Wuhan area, with another 80,000 around Guangzhou. The Guomindang afterwards complained that ten Japanese divisions from northern Hebei were enabled to join the Hunan battle without interference by the Communist guerrillas because the Red armies were helping the Japanese as a consequence of the Russo-Japanese pact.

The battle of central Hunan started on 25 May along a front of more than 150 miles along the Hubei–Hunan border. The Japanese drove south into Hunan in a pincer movement from northern Jianxi and southern Hubei.

On the westernmost front the Chinese repelled the Japanese at the beginning of June, recapturing Anxiang and Doushi on the Yangzi River. This was the same terrain over which the two sides had fought with such ferocity six months earlier, in the battle for Changde. The Japanese flanks at Gugang and Yiyang were turned by the Chinese defenders.

But the Japanese Eleventh Army columns nevertheless marched relentlessly on Changsha, the provincial capital and the city where Mao Zedong went to school, from all points of the compass save the south. The first Japanese soldiers reached Changsha on 5 June, and after two weeks of bitter combat the Chinese defenders had to give it up. During this battle the Generalissimo telephoned General Xue Yue, the 'Tiger of Hunan', in the middle of the fighting to order the transfer of some of his troops – as a result of which, in the field commander's opinion, Changsha was lost. General Xue pointedly disregarded Jiang's order to withdraw to western Hunan, taking his men instead to Jiangxi. Asked why, he explained: 'I wanted to get so far away that he could make no more telephone calls.'

Having on their third attempt reduced Changsha, the Japanese continued their drive to the south on both sides of the Xiang River, capturing all the major cities one by one.

These triumphs led them to Hengyang, the vital railway junction from which the feeder line from Guangxi, Yunnan and Vietnam comes to join the north–south Beijing–Guangzhou trunk railway. As long as the railway was an important mode of moving troops and materials, it could be said that whoever controlled this city controlled all of south China. The Chinese National Military Council in Chongqing decided on a desperate engagement with the Japanese at Hengyang in order to stop their advance and hold the city.

The task of defending Hengyang fell to the Tenth Corps under the gallant General Fang Xianjue, and his men stood their ground against better-armed attackers for no fewer than forty-seven days, in the course of which over 15,000 of the 16,275 Chinese defenders perished – at a cost of some 20,000 Japanese casualties. The siege began on 23 June, though another Japanese column meanwhile moved south towards the next major city on the railway to Guangzhou, Leiyang.

The Chinese recaptured Leiyang at the end of July, as part of the general counter-attack ordered by Jiang Jieshi. Cities and strategic positions on both banks of the Xiang River changed hands repeatedly. General Fang could not, however, take decisive advantage of these counter-offensive moves outside the beleaguered city of Hengyang. The Chinese co-ordination failed, and Hengyang fell on 8 August.

The Japanese were extremely disappointed over the delay in

capturing Hengyang, without which they could not control the Guangzhou–Wuhan railway. The reason given by the Japanese military historians was the familiar one of inadequate supplies reaching the front over the long lines of communications.

By the time Hengyang fell, the Japanese ammunition supply in this sector had come down to less than one round per man, and motor fuel was enough to last only two months. The Japanese lost many horses because they had to send them out to forage for their own food. The railway lines between the front and the Japanese main bases were constantly sabotaged and on top of all this the Japanese Fifth Air Army responsible for the Guangzhou and Wuhan sectors had only 252 pilots on its strength.

The fighting around Hengyang subsided in the middle of August, and Operation To-go moved into its more spectacular second phase. In this engagement, which became known as the battle of Guangxi–Guizhou, and which included movements over four provinces covering an area equal to France, Germany and Italy combined, the Japanese sought to open an overland corridor which would connect their troops in Vietnam with their main forces in China.

For this purpose a new force called the Sixth Area Army was set up on 26 August under the command of General Okamura. It embraced the unprecedented number of 350,000 soldiers in the Eleventh, Thirty-Fourth and Twenty-Third armies, reinforced by three air regiments because, as one of the Japanese commanders complained, their own fighters were 'almost totally exhausted'. These reinforcements included the Type 4 fighters which allowed the Japanese to reactivate their river craft for use during the coming campaign.

It was now the middle of the rainy season in south China, meaning that more use could be made of river vessels and also that the Japanese were subject to less harassment by Chinese and American aircraft. There was a tank brigade, but once the tanks had reached the deep interior where this campaign was carried out, 'it was estimated', according to a Japanese account, 'that they would probably lose most of their mobility due to the lack of fuel'. In any case many roads and bridges were destroyed, and once the rains ceased in the autumn the tanks became vulnerable to air attack.

At the end of September, still in the early stages of the battle of Guangxi–Guizhou, heavy rain prevented road movements of all kinds. In this particular year the rainy season was unusually long, turning the operations of the Japanese air force at Wuhan airfield in September and October into a sea of mud. The Japanese Fifth Air Army had only 152 planes flying, against about 800 operated by the Chinese and Americans.

The Japanese began on 26 August to advance on Liuzhou from three directions, and also marched westwards from Hengyang and Xiangtan towards Shaoyang in western Hunan. It was during this part of the operation that disagreement developed between the Japanese Eleventh Army and the overall Sixth Area Army Headquarters. The Eleventh Army had been the victor at Changsha in June, and was now eager to win further glories, regardless of the difficulties which the rear units were having in maintaining supplies, especially of ammunition and artillery. Instead of waiting for the other units in the grand plan, the Eleventh Army wanted to race ahead of the timetable.

On 29 August the Eleventh Army told HQ it was going after the Chinese, contrary to original instructions, in the area of Hengyang. In a telegram on the following day, HQ underlined that the primary objective was merely for the Japanese to utilize the airfield at Hengyang.

'At the time,' it warned, 'when the army cannot push the rear forward satisfactorily and constantly, it is not advisable to consider the enemy situation lightly, or to advance troops far into Lingling and its vicinity, which will result in waste of fighting power....' Headquarters ordered the Eleventh Army to postpone its advance, but too late; it had already started. The Eleventh Army took Lingling on 7 September.

On 18 September a staff officer of the Sixth Area Army went to rebuke the rash Eleventh Army at Hengyang, and new plans were made by which joint operations against Guilin and Liuzhou would begin on 29 September.

'The main objective of this kind of operation,' General

Okamura told the Eleventh Army commanders at Hengyang airfield at the beginning of October, 'is ... the annihilation of the enemy. However, Guilin and Liuzhou are vital strategic objects.' It was the Twenty-Third Army which would capture Liuzhou, 'therefore it is requested that the Eleventh Army direct its operations towards annihilation of the outlying enemy'.

Alas, just when the Japanese armies were openly quarrelling, the precious three air regiments were withdrawn by Tokyo for use in other theatres, thus enabling the Chinese to dominate the air.

There were four separate major movements in the Japanese offensive in Guangxi–Guizhou in the second half of 1944. The first was a strong eastward thrust to Shaoyang in Hunan Province. Chinese troops held the city of Shaoyang for thirty-eight days but finally surrendered on 3 October.

Meanwhile the main part of the Japanese forces drove towards Liuzhou from three directions. One column advanced along the Hunan–Guangxi railway from Hengyang to Guilin, where the Japanese Eleventh Army defeated a Chinese garrison described by the Japanese as comprising five or six divisions, but claimed in Chinese accounts to include twenty divisions.

Another column advanced slightly southwards of the first one from the same base, swinging through eastern Guangxi to Liuzhou.

The third column in this enormous campaign advanced from Guangzhou along the Xi River to capture Wuzhou and then drive northwards to Liuzhou. This was the famous Twenty-Third Army, of which a neutral staff officer, Colonel Miyazaki, commented about this time that although it 'traditionally had a reputation of implicit obedience to the Emperor, it was feared that prolonged garrison duty had undermined their discipline'.

Disciplined or not, it ran into severe difficulties in this campaign. At the end of October it was held up by a damaging Chinese attack at Guiping, and then in the roadless primeval forest of these parts it lost contact with HQ during the crucial period between 3 and 14 November.

It was in these circumstances, following the Eleventh Army's encirclement of Guilin, that the Eleventh Army decided to send an advance unit towards Liuzhou with the evident hope of adding a double laurel to its wreath of victories and snatching the prize of Liuzhou from the Twenty-Third Army's grasp. On learning of this insubordination, the Sixth Army HQ ordered the advance unit to be placed temporarily under the command of the Twenty-Third Army, but this was when radio contact cut out, and HQ's intentions could not be carried out.

With the two main targets of Liuzhou and Guilin effectively in their hands, the Japanese advanced northwards along the railway from Liuzhou into Guizhou province to reduce in rapid succession Nandan and Dushan, the terminus at that time of the railway into Guizhou. Here the Eleventh Army, with its supplies fully stretched, had come to a halt. Some vanguard units moved forward as far as Duyun, on the road to the provincial capital of Guiyang where US air force facilities constituted an important Japanese target.

The Japanese field commanders were not at all sure of their strategic premises. They had checked the Chinese temporarily, but not necessarily fatally. 'Our speed and limited scale of operations...,' one of them commented, 'could hardly cope with the enemy's speed in changing and equipping airfields. The only practical result of this operation was the expansion of a larger zone extending from north China to French Indochina for ... observation of enemy air activities.' The Chinese were nevertheless estimated by Japan to have lost almost one-sixth of the men of their more than thirty divisions engaged in the campaign.

The position now began to deteriorate for Japan, with virtually no new military supplies arriving after November, and with salt, the principal Japanese collateral for buying local goods, and coal for firing their trains, both very short.

Meanwhile Chinese reinforcements arrived from Sichuan and the northwestern provinces, some flown in American transports although many marched on foot or rode in trucks.

It should not be imagined, however, that the large numbers of conscripts who became available to the Chinese army were sound fighting men. So poor was the medical condition of the average conscript that, for example, more than a third of the 60,000 hand-picked men whom Jiang put at the disposal of General Wedemeyer, Stilwell's successor, were eliminated in medical examinations. When it came to sending replacements to India for the American training programme, more than two in three of the Chinese recruits were rejected on physical grounds.

There was a telling incident in these final stages of the war when the Generalissimo was told by his son, General Jiang Jingguo, that several recruits at a certain base had committed suicide while locked in their barracks. The Gimo went to inspect these barracks himself, and when he saw the unbearable conditions under which the conscripts had to live with the minimum of care or attention, he broke down and cried. In his anger he hit the chief of the Conscription Board, who was with him on the inspection, with his cane and shouted: 'You are murdering my soldiers.'

He sentenced to death the officer responsible on the spot.

Meanwhile he tried to stiffen military leadership by putting in General Tang Enbo as the supreme commander of the Guizhou–Guangxi theatre, and Tang came down to Guiyang from Henan with his Thirteenth Army and other units. But Jiang also allowed the War Minister and Chief of Ground Staff, General He Yingqin, to remain in Guiyang to direct the war as supreme commander in southwest China, in the hope that his troops would remain loyal to the central government in spite of their grievances.

At about this time the American army found a vast cache of arms at Dushan in Guizhou province. Fifty new field guns and 50,000 tons of shells, other weapons and ammunition had been stored by the central government in twenty warehouses in case of need. Yet they had never been used, even though Japan had taken almost the whole country.

The reinforced Chinese now began to recapture the forward Japanese positions in Guizhou–Guangxi, beginning with Dushan on 8 December. By the end of the year they had driven the Japanese to a stalemate near Hechi in northern Guangxi, with neither side able to move the other.

Meanwhile the Japanese in Vietnam sent a column into western Guangxi which was on 10 December united with Japanese units near Longzhou. At last Tokyo had won its prize of creating a 'continental corridor' into southeast Asia.

That corridor was not to last long, however. In May 1945 the Chinese recaptured Nanning in a surprise attack and then went on, pushing out on both flanks, to recapture Longzhou and Pingyang by the beginning of June. By late June southwestern Guangxi had been cleared of Japanese forces, and one Chinese column even crossed the Vietnam border to attack the Japanese there (a few Chinese and French elements were already operating in the border region).

One by one all the positions won at such cost by the Japanese in the battle of Guangxi–Guizhou were reoccupied by the Chinese – Hechi in May, Liuzhou at the end of June. When the Japanese surrendered to the Allies that summer, the Chinese were fast closing on Guilin itself.

16

Surrender

The failure of the Japanese Ichi-go offensive during 1944 sent waves of relief over those parts of China still untouched by the invader. A British teacher in Kunming, in China's deep south, wrote in his diary on 19 January 1945: 'We felt in December that the Japanese could do with us as they pleased. With ten more men at the right place they might have thrust down to Kunming; with another ten men they might have thrust through Sichuan....' But now, 'we know in our bones that the Japanese have lost the war'.

The Japanese commanders in China indeed showed signs of loss of nerve. The new commander-in-chief of the Japanese Expeditionary Forces in China sent his chief of staff to the Imperial GHQ in Tokyo at the beginning of January to win its assent yet again to a plan to invade Sichuan, Generalissimo Jiang's last fortress. 'This', his memo pleaded, 'is our last opportunity to destroy the enemy separately.'

Imperial GHQ which had far more pressing problems to consider, said it would have to have more information and would wait for further developments before authorizing the new campaign. Actually the Japanese generals in China knew in their hearts that they did not have enough men, time or materials to conquer Sichuan. They settled for a more limited set of campaigns during 1945, concentrating in particular on the destruction of two deadly air bases being used by the Americans at Zhijiang in Hunan and Laohekou in Hubei.

But the logistics were extremely doubtful. Having opened up the main railway to the north at such cost of blood, the Japanese army in China now found itself without enough rolling stock.

During the month of April 1945 only one train ran from Guangzhou to Wuhan, and a chastened Japanese officer still complained that 'foot movement was the only means of transporting troops'.

The Japanese offensives in the last six months of the war were in two theatres, one in Henan–Hubei and the other in western Hunan. The battle of Henan–Hubei opened on 21 March when 80,000 Japanese troops in those two provinces drove towards the Laohekou air base on the Han River in northernmost Hubei. One Japanese column marched north from Jingmen, another westwards from the Lushan–Wuyang line, a third westwards from Suixian and a fourth westwards from Luoning in western Henan.

They all made fairly rapid progress at first. Nanyang was bitterly contested for eleven days by two Chinese regiments holding out against a Japanese division of the Twelfth Army, but fell on 4 April after intensive street fighting.

Laohekou, the air base used for Chinese and American strikes against central and north China targets, was captured by the Japanese Twelfth Army after seven days of hand-to-hand fighting. But the Chinese rallied at this point, strengthened by reinforcements, and in a counter-attack they recaptured Laohekou on 12 April. This was a signal for a general Chinese counter-attack in northwestern Hubei, recapturing Xiangyang on 14 April and restoring the original Chinese position along the Han River a week later.

Meanwhile the Japanese had driven as far west as Xixia, and here there were fierce clashes with the Chinese under General Wang Zhonglian, in co-operation with local militia. Xixia itself and other towns changed hands many times, and General Wang's men fought four 'annihilation battles' in five weeks between 7 April and 18 May. The first victory on 7 April stopped the Japanese drive and gained the Chinese a valuable initiative in the campaign.

In May other Japanese forces at Sanmenxia, where the huge Yellow River dam now stands, marched southwest in a delayed diversionary movement to support their comrades. But Chinese forces under General Hu Zongnan engaged these Japanese and threw them back after several bitter fights.

The second big battle of 1945 – the last of the war – was the western Hunan campaign which opened on 9 April. Here the Japanese objective was to neutralize the Chinese–American air base at Zhijiang near the Guizhou border, and also to protect the Guangzhou–Wuhan railway.

For this campaign the Japanese put 80,000 men into the field, attacking on a 250-mile-long front along the Zi River from Yiyang to Xinning. There was some confusion over this, some of the senior Japanese staff officers believing that it would be better to aim merely for the Yuan River and bank on the Americans destroying the Zhijiang base if they reached thus far, rather than attempting to take Zhijiang itself.

But the Japanese Twentieth Army, confident as ever, felt certain it could reach the objective and it set out determinedly from Shaoyang on 15 April. Ominously, it was able to march only at night and in the mountains because of the American aircraft constantly overhead during the day.

The US air force did more than harass the Japanese. As soon as this offensive opened it airlifted the entire Chinese Sixth Army from Kunming to Zhijiang, carrying a division every four days. These men had fought successfully in the Burma campaign and their presence in Hunan was good for the morale of the other Chinese troops at the front.

By contrast, when the Japanese troops needed help their air force was often incapable. The Takidera Battalion of the 116th Division, for example, near Guidong, was encircled in mountainous terrain and called for reinforcements. The answer from HQ was that there was no possibility of withdrawing Japanese soldiers from the southern fronts, and that if Takidera and other Japanese Sixth Army units could not make headway, they should pull out.

At the beginning, during April, the Japanese made rapid gains, reaching Dongkou. But in evacuating the area the Chinese left enough units behind Japanese lines to hold strategic points and delay the Japanese advance.

From 29 April, the birthday of their Emperor, the Japanese made an all-out westward drive, reaching Jiangkou, only twenty miles from the vital Zhijiang airfield. They met with very strong Chinese resistance, especially east of the Snow Peak mountains. Three days later the Japanese 217th Regiment was routed by the Chinese and other units thrown back by the defenders.

By the beginning of June the Chinese were back where they had begun. They pressed forward to Shaoyang, the key Japanese base in western Hunan, and were attacking it by the end of June. But on 9 May Japanese HQ had already ordered the Twentieth Army to withdraw from its hopeless campaign. The six-week operation in Hunan had failed.

The war now came to its conclusion, events outside China overtaking the Chinese battlefields. Germany surrendered in Europe on 17 May. In July the Generalissimo joined with his fellow leaders of the Allies in calling on Japan to make unconditional surrender. The atom bomb was dropped on Hiroshima on 6 August, another on Nagasaki on 9 August, and the Russians declared war on Japan on the same day.

The Japanese government surrendered unconditionally on 10 August. Unaware of this, the Japanese Eleventh Army began a counter-attack on that very day.

On 15 August the Chinese Foreign Minister formally received the Japanese surrender text, and Generalissimo Jiang cabled the Japanese Supreme Commander in China, General Okamura, detailing the principles on which the surrender would be organized. He proclaimed to the Chinese people over the radio that, 'our faith in justice through the black and hopeless days of eight long years of struggle have been rewarded....' Crowds wept with joy in Chongqing as fireworks exploded and searchlights played, and Allied soldiers were carried shoulder-high through the streets. In Tokyo people were stunned. Two days later Prince Asaka Yasuhiko, of the Imperial family, arrived at the Japanese Expeditionary Army Headquarters in China to convey personally the Emperor's humiliating orders. Eight Japanese peace emissaries flew to Zhijiang, where only weeks before there had been desperate fighting by the Japanese to capture the airfield, to deal with Chinese representatives about the surrender of the Japanese troops. British marines landed in Hong Kong to engage a Japanese 'suicide squad'.

In September in Nanjing General He Yingqin, Supreme Commander of the Chinese Armies, presided at the Japanese surrender ceremony for the Chinese theatre. Before the Chinese high command, as well as representatives of China's allies – the US, Britain, Russia, Australia and Holland – the Japanese acknowledged 'complete military defeat'. Some 1,283,140 Japanese soldiers surrendered to China. Most of them were repatriated on American navy ships between October 1945 and June 1946. Their mission had failed, the war was over and China was free.

The Chinese generals then set about fighting each other in a bloody civil war which ate up the rest of the decade and led to a Communist People's Republic in 1949. The Japanese generals were tried by an Allied Tribunal for their war crimes and most were either hanged – like Itagaki, Doihara and Matsui – or else committed ritual *hara-kiri*, like Anami, or suicide, like Sugiyama.

Epilogue

China won the war in the end through the unexpected agency of the Americans, although her own capacity simply to absorb the Japanese invasion played its part. As for the Japanese, they believed that they would have won their China war if other business had not competed.

All this was reflected in the post-war era. Japan went on to become, in spite of the destruction of her industries by American bombs, the third largest economy in the world after the two superpowers, with an income per head comparable to that of the USA. China, by contrast, fell back into a civil war which led to three decades of shared poverty under a Maoist government, and isolation from the world mainstream of economic development.

Even before the Japanese surrendered, the rival Chinese forces were chasing the Japanese heels in order to occupy as much territory as possible. In the end, as Japan lay down its arms, the Chinese Nationalist armies under Generalissimo Jiang controlled about 60 per cent of China's population, mostly in the south and west. Mao Zedong and his Chinese Communists held sway over only 20 per cent in the northwest and east, while the Japanese also retained about 20 per cent along the coasts and around the big cities.

To complicate matters, Stalin decided at the last moment to join in the war against Japan, and in a single week of marching his men managed by the time of Japan's surrender to occupy most of Manchuria. Under the peace terms the Japanese were to hand over their arms to the USSR in Manchuria and to the Nationalist armies in China itself. General He Yingqin ordered the Japanese, in view of the concentration of his own forces in the southwest, to stay put in other areas, where the Chinese Nationalists would 'retain and utilize' them to 'do liaison work'. Ideology thus proved thicker than blood, and before the powder was even dry the Japanese were willy-nilly involved in the ravaging civil war which followed their failure in China.

Just as the Russians helped Mao Zedong by allowing his Red armies to flow across Manchuria, so the Americans helped Jiang Jieshi by airlifting half a million Nationalist soldiers to Beijing, Shanghai, Nanjing and other cities of northern and coastal China by mid-October 1945. But the Chinese Communists had, for the most part, got to those areas first, and when the Russians went home Mao and his men were able to take over their positions. All was not sweetness and light between the Chinese and Russian Communists, however, because of the latter's systematic stripping of industrial plant in Manchuria for transportation back to the Soviet Union to buttress the ailing Russian economy.

In these circumstances it can be imagined how the fate of the Japanese prisoners varied. Some were taken by the Russians to the Soviet Union and never returned, or returned to Japan many years later. Others made themselves useful in the Chinese Civil War, but most waited patiently for repatriation. Some of them had to sit it out for ten months.

It took decades to pick up all the pieces of the war. The Japanese secured an early peace treaty with Jiang Jieshi, only to find that it was not recognized by the successor Communist government after 1949. Jiang, incidentally, generously gave up China's rights to war reparations, following the example of India and other British Commonwealth countries. All the same, Japan later carried out a large economic aid programme, first to Taiwan (which the Allies, of course, restored to China) and later to the People's Republic of China, on a scale which suggested a surviving sense of guilt.

Even as late as the 1980s the respective authorities were negotiating visits to Japanese war graves in China and the return of residual Japanese personnel from China. Pathetic groups of children of Japanese parents lost in the scuttle home in 1945 have visited Japan, thirty-five years older, in desperate efforts to trace their parents and prove their claim to Japanese citizenship. Japan and Communist China recognized each other only in 1972, and it took a few more years to negotiate a Treaty of Amity.

On that occasion, when the Chinese statesman Vice-Premier Deng Xiaoping visited Tokyo, the Emperor Hirohito – himself one of the survivors of the war – went as near to a formal apology as protocol allowed, expressing regret for 'unfortunate things' which had happened in a certain period of the past. For his part, Deng preferred to regard the past as done with, looking forward instead 'towards the future in building up peaceful relations between our two countries'. The scars of the war are healing.

A Chinese Christian had put the impact of the war on China's image of Japan in this way: 'Before this war many of us had a sort of affection for the Japanese. Our students had studied in Japan; our revolutionary leader, Sun Zhongshan, and his friends had often sheltered there. We'd done business with them. They seemed more akin to us than all the other foreigners. Now from their fighting, their ravages, their bombing and their harshness, there is no one of our people that looks on them with anything but fear and repulsion. Yet my son and grandson both agree that what we see now is not the real Japan. The Japanese at home, they say, are mostly poor, hard-working, courteous folk, much like the Chinese people in their daily life. When Japan is overthrown, as all know she will be overthrown, we hope the true Japan will appear again. . . . Her wild dreamers have an ambition to seize China and conquer all the world. They are hardly aware of the atrocities of their soldiers, or else assume that this is the sort of thing that always occurs in war, and that they are no worse than other people.'

China came out of the Japan war with enhanced recognition as a world power, with an automatic seat at world summits, a permanent veto-carrying seat in the United Nations Security Council and the ability to call upon both Soviet and American aid. But, as so often in the past, China was torn by her own internal divisions. Mao Zedong's Communist Party owed its survival to Japanese intervention, without which it would have been crushed by Jiang Jieshi: the ironical result of Japan's quest to save China from Marxism was a Communist China.

As for Japan, the failure in China was a key to the collapse of Japan's global ambitions. These now rearranged themselves to become expressed in economic terms. But so appalling was the impact of Japan's defeat in 1945 that even today the pacifist lobby can still ensure that the Japanese defence forces are wholly inadequate, laughably ill-equipped and lacking any political leverage. Without H-bombs and without a credible self-defence force, Japan stands naked in the international politics of the 1980s, because of her memories of the political uses to which the army leaders put their men and materials in the late 1930s. The Japanese continue to feel guilty about their actions in China, unable to conduct a rational and detached foreign policy towards that country. In the opinion polls China is regularly picked out as the country which most Japanese love best and fear least.

As for the outsiders, the war did indeed, as Japan had intended, end European domination of the Asian mainland, and cut the Gordian knot of what to do with Europe's unequal treaties with China. Both China and Japan were bled white by their fighting and had to receive massive post-war injections of American aid. But in China's case this was contested by the two sides in her civil war, and the winning Communist Party in 1949 had to do without it. Hence the continued weakness of the self-reliant Chinese economy.

Jean Escarra argued in *L'Honorable paix japonaise* that the war had occurred two years too early for China, but two years too late for Japan. If it had come a little later, then China might have beaten off the Japanese on her own. If it had come two years earlier, Japan might have been able to complete the defeat of China before having to take on the western powers as well.

Whatever damaging things a modern war may do, it also brings together people from different countries, different races and cultures, and out of this enforced intimacy sometimes comes a new understanding. Such was the case in Europe.

Sadly, however, this kind of consequence of the Sino-Japanese War was aborted. Japan and China in the post-war decades went their own separate ways, attaching themselves initially to rival superpowers, following totally different paths of economic and social development.

Japan hardly existed to the Chinese of the 1950s and 1960s, while the Japanese had largely to ignore China. Only in the late 1970s was a true interchange of people and minds begun, and even now that interchange is far less than what obtains between Britain and France, for example, or between Britain and Germany. All that human knowledge of the other side, those scraps of language and shared wartime experiences, gradually died away, unnourished by new opportunities for peacetime exchanges.

It seems, then, that the war did little good for anybody. Japan failed to keep China safe from Communism or from Russian influence. She did leave an East Asia free from the superficially irritating manifestations of western imperialism, but only at the price of herself having to live under an American shadow for all these post-war decades.

And in her ties with China, Japan finds herself no further forward than in the 1930s, having to cultivate the basic conditions for a relationship from almost the same point as when she substituted force for argument in the earlier decades of the century. China did indeed secure her independence, only to carry it too far for her own good in the Maoist period.

As their new Treaty of Amity shows, Japan and China will collaborate in some degree to keep East Asia from becoming someone else's playground. But in their different ways they are both incapable of enforcing their aims – China because of its debilitating civil war and wasteful Communist experiments, Japan because of its profound loss of self-confidence and almost paranoid insistence on never trusting its generals again.

The Sino-Japanese war is thus a one-off phenomenon, a tragic and wasteful episode which did no good to anyone, a negative example of the unwise use of military power. The fight of the tigers was an extraordinary event, a contest of technology and tradition on a continental scale. But it achieved nothing.

Acknowledgements

The author wishes to thank the many friends whose help in following this complex story has been invaluable, not only in identifying sources and materials, and translating from Japanese and Chinese, but also, in some cases, giving their first-hand recollections of the war. I am especially grateful to Jacques Guillermaz and David Steeds for giving me wonderfully detailed critiques of earlier drafts of certain chapters, and also to Adam Baillie, Steve Lewis, Janet Marks, Caroline Mason, Matsumoto Shigeharu, Caroline E. Smith, Shinya Sugiyama, Kayser Sung and Joseph Yen for their varied contributions to this book.

Notes on Sources

This book is written for the general reader who does not know very much about the war but seeks a reliable general account of it. For the benefit of the few who may wonder what is the precise origin of a quoted statement or piece of information, limited notes follow on sources for particular episodes or quotations in each chapter, with a list of the books and periodicals most frequently cited. A book cited only once is set out in all its detail within the relevant note, but books so frequently cited as to be on the list are referred to in the notes by an abbreviation or code-name.

In order to make these notes as brief as possible, each one is introduced by a key word or phrase of which one word is printed in bold type, to allow the eye to pick it out more easily. The next word or words which follow represent the abbreviated source, usually a single word or name in italics representing a book. The next piece of information is a page number; if there are further references within the same note there is a comma, followed by the other references. The end of the note is indicated by a semi-colon, after which another key word or phrase introduces the next note. Thus the first note of the introduction reads: **Lin** *Vigil* 637;. This means that the quotation from Lin Yutang is taken from his book called *Vigil of a Nation*, on page 637.

These notes have not been compiled for every single fact cited, but only for the quotations in the main text, for specific episodes of particular interest and for anything controversial.

The most used sources have been the principal official accounts left by the two sides, notably Hu Pu-yu's *Brief History* on the Chinese side, and the *Japan Monographs*, based on the memoirs of Japanese staff officers and published by the American occupation authorities in Japan after the war, on the other. The official or semi-official year books and other periodicals of the two sides at the time were also used, along with the reports of the many foreign correspondents who covered the various stages of the war. Almost all of these wrote books, sometimes several books, on their experiences and impressions, as well as contributing to their home newspapers.

Several of the soldiers who participated in the war left behind vivid recollections, from the commanding generals and staff officers like Li Zongren or Imai Takeo to lower-ranking soldiers who kept graphic diaries of their experiences.

Works cited more than once in Notes

Abend: Hallett Abend, *Chaos in Asia*, Washburn, New York, 1939.

Andersson: Johan G. Andersson, *China Fights for the World*, Kegan Paul, London, 1939.

Awake: Robert Payne, *China Awake*, Heinemann, London, 1947.

Battle: Agnes Smedley, *Battle Hymn of China*, Gollancz, London, 1944.

Bertram: James Bertram, *Unconquered*, John Day, New York, 1939.

Booker: Edna Lee Booker, *News is my Job*, MacMillan, New York, 1940.

Carlson: Evans Fordyce Carlson, *Twin Stars of China*, Hyperion Press, Connecticut, 1940.

Chungking: Robert Payne, *Chungking* Diary, Heinemann, London, 1945.

CQ: The China Quarterly, London.

CWR: China Weekly Review, Shanghai.

Dempo: Japan Illustrated 1938, Nippon Dempo Tsusinsha, Tokyo, 1938.

Die: Jack Belden, *Still Time to Die*, Blakiston, Philadelphia, 1944.

Ekins: H. R. Ekins and Theon Wright, *China Fights for her Life*, McGraw-Hill, New York, 1938.

Epstein: Israel Epstein, *The People's War*, Gollancz, London, 1939.

Fights: Agnes Smedley, *China Fights Back*, Vanguard Press, New York, 1938.

Fitch: George A. Fitch, *My Eighty Years in China*, Mei Ya Publications, Taipei, 1967.

Forman: Harrison Forman, *Report From Red China*, Robert Hale, London, 1946.

Gelder: Stuart Gelder, *The Chinese Communists*, Gollancz, London, 1954.

Goette: John A. Goette, *Japan Fights for Asia*, London, 1945.

Hahn: Emily Hahn, *China to Me*, Doubleday, New York, 1944.

Hana: Hino Ashihei, *Hana to Heitai*, Shinchosha, Tokyo, 1953.

Hedin: Sven Hedin, *Chiang Kai-shek, Marshal of China:* John Day, New York, 1940.

Hu: Hu Pu-yu, *A Brief History of the Sino-Japanese War 1937–45*, Chungwu, Taipei, 1974.

Imai: Imai Takeo, *The Intrigues of Showa*, Harashoba, Tokyo, 1967.

Inside: Helen Foster Snow (Nym Wales), *Inside Red China:* Doubleday, New York, 1939.

Isherwood: W. H. Auden and Christopher Isherwood, *Journey to a War*, Faber, London, 1938.

JM: Japan Monographs, numbered series of Japanese commanders' reminiscences published by the US armed forces in Japan after 1946.

Kalyagin: Aleksandr Ya. Kalyagin, *Along Alien Roads* (to be published 1981, page numbers from typescript).

Liang: Liang Chin-tung, *General Stilwell in China 1942–44: The Full Story*, St John's University Press, New York, 1972.

Li: Li Tsung-jen and Tek-kong Tong, *The Memoirs of Li Tsung-jen*, Dawson, Folkestone, 1980.

Liu: F. F. Liu, *A Military History of Modern China 1924–49*, Princeton University Press, 1956.

Lory: Hillis Lory, *Japan's Military Masters*, Viking Press, New York, 1943.

Maurer: Herryman Maaurer, *The End is Not Yet*, Stratford, New York, 1941.

Mowrer: Mowrer in China, Penguin, London, 1938.

Mugi: Hino Ashihei, *Mugi to Heitai*, Kaizosha, Tokyo, 1938.

Payne: Robert Payne, *Chiang Kai-shek*, Weybright & Talley, New York, 1969.

Peck: Graham Peck, *Through China's Wall*, Collins, London, 1941.

Quigley: Harold S. Quigley, *Far Eastern War 1937–41*, Greenwood Press, Connecticut, 1973.

Saga: Saga of Resistance to Japanese Invasion, Foreign Languages Press, Peking, 1959.

Sisters: Emily Hahn, *The Soong Sisters*, Robert Hale, London, 1942.

Scorched: Edgar Snow, *Scorched Earth*, 2 volumes, Gollancz, London, 1941.

Tsuchi: Hino Ashihei, *Tsuchi to Heitai*, Shinchosha, Tokyo, 1953.

Tuchman: Barbara Tuchman, *Sand Against the Wind, Stilwell and the American Experience in China 1911–45*, MacMillan, London, 1970.

Timperley: Harold J. Timperley, *What War Means: The Japanese Terror in China*, Gollancz, London, 1938.
Utley: Freda Utley, *China At War*, Faber, London, 1939.
Vigil: Lin Yutang, *Vigil of a Nation*, Heinemann, London, 1946.
Wampler: Ernest M. Wampler, *China Suffers*, Brethren Publishing, Illinois, 1945.

Introduction (pages 1–10)

Lin *Vigil* 637; **Hedin** Chiang 132–3; **Fukuda** and Ohira *Guardian* 5 Dec. '79; **Hua** *Cheng Ming* Oct. '78 and *CQ* 77 of Mar. '79 p. 174; **Matsuoka** *Quigley* 59; **Gunther** *Booker* 295; **Hino** *Tsuchi* and *Mugi* 104–5, *Hana* 131, 138, 141; **Ishihara** Tamura Masasaku *Miaoping Jinken* 1953 Tokyo 22–5, 33–41; **British** observer H. Vere Redman in *Oriental Affairs*, vol. 8, no. 3, Sep. '37 p. 163; **Kuga** *Lory* 82; **pamphlet** *Lory* 201; **Jiang** on Liu *Li* 428; Chinese **generals** *Hedin* 182, *Scorched I* 118; **Russian** story *Kalyagin* 372.

1 Marco Polo Bridge (pages 13–29)

Bridge *The Travels of Marco Polo* (Dent, London, 1907) 222–3, *Hedin* 165; **Wanping** shooting *JM 178* 15–16, *Dempo* 133, *Imai* 111, *Bertram* 34–7, *Payne* 224–6, *Goette* 11, Hara Fumiyasu's 'Rokokyo kara Isshukan' in *Ichiokunin no showashi* (Tokyo, Mainichi Shimbunsha, 1975) vol. 2, pp. 115–21 [the view that Japanese army rightists fired the first shot in order to start the war is, of course, supported by many Japanese writers including e.g. Saito Heiguro who commanded the Police Guard Division in north China at the time (*Maru*, no. 216, May 1965, Tokyo, p. 125): Imai, the Japanese assistant military attaché in Beijing at the time declares that the local Chinese commandant had objected to these particular manoeuvres on the day before, i.e. 6 July, so that the incident should be seen as Japanese provocation (*Imai* 111) – each witness seems to have his *idée fixe*]; **golf** *Peck* 264; **Jiang** *Payne* 204–5, Lin *Vigil* 63–4; Don't **bother** Jiang Jingguo *Calm in the Eye of the Storm* Li Ming 1978 Taibei 124; Sung-Katsuki **negotiations** *JM 178* 17; **Langfeng** incident *JM 70* 2–3; **Tongxian** incident Foreign Affairs Association of Japan *What Happened at Tungchow* [*Tongxian*]?; Tokyo n.d., *Dempo* 142, *Vigil* 647, *Bertram* 48–53; **Zhang** Zhiyong *Epstein* 45–6, Smedley *Battle* 309; **diary** *Bertram* 176; Teng's **escape** *Scorched I* 14–15, 29; **'please kill'** *Hana* 59; five Japanese **motives** *Scorched I* 24; **Red Cross** evidence *Peck* 286–304.

2 Shanghai Falls (pages 30–48)

Brothel *Peck* 307; **Oyama** incident *Epstein* 83; **Woodhead** *Oriental Affairs*, vol. 8, no. 3, 130; Chinese **upstage** *ibid.* 131, *Quigley* 71–2; Izumo **jewels** *Andersson* 168; **Yan** Haiwen *Hu* 143; war between **races** *Ekins* 232; **Verdun** *Liu* 104; men before **tanks** *Maurer* 17; Chinese soldiers' **motives** *Carlson* 10–11; **cannibalism** *Li* 335; Japan's eighty-five **divisions** *JM 179* 15; **Baoshan** *Hedin* 168; **Konoye** *Dempo* 78; Madame **Jiang Jieshi** *Payne* 229–30, *Fitch* 228–9, *Sisters* 218–19; **Dachang** and air bombardment *Epstein* 112; **Auden** *Collected Poetry* 338; **Zhapei** *Isherwood* 242–3, *Epstein* 112–13; **Suzhou creek** air gunning *Timperley* 123; **Hangzhou** Bay *JM 179* 17 and *JM 70* 13–14, *Carlson* 26; **Falkenhausen** on Bai *Scorched I* 178; his **language** *Andersson* 73; Snow on **Bai** *Battle for Asia* 184; Japanese **diary** *Tsuchi* 89–91; **Stephens** *Scorched I* 57–8; **casualties** *Carlson* 31–3, *Liu* 198, Guillermaz; **damage** *CWR* 19 Mar. 38, *Timperley* 149, 151 and 153; China's officer **losses** *Liu* 148; **Russian** criticism *Kalyagin* 309; **Japanese faults** *Carlson* 31–2; **Snow** *Scorched I* 54.

3 Down to the Yellow River (pages 49–65)

Nankou Smedley *Fights* 51–2, *JM 178* 27; **Terauchi** arrival *JM 178* 28; **air** engagements *JM 76*; **Katsuki**–Feng pact *Imai* 193; **Baoding** and Stilwell *Tuchman* 171–2; Itagaki **bodyguard** *Bertram* 184; **Pingxingguan** battle *Hu* 136, *Carlson* 70–1, *Saga* 13–23, *Bertram* 83–4; **He** Long comment *Forman* 128; **Zhou** Enlai *Bertram* 157; Japanese Shanxi **diaries** Smedley *Fights* 38–9; 'your **ashes**' *Payne Awake* 247; **He** Long *Bertram* 196; **Niangziguan** *Hu* 146, *JM 178* 85–90; **Lin** Biao Smedley *Fights* 133; **horses** short *JM 178* 94.

4 The Rape of Nanjing (pages 66–85)

Jiang's call *China Yearbook 1939* 410; **bombing** J. B. Powell *CWR* 30 Oct. '37; **Mizuno** *Dempo* 111; **Wuxi** *CWR* 19 Mar. '38 or *Timperley* 111–15; Japanese **attack** plans *JM 179* 21–3; **Tang** and surrender *Andersson* 176–81, *Carlson* 49; perfect **pattern** *Fitch* 100; Japan **losses** *Timperley* 26; **Xiaguan** gate *Scorched I* 60, *Fitch* 101–2; **Swede** *Hedin* 22–3; **Auden** *Collected Poetry* 328; **contest** to kill 100 *Japan Advertiser* 7 & 14 Dec. '37 or *Timperley* 284–5; Western witnesses and **atrocity** reports *Timperley passim* especially 20–2, 44, 68–9, 181–2 and 195, *Booker* 353, *Fitch* 430 and 445; house of **consolation** *Booker* 354–5;

Japanese **explanations** *Bertram* 307; **noses** or ears Smedley *Battle* 187; **Nakamura** diary *Battle* 185–6; **Ito** Smedley *Battle* 283; **Matsumoto** Hahn 54–5; horrible but **calculated** A. Morgan Young *Imperial Japan 1926–38* (Allen & Unwin, London, 1938) 298; **rape** as duty *Hahn* 288; the **survivor** *Awake* 271; **use of dogs** *Forman* 118; **bayoneting** *Forman* 119; **syringe** and iron *Honda* 245, *Forman* 118–19; **Endo** *The Sea and Poison* (Quartet, London, 1979) 17–18 and 129–30; **Wuhu** Shusi Hsü *A New Digest of Japanese War Conduct* (Kelly, Hong Kong, 1941) 49; Japanese **writer** Honda Katsuichi of *Asahi Shimbun*; **casualty** figures Japanese correspondent Matsumoto, GMD *Hu* 138, see also *Timperley* 61 (*Payne* 230 estimates 150,000); **rape** order, hosing and scalping *Honda* 201–4 and 259–87; **Auden** *Isherwood* 101; **Loti** in Henry McAleavy *The Modern History of China* (Weidenfeld & Nicolson, London, 1967) 166; **Matsui** reprimand (correspondent was Matsumoto) *Goette* 52–3, personal interview, Hallett Abend *Chaos in Asia* (Washburn, New York, 1939) 191, Lord Russell *The Knights of Bushido* (Cassell, London, 1958) 294–5, and Christopher Chancellor in *International Affairs* vol. 18, no. 5, p. 606; **Mitsunami** Hallett Abend *My Years in China* (Lane, London, 1944) 269; **Hashimoto** *Payne* 229; Japan **reorganization** *JM 179* 25–6, *Hedin* 172.

5 Battle for Xuzhou (pages 86–113)

Wuhan conference *Epstein* 142–7; **Zhou** *Epstein* 148; **Li** praying *Li* 334; **Canadian** *Hedin* 185; **Linyi** battle *Epstein* 164–5, *JM 178 passim*; General **Li** *Epstein* 167; **Sun** Lianzhong *Epstein* 170, *Carlson* 140–1; **Taierzhuang** battle *JM 178 passim*, *Hu* 139–41, *Die* chapter on 'The Retreat from Hsuchow'; Japanese **poem** and diary *Epstein* 173; **Sakamoto**-Seya muddle *JM 178* 140–6; press party & **Sun** *Epstein* 169–74; **Asahi** *Shimbun* 7 Apr. '38; **numbers** at Taierzhuang *Li* 356 says 100,000 Chinese; **Carlson** 143–4; **Hedin** 174–5; von **Falkenhausen** *Carlson* 151–2; **Bai** and Stilwell *Tuchman* 187; **Hashimoto** mission *JM 178* 151–4; **Prince** Higashikuni *JM 178* 162; message to **economize** *Epstein* 196; lieutenant's **diary** and poem *Mugi* 33–4 and 49–50; **pomegranate** diary *Mugi* 201–2; Chinese **escape** *Die* 78–91; **retreat** description *Mowrer* 107; **Umemoto's** mix-up *Mugi* 220–2; fountain **pens** *Die* 108; neutral description Xuzhou **occupation** *Mowrer* 50–1; **Germans** *Liu* 163–4, *Carlson* 287–8, *Andersson* 219–20; **Chen** *Utley* 8–9; **Italians** Claire C. Chennault *Ways of a Fighter* (Putnam, New York, 1949) 38; **Stennes** *Utley* 9; **Zhukov** *Liu* 170.

6 Wuhan Captured (pages 114–133)

Doihara and Yellow River *Die* 123, *Goette* 94, *Chungking Diary*, 64; **Gui** *Die* 157–73; **dykes** – funny moment *Mowrer* 115, also *Maurer* 28–9, *Die* 177–80, *JM 70* 21 and *Battle* 156; Japanese **diary** *Utley* 111; Sichuan **recruits** *Utley* 46; **Auden** *Isherwood* 175; another foreign **visitor** *Utley* 44; **Kobayashi** *Kalyagin* 70; **Madrid** *Kalyagin* 221; **Wuhan** battle *Epstein* 305–20, *JM 179* 32–86, *Hu* 148 *et seq*; **Tang** *Utley* 170; **Madang** *Kalyagin* 148; Japanese **captain** diary *Utley* 112; **Stilwell** in *Utley* 156–7; **Jiang** Jingguo *Hedin* 179; Minsheng **ferry** in Lin *Vigil* 71–2; **Guangzhou** landing and rumours *JM 70* 25, *Carlson* 294, *Imai* 195; Guangzhou **bombing** *Booker* 323.

7 The Partisans (pages 134–146)

Domei apes *Maurer* 75; **Carlson** *Epstein* 199–203; **Hanson** *Epstein* 203–4 and 224–5; **Peng** Wales *Inside* 314–15; **head-splitting** by sword, *Fights* 147; **Ma** *Carlson* 198; **girls** burned *Battle* 177; Ishiguro **diary** *Booker* 336–7; **Zhu** Bertram 161–2, *Fights* 155; **peanuts** *Maurer* 96; **Brown** *Utley* 137–9; too many **killed** Michael Lindsay, *The Unknown War* (Bergström & Boyle, London, 1975); **newspaper** *Goette* 89; **flannels** *Forman* 144; **Ye** *Epstein* 261, *Battle* 182–3; mutual **betrayal** *Bertram* 290–1, *Battle* 312–13; **flags** *Die* 105; **puppets** *Goette* 89; **Aoyama** *Scorched I* 187, see also *Epstein* 157 for Kaji Wataru and *Battle* 452 for Shiomi Saisaku; **missionary** *Wampler* 113; **Zhao** Epstein 59–70; **cavalry** *Saga* 39; **warlord** conversion *Maurer* 69–72; **Kaifeng** *Hedin* 204; **Fu** *Maurer* 40–1.

8 China Wins at Changsha (pages 147–164)

Planning *Kalyagin* 234; **prisoners** *Kalyagin* 334; **clothes lines** *Mowrer* 136; **Mao** *Carlson* 168; **Wales** *Inside* 316–17; **air forces** *JM 76*; **Chen** *Utley* 8; **Chongqing** bombing raids *Battle* 344, *Maurer* 103–10, *Fitch* 138, *Hahn* 255–6; diminishing **returns** *Maurer* 106–7; **Zaoyang** battle *JM 178* 224–41; **Li-Tang** campaign *Li*; **graffiti** *Battle* 209; He **gassed** *Gelder* 75; **Fuzhou** *Hedin* 210; **Tianjin** Hugh Borton *Japan's Modern Century* (Ronald Press, New York, 1955) 356–7 and *Hedin* 210–12; **Changsha** battle *JM 179* 146–59, *Hu* 156–7, *JM 70* 56; **Kunlun** pass Lt.-Col. Ishiwara Heizo in *JM 74* 6, *Hu* 157–8; **Genghis** *Kalyagin* 383.

264   *When Tigers Fight*

9 The Hundred Regiments (pages 165–178)

Megaphone propaganda *Battle* 285; **mutiny** letter *Battle* 332; **leaflets** *Maurer* 283; 'most **annoying**' *JM 178* 218; winter 1939–40 **offensive** *Hu* 161–5, *Battle* 309, *JM 179 passim*; **Zhang** *Battle* 311; **Fu** *JM 178* 293–9; **Yan** in S. W. Shansi *JM 178* 303; Tada's **cage** *Gelder* 162; **Yichang** battle *JM 179* 191–219; **Hundred** Regiments *JM 178* 291 *et seq.*, Peng in *Gelder* 162.

10 No End in Sight (pages 179–187)

New Fourth Army *Hu* 167–70, *Battle* 257 and 313–14; contents of **kitbag** *Battle* 225–6; **West Point** graduate *ibid.* 240; **Zhongtiao** battle *Hu* 167, *JM 178* 333–43; Western **correspondent** *Goette* 47; **Okamura**, Peng Dehuai in *Gelder* 162–3; **Operation 102** *JM 76* 97–8; Changsha II battle *Hu* 167–8, *JM 179* 229–65 and *JM 70* 58–9; **casualties** Wellington Koo *China after Five Years of War* (Gollancz, London, 1943) 58; '**finish** the job' *Goette* 48.

11 Allies at Last (pages 188–202)

Hong Kong *JM 76* 103–6, Oliver Lindsay *The Lasting Honour: The Fall of Hong Kong 1941* (Hamilton, London, 1978); **swimmers** *Lory* 101; **rape** *Hahn* 289–90; **spy** He *Li* 315–17 and 378–80; Jiang on **India** *Hu* 173; **Stilwell** *Goette* 79; **Gandhi** *Liang* 60; **sedan** chair general *Awake* 49–51; **Kyaukse** conference *Tuchman* 289; **loss** of two armies *Liu* 123.

12 The Flying Tigers (pages 203–214)

Changsha III battle *Hu* 171, *Chungking* 39 *et seq.*; **Jiang**'s claims *Payne* 241–2; **Doolittle** and retaliation *JM 76* 107–10, *Hu* 175–6; **Ye** *Gelder* 76–7; **Zhu** *Battle* 259; **Xiangyangdian** *Saga* 177–84; **mimicking** Japanese *Jiefang Ribao* Yan'an 10 Feb. 45 and *Saga* 210–11.

13 Defence of Changde (pages 215–222)

Taihang trap Lin *Vigil* 114; **Asahi** *Shimbun* 15 Jan. '44 (see *Gelder* 103); **Ye** *Gelder* 77; **Miyazaki** *JM 129* 2 *et seq.*; **tunnels** *Awake* 405–6; Japan **air** arguments *JM 129* 4–6; second **Burma** campaign *Hu* 185–6; **Changde** battle *Hu* 182, *Gelder* xvi; **Cairo** *Hu* 179–81; Stilwell and Roosevelt *Liang* 233.

14   Second Try in Burma (pages 223–233)

Second Burma **campaign** *Hu* 185–6, *Dupont* 39–40, Li *Li* 427; **Tojo** *Liu* 188; **weak recruits** *Lin* 141; **tails** up *The Stilwell Papers* (William Sloane, New York, 1948) 300; **Sun** *Liu* 189; **Zeng** *Tuchman* 508; **road** name Jiang's 28 Jan. '45 broadcast to American people in *Liu* 183.

15   The Ichi-go Offensive (pages 234–245)

Japanese **goals** *JM 129* Appendix 1; **Henan** battles *JM 76* 143–84, *Hu* 183; **Communist**-Guomindang tension in Henan *Liu* 220; **Hunan** battles *JM 129* 49, *Hu* 183–4; **Gimo telephones** Xue *Li* 429; Japanese **shortages** *JM 130* 5; **Guangxi**–Guizhou battle *Hu* 184, *JM 130* 19–45; Japan **dissensions** *JM 129* Appendix 8 vi; Chinese recruits' **health** *Liu* 141; Jiang and **conscripts** *Liu* 137–8; arms **cache** *Tuchman* 489.

16   Surrender (pages 246–250)

Teacher *Awake* 36; Japanese **C-in-C** *JM 129* 89–98; **trains** *JM 130* 72 and 100; **Henan** and Hubei campaign *Hu* 197; **western Henan** campaign *JM 130* 90–105; **surrender** *Hu* 203 5.

Epilogue (pages 251–255)

Lost **children** *Japan Times* 14 Apr. '81; He's **liaison** *China Handbook 1937–45* (MacMillan, New York, 1947) 765; **Hirohito** and Deng *CQ* 77 pp. 191–2; **Christian** in Harold Rattenbury *Through Chinese Eyes* (Livingstone Press, London, 1945) 127–8.

Index